Home Life in Colonial Days

AMERICAN CLASSICS™

Home Life in Colonial Days

Written by

ALICE MORSE EARLE

Author of *Child Life in Colonial Days*

Foreword by
James Baker

Berkshire House Publishers
Lee, Massachusetts

AMERICAN CLASSICS ™

HOME LIFE IN COLONIAL DAYS
by Alice Morse Earle

Originally published in 1898
American Classics ™ edition © 1993
by Berkshire House Publishers
Illustrations © 1974 by Berkshire Traveller Press
Foreword © 1992 by Berkshire House, Publishers
All rights reserved.

Front cover art © 1993 by Michael McCurdy
Cover design by Joyce C. Weston

Library of Congress Cataloging-in-Publication Data
Earle, Alice Morse, 1851-1911.
Home life in colonial days / written by Alice Morse Earle ;
foreword by James Baker.
p. cm. -- (American Classics)
Originally published: New York : Grosset & Dunlap, 1898.
Includes index.
ISBN 0-936399-22-8 (pbk.)
1. United States--Social life and customs--To 1775. I. Title.
II. Series: American classics (Stockbridge, Mass.)
E162.E18   1993   93-34515

Berkshire House Publishers
480 Pleasant Street, Suite 5
Lee, MA 01238
800-321-8526
www.berkshirehouse.com

Printed in the United States of America
10 9 8 7

FOREWORD

It is gratifying to find that Alice Morse Earle's *Home Life in Colonial Days* will remain in print. This much-requested sourcebook on colonial life has been in continual demand since its original publication in 1898. Although *Home Life* is nearly a century old, it has yet to be superseded by as rewarding and accessible an introduction to colonial life. Few scholarly works have a useful life even half so long. Mrs. Earle's engaging style and thorough immersion in her sources have made *Home Life in Colonial Days* a true American classic, as are other of her works on the material and social culture of the colonial period.

A century ago the United States was caught up in a widespread fascination with everything colonial. Years of industrial progress and social turmoil, not to mention the Civil War, had disrupted the traditional patterns of American life. The challenge of immigration and national expansion called into question the old WASP verities that had been unquestioned earlier in the century. Enthusiasm for the future was offset by a sense of loss that caused people to look back at what was felt to be a simpler time, when life was more predictable and certain. The Philadelphia Centennial Exposition of 1876, in celebrating a hundred years of American events and accomplishments, aroused the public's interest in life as it was at the time of the Revolution and earlier. By the time of the Columbian Exposition in 1893, an elegiac sensibility about the past had become firmly established, resulting in a fashion for antiquarianism, historical novels, pageants, period room exhibits, neo-Georgian architecture, antique collecting, and village handicrafts. This movement became known as the Colonial Revival.

The Colonial Revival had its most evident effect on American architecture. The colonial theme can be seen today in school and business structures and in public buildings, while not only the style but even the very concept of the suburban single-family home owes a debt to this sensibility. However, the enthusiasts of the Revival were as interested in the inside of the house as the outside. The lure of the vernacular antique, whether it was old blue and white china, spinning wheels, or early pine furniture, turned the stock of East Coast attics into treasure-troves, and spurred a craze for collecting that, if anything, has intensified since that time. The fascination with the *things* of the past in turn reflected a profound curiosity about the society which made and used those artifacts. Old customs and old manners were recalled as part of the romantic evocation of the "nation's childhood." The public demand for information about life in the days of America's "forefathers" (or, more often, "foremothers") was met by a number of writers on colonial topics, of which Alice Morse Earle (1853 - 1911) was a leading example.

Alice Morse Earle's entry into authorship began with a modest article on old Sabbath customs, which she had learned from her grandfather. First published in *Youth's Companion*, it led to an enlarged article in the *Atlantic Monthly* in 1890, and then grew into her first book, *The Sabbath in Puritan New England* (1891). This book was quickly followed by other works on china collecting, biography, costume, local history, travel, childhood, and other subjects largely focused on the later colonial period. Mrs. Earle herself considered her final work, *Two Centuries of Costume* (1903), to be her most significant accomplishment.

Her intimate knowledge of the domestic, daily life of the past is what makes Mrs. Earle's work relevant even today. She was not original in the sense of discovering new sources or creating ground-breaking analyses, but she brought together a mass of obscure and diverse information in a form people could and did enjoy. Alice Morse Earle mastered the sources of her subject of study with a thoroughness that is all the more impressive when one considers that it was a time before the advent of modern communications and research facilities. It is not uncommon for a researcher to come across in her books a casual clue to some important fact that might otherwise only have been found after considerable digging in some obscure source. Her work is social rather than political history, full of imaginative detail, and far more lively than the didactic texts of many of her masculine counterparts. Like them, however, she was a citizen of her own age, and that, at times, causes a conflict between the facts she uncovered and the connotation she unconsciously imposed on them. As Karal Marling notes in *George Washington Slept Here*, Mrs. Earle's contemporary ideology is revealed by illustrations that stress women's hermetic isolation in the household (in the late 19th-century ideal) even as her text reveals evidence to the contrary.

Alice Morse Earle's books were published at a time when historians commonly wrote for a popular audience, and the professionalization of the discipline had just begun. In the years to follow, historians became highly qualified academics writing for their peers in small areas of intensive concentration. The discursive "antiquarian" style of *Home Life* went out of fashion, as did the domestic subject matter, which caused the book to be dismissed by academic critics as amateur "pots-and-pans" history. Professional historians also came to neglect the popular audience, leaving older works by antiquarians such as Mrs. Earle as the most accessible sources for ordinary readers interested in colonial life. In the past twenty years or so, however, there has been a revival of interest in social history, in the lives and roles of women and the artifacts of everyday life (now referred to as "material culture studies") — in other words, the very areas in which Alice Morse Earle excelled. The antiquarian writers, although now outdated, have begun to receive a more respectful reception as worthy forebears of contemporary scolarship. Laurel Thatcher Ulrich honored the precedent of Mrs. Earle's books in her *Good Wives*, a highly acclaimed work on colonial women: "These were pioneering works, important but limited, primarily anecdotal rather than analytical, heavily weighed toward the 18th century, and, of course, untuned to the sorts of economic and social distinctions that later historians would find essential. Their insights were not pursued in later works." Today, those are being once again explored by a new generation of social historians, and a new audience is still able to find in Alice Morse Earle an impressionistic wealth of information that can point the way to a greater knowledge of the formative years of American society.

James Baker
Plimoth Plantation
September 1991

THIS BOOK IS BEGUN

AS IT IS ENDED

IN MEMORY OF MY MOTHER

PREFACE

The illustrations for this book are in every case from real articles and scenes, usually from those still in existence — rare relics of past days. The pictures are the symbols of years of careful search, patient investigation, and constant watchfulness. Many a curious article as nameless and incomprehensible as the totem of an extinct Indian tribe has been studied, compared, inquired and written about, and finally triumphantly named and placed in the list of obsolete domestic appurtenances. From the lofts of woodsheds, under attic eaves, in dairy cellars, out of old trunks and seachests from mouldering warehouses, have strangely shaped bits and combinations of wood, stuff, and metal been rescued and recognized. The treasure stores of Deerfield Memorial Hall, of the Bostonian Society, of the American Antiquarian Society, and many State Historical Societies have been freely searched; and to the officers of these societies I give cordial thanks for their coöperation and assistance in my work.

The artistic and correct photographic representation of many of these objects I owe to Mr. William F.

Halliday of Boston, Massachusetts, Mr. George F. Cook of Richmond, Virginia, and the Misses Allen of Deerfield, Massachusetts. To many friends, and many strangers, who have secured for me single articles or single photographs, I here repeat the thanks already given for their kindness.

There were two constant obstacles in the path: An article would be found and a name given by old-time country folk, but no dictionary contained the word, no printed description of its use or purpose could be obtained, though a century ago it was in every household. Again, some curiously shaped utensil or tool might be displayed and its use indicated; but it was nameless, and it took long inquiry and deduction, — the faculty of " taking a hint," — to christen it. It is plain that different vocations and occupations had not only implements but a vocabulary of their own, and all have become almost obsolete; to the various terms, phrases, and names, once in general application and use in spinning, weaving, and kindred occupations, and now half forgotten, might be given the descriptive title, a "homespun vocabulary." By definite explanation of these terms many a good old English word and phrase has been rescued from disuse.

ALICE MORSE EARLE.

CONTENTS

		Page
I.	Homes of the Colonists	1
II.	The Light of Other Days	32
III.	The Kitchen Fireside	52
IV.	The Serving of Meals	76
V.	Food from Forest and Sea	108
VI.	Indian Corn	126
VII.	Meat and Drink	142
VIII.	Flax Culture and Spinning	166
IX.	Wool Culture and Spinning, with a Postscript on Cotton	187
X.	Hand Weaving	212
XI.	Girls' Occupations	252
XII.	Dress of the Colonists	281
XIII.	Jack-knife Industries	300
XIV.	Travel, Transportation, and Taverns	325
XV.	Sunday in the Colonies	364
XVI.	Colonial Neighborliness	388
XVII.	Old-time Flower Gardens	421

Home Life in Colonial Days

Home Life in Colonial Days

CHAPTER I

HOMES OF THE COLONISTS

WHEN the first settlers landed on American shores, the difficulties in finding or making shelter must have seemed ironical as well as almost unbearable. The colonists found a land magnificent with forest trees of every size and variety, but they had no sawmills, and few saws to cut boards; there was plenty of clay and ample limestone on every side, yet they could have no brick and no mortar; grand boulders of granite and rock were everywhere, yet there was not a single facility for cutting, drawing, or using stone. These homeless men, so sorely in need of immediate shelter, were baffled by pioneer conditions, and had to turn to many poor expedients, and be satisfied with rude covering. In Pennsylvania, New York, Massachusetts, and, possibly, other states, some reverted to an ancient form of shelter: they became cave-dwellers; caves were dug in the side of a hill, and lived in till the settlers could have time to chop down and cut up trees for log houses. Cornelis Van Tienhoven, Secretary of the Province of New Netherland, gives a description of these cave-dwellings, and says that "the wealthy and principal men in New England lived in this fashion for two reasons : first, not to waste time building; second, not to discourage poorer laboring people." It is to be doubted whether wealthy men ever lived in them in New England, but Johnson, in his *Wonder-working Providence*, written in 1645, tells of the occasional use of these "smoaky homes." They were speedily abandoned, and no records remain of permanent cave-homes in New England. In Pennsylvania caves were used by newcomers as homes for a long time, certainly half a century. They generally were formed by digging into the ground about four feet in depth on the banks or low cliffs near the river front. The walls were then built up of sods or earth laid on poles or brush; thus half only of the chamber was really under ground. If dug into a side hill, the earth formed at least two walls. The roofs were layers of tree limbs covered over with sod, or bark, or rushes and bark. The chimneys were laid of cobblestone or sticks of wood mortared with clay and grass. The settlers were thankful even for these poor shelters, and declared that they found them comfortable. By 1685 many families were still living in caves in Pennsylvania, for the Governor's Council then ordered the caves to be destroyed and filled in. Sometimes the settler used the cave for a cellar for the wooden house which he built over it.

These cave-dwellings were perhaps the poorest houses ever known by any Americans, yet pioneers, or poor, or degraded folk have used them for homes in America until far more recent days. In one of these miserable habitations of earth and sod in the town of Rutland, Massachusetts, were passed some of the early years of the girlhood of Madame Jumel, whose beautiful house on Washington Heights, New York, still stands to show the contrasts that can come in a single life.

The homes of the Indians were copied by the English, being ready adaptations of natural and plentiful resources. Wigwams in the South were of plaited rush or grass mats; of deerskins pinned on a frame; of tree boughs rudely piled into a cover, and in the far South, of layers of palmetto leaves. In the mild climate of the Middle and Southern states a " half-faced camp," of the Indian form, with one open side, which served for windows and door, and where the fire was built, made a good temporary home. In such for a time, in his youth, lived Abra-

ham Lincoln.   Bark wigwams were the most easily
made of all; they could be quickly pinned together
on a light frame.   In 1626 there were thirty home-
buildings of Europeans on the island of Manhattan,
now New York, and all but one of them were of bark.

Though the settler had no sawmills, brick kilns,
or stone-cutters, he had one noble friend, — a firm

Log Cabin

rock to stand upon, — his broad-axe.   With his axe,
and his own strong and willing arms, he could take
a long step in advance in architecture; he could build
a log cabin.   These good, comfortable, and sub-

stantial houses have ever been built by American pioneers, not only in colonial days, but in our Western and Southern states to the present time. A typical one like many now standing and occupied in the mountains of North Carolina is here shown. Round logs were halved together at the corners, and roofed with logs, or with bark and thatch on poles; this made a comfortable shelter, especially when the cracks between the logs were "chinked" with wedges of wood, and "daubed" with clay. Many cabins had at first no chinking or daubing; one settler while sleeping was scratched on the head by the sharp teeth of a hungry wolf, who thrust his nose into the space between the logs of the cabin. Doors were hung on wooden hinges or straps of hide.

A favorite form of a log house for a settler to build in his first "cut down" in the virgin forest, was to dig a square trench about two feet deep, of dimensions as large as he wished the ground floor of his house, then to set upright all around this trench (leaving a space for a fireplace, window, and door), a closely placed row of logs all the same length, usually fourteen feet long for a single story; if there was a loft, eighteen feet long. The earth was filled in solidly around these logs, and kept them firmly upright; a horizontal band of punch-eons, which were split logs smoothed off on the face with the axe, was sometimes pinned around within the log walls, to keep them from caving in.   Over this was placed a bark roof, made of squares of chestnut bark, or shingles of overlapping birch-bark.   A bark or log shutter was hung at the window, and a bark door hung on withe hinges, or, if very luxurious, on leather straps, completed the quickly made home.   This was called rolling-up a house, and the house was called a puncheon and bark house.   A rough puncheon floor, hewed flat with an axe or adze, was truly a luxury.   One settler's wife pleaded that the house might be rolled up around a splendid flat stump; thus she had a good, firm table.   A small platform placed about two feet high alongside one wall, and supported at the outer edge with strong posts, formed a bedstead.   Sometimes hemlock boughs were the only bed.   The frontier saying was, "A hard day's work makes a soft bed."   The tired pioneers slept well even on hemlock boughs.   The chinks of the logs were filled with moss and mud, and in the autumn banked up outside with earth for warmth.

These log houses did not satisfy English men and women.   They longed to have what Roger Williams called English houses, which were, however, scarcely different in ground-plan. A single room on the ground, called in many old wills the fire-room, had a vast chimney at one end. A so-called staircase, usually but a narrow ladder, led to a sleeping-loft above. Some of those houses were still made of whole logs, but with clapboards nailed over the chinks and cracks. Others were of a lighter frame covered with clapboards, or in Delaware with boards pinned on perpendicularly. Soon this house was doubled in size and comfort by having a room on either side of the chimney.

Each settlement often followed in general outline as well as detail the houses to which the owners had become accustomed in Europe, with, of course, such variations as were necessary from the new surroundings, new climate, and new limitations. New York was settled by the Dutch, and therefore naturally the first permanent houses were Dutch in shape, such as may be seen in Holland to-day. In the large towns in New Netherland the houses were certainly very pretty, as all visitors stated who wrote accounts at that day. Madam Knights visited New York in 1704, and wrote of the houses,— I will give her own words, in her own spelling and grammar, which were not very good, though she was the teacher of Benjamin Franklin, and the friend of Cotton Mather: —

Suydam House, Bushwick, Long Island, 1700.   From an old print

" The Buildings are Brick Generaly very stately and high: the Bricks in some of the houses are of divers Coullers, and laid in Checkers, being glazed, look very agreable.   The inside of the houses is neat to admiration, the wooden work; for only the walls are plaster'd; and the Sumers and Gist are planed and kept very white scour'd as so is all the partitions if made of Bords."

The " sumers and gist " were the heavy timbers of the frame, the summer-pieces and joists.   The summer-piece was the large middle beam in the middle from end to end of the ceiling; the joists were cross-beams.   These were not covered with plaster as nowadays, but showed in every ceiling;

and in old houses are sometimes set so curiously and fitted so ingeniously, that they are always an entertaining study. Another traveller says that New York houses had patterns of colored brick set in the front, and also bore the date of building. The Governor's house at Albany had two black brick-hearts. Dutch houses were set close to the sidewalk with the gable-end to the street; and had the roof notched like steps, — corbel-roof was the name; and these ends were often of brick, while the rest of the walls were of wood. The roofs were high in proportion to the side walls, and hence steep; they were surmounted usually in Holland fashion with weather-vanes in the shape of horses, lions, geese, sloops, or fish; a rooster was a favorite Dutch weather-vane. There were metal gutters sticking out from every roof almost to the middle of the street; this was most annoying to passers-by in rainy weather, who were deluged with water from the roofs. The cellar windows had small loop-holes with shutters. The windows were always small; some had only sliding shutters, others had but two panes or quarels of glass, as they were called, which were only six or eight inches square. The front doors were cut across horizontally in the middle into two parts, and in early days were hung on leather hinges instead of iron.

In the upper half of the door were two round bull's-eyes of heavy greenish glass, which let faint rays of light enter the hall. The door opened with a latch, and often had also a knocker. Every house had a porch or "stoep" flanked with benches, which were constantly occupied in the summer time; and every evening, in city and village alike, an incessant visiting was kept up from stoop to stoop. The Dutch farmhouses were a single straight story, with two more stories in the high, in-curving roof. They had doors and stoops like the town houses, and all the windows had heavy board shutters. The cellar and the garret were the most useful rooms in the house; they were storerooms for all kinds of substantial food. In the cellar were great bins of apples, potatoes, turnips, beets, and parsnips. There were hogsheads of corned beef, barrels of salt pork, tubs of hams being salted in brine, tonnekens of salt shad and mackerel, firkins of butter, kegs of pigs' feet, tubs of souse, kilderkins of lard. On a long swing-shelf were tumblers of spiced fruits, and "rolliches," head-cheese, and strings of sausages — all Dutch delicacies.

In strong racks were barrels of cider and vinegar, and often of beer. Many contained barrels of rum and a pipe of Madeira. What a storehouse of plenty and thrift! What an emblem of Dutch character! In the attic by the chimney was the smoke-house, filled with hams, bacon, smoked beef, and sausages.

In Virginia and Maryland, where people did not gather into towns, but built their houses farther apart, there were at first few sawmills, and the houses were universally built of undressed logs. Nails were costly, as were all articles manufactured of iron, hence many houses were built without iron; wooden pins and pegs were driven in holes cut to receive them; hinges were of leather; the shingles on the roof were sometimes pinned, or were held in place by "weight-timbers." The doors had latches with strings hanging outside; by pulling in the string within-doors the house was securely locked. This form of latch was used in all the colonies. When persons were leaving houses, they sometimes set them on fire in order to gather up the nails from the ashes. To prevent this destruction of buildings, the government of Virginia gave to each planter who was leaving his house as many nails as the house was estimated to have in its frame, provided the owner would not burn the house down.

Some years later, when boards could be readily obtained, the favorite dwelling-place in the South was a framed building with a great stone or log-and-clay chimney at either end. The house was usually set on sills resting on the ground. The partitions were sometimes covered with a thick layer of mud which dried into a sort of plaster and was white-washed. The roofs were covered with cypress shingles.

Hammond wrote of these houses in 1656, in his *Leah and Rachel*, "Pleasant in their building, and contrived delightfull; the rooms large, daubed and whitelimed, glazed and flowered; and if not glazed windows, shutters made pretty and convenient."

When prosperity and wealth came through the speedily profitable crops of tobacco, the houses improved. The home-lot or yard of the Southern planters showed a pleasant group of buildings, which would seem the most cheerful home of the colonies, only that all dearly earned homes are cheerful to their owners. There was not only the spacious mansion house for the planter with its pleasant porch, but separate buildings in which were a kitchen, cabins for the negro servants and the overseer, a stable, barn, coach-house, hen-house, smoke-house, dove-cote, and milk-room. In many yards a tall pole with a toy house at top was erected; in this bird-house bee-martins built their nests, and by bravely disconcerting the attacks of hawks and crows, and noisily notifying the family and servants

of the approach of the enemy, thus served as a
guardian for the domestic poultry, whose home
stood close under this protection. There was seldom an ice-house. The only means for the preservation of meats in hot weather was by water
constantly pouring into and through a box house
erected over the spring that flowed near the house.
Sometimes a brew-house was also found in the yard,
for making home-brewed beer, and a tool-house for
storing tools and farm implements. Some farms
had a cider-mill, but this was not in the house yard.
Often there was a spinning-house where servants
could spin flax and wool. This usually had one
room containing a hand-loom on which coarse bag-

Sabin Hall

Slave Quarters, Upper Brandon

ging could be woven, and homespun for the use of the negroes. A very beautiful example of a splendid and comfortable Southern mansion such as was built by wealthy planters in the middle of the eighteenth century has been preserved for us at Mount Vernon, the home of George Washington.

Mount Vernon was not so fine nor so costly a house as many others built earlier in the century, such as Lower Brandon — two centuries and a half old — and Upper Brandon, the homes of the Harrisons ; Westover, the home of the Byrds ; Shirley, built in 1650, the home of the Carters ; Sabin Hall, another Carter home, is still standing on the Rappahannock with its various and many quarters and outbuildings, and is a splendid example of colonial architecture.

As the traveller came north from Virginia through Pennsylvania, "the Jerseys," and Delaware, the negro cabins and detached kitchen disappeared, and many of the houses were of stone and mortar. A clay oven stood by each house. In the cities stone and brick were much used, and by 1700 nearly all Philadelphia houses had balconies running the entire length of the second story. The stoop before the door was universal.

For half a century nearly all New England houses were cottages. Many had thatched roofs. Seaside towns set aside for public use certain reedy lots between salt-marsh and low-water mark, where thatch could be freely cut. The catted chimneys were of logs plastered with clay, or platted, that is, made of reeds and mortar; and as wood and hay were stacked in the streets, all the early towns suffered much from fires, and soon laws were passed forbidding the building of these unsafe chimneys; as brick was imported and made, and stone was quarried, there was certainly no need to use such danger-filled materials. Fire-wardens were appointed who peered around in all the kitchens, hunting for what they called foul chimney hearts, and they ordered flag-roofs and wooden chimneys to be removed, and replaced with stone or brick ones.   In Boston every housekeeper had to own a fire-ladder ; and ladders and buckets were kept in the church.   Salem kept its "fire-buckets and hook'd poles" in the town-house.   Soon in all towns each family owned fire-

Fire-buckets

buckets made of heavy leather and marked with the owner's name or initials.   The entire town constituted the fire company, and the method of using the fire-buckets was this. As soon as an alarm of fire was given by shouts or bell-ringing, every one ran at once towards the scene of the fire.   All who owned buckets carried them, and if any person was delayed even for a few minutes, he flung his fire-buckets from the window into the street, where some one in the running crowd seized them and carried them on.   On reaching the fire, a double line called lanes of persons was made from the fire to the river or pond, or a well.   A very good representation of these lanes is given in this fireman's certificate of the year 1800.

Fireman's Certificate, 1800

The buckets, filled with water, were passed from hand to hand, up one line of persons to the fire, while the empty ones went down the other line. Boys were stationed on the *dry lane*. Thus a constant supply of water was carried to the fire. If any person attempted to pass through the line, or hinder the work, he promptly got a bucketful or two of water poured over him. When the fire was over, the fire-warden took charge of the buckets; some hours later the owners appeared, each picked out his own buckets from the pile, carried them home, and hung them up by the front door, ready to be seized again for use at the next alarm of fire.

Many of these old fire-buckets are still preserved, and deservedly are cherished heirlooms, for they

c

represent the dignity and importance due a house-
holding ancestor.   They were a valued possession
at the time of their use, and a costly one, being
made of the best leather.   They were often painted
not only with the name of the owner, but with
family mottoes, crests, or appropriate inscriptions,
sometimes in Latin.   The leather hand-buckets of
the Donnison family of Boston are here shown ;
those of the Quincy family bear the legend *Impavadi
Flammarium* ; those of the Oliver family, *Friend and
Public*.   In these fire-buckets were often kept, tightly

First Fire-engine used in Brooklyn, 1785

rolled, strong canvas bags, in which valuables could be thrust and carried from the burning building.

The first fire-engine made in this country was for the town of Boston, and was made about 1650 by Joseph Jencks, the famous old iron-worker in Lynn. It was doubtless very simple in shape, as were its successors until well into this century. The first fire-engine used in Brooklyn, New York, is here shown. It was made in 1785 by Jacob Boome. Relays of men at both handles worked the clumsy pump. The water supply for this engine was still only through the lanes of fire-buckets, except in rare cases.

By the year 1670 wooden chimneys and log houses of the Plymouth and Bay colonies were replaced by more sightly houses of two stories, which were frequently built with the second story jutting out a foot or two over the first, and sometimes with the attic story still further extending over the second story. A few of these are still standing : The White-Ellery House, at Gloucester, Massachusetts, in 1707, is here shown. This "overhang" is popularly supposed to have been built for the purpose of affording a convenient shooting-place from which to repel the Indians. This is, however, an historic fable. The overhanging second story was a common form of building in England in the time of Queen Elizabeth, and the Massachu-

White-Ellery House, Gloucester, Massachusetts, 1707

setts and Rhode Island settlers simply and naturally copied their old homes.

The roofs of many of these new houses were steep, and were shingled with hand-riven shingles. The walls between the rooms were of clay mixed with chopped straw. Sometimes the walls were whitened with a wash made of powdered clamshells. The ground floors were occasionally of earth, but puncheon floors were common in the better houses. The well-smoothed timbers were sanded in careful designs with cleanly beach sand.

By 1676 the Royal Commissioners wrote of Boston that the streets were crooked, and the houses
usually wooden, with a few of brick and stone.   It
is a favorite tradition of brick houses in all the colonies that the brick for them was brought from
England.   As excellent brick was made here, I cannot believe all these tales that are told.   Occasionally a house, such as the splendid Warner Mansion,
still standing in Portsmouth, New Hampshire, is
proved to be of imported brick by the bills which
are still existing for the purchase and transportation
of the brick.   A later form of many houses was

Boardman Hill House, North Saugus, Massachusetts, 1650

two stories or two stories and a half in front,
with a peaked roof that sloped down nearly to the
ground in the back over an ell covering the kitchen,

added in the shape known as a lean-to, or, as it was called by country folk, the linter.   This slop-ing roof gave the one element of unconscious pict-uresqueness which redeemed the prosaic ugliness of these bare-walled houses.   Many lean-to houses are still standing in New England.   The Boardman

Birthplace of John Adams and John Quincy Adams

Hill House, built at North Saugus, Massachusetts, two centuries and a half ago, and the two houses of lean-to form, the birthplaces of President John Adams and of President John Quincy Adams, are typical examples.

The next roof-form, built from early colonial days, and popular a century ago, was what was known as the gambrel roof.   This resembled, on two sides, the mansard roof of France in the seventeenth century, but was also gabled at two ends. The gambrel roof had a certain grace of outline, especially when joined with lean-tos and other additions. The house partly built in 1636 in Dedham, Massachusetts, by my far-away grandfather, and known as the Fairbanks House, is the oldest gambrel-roofed house now standing. It is still occupied by one of his descendants in the eighth generation. The rear view of it, here given,* shows the picturesqueness of roof outlines and the quaintness which comes simply from variety. The front of the main building, with its eight windows, all of different sizes and set at different heights, shows equal diversity. Within, the boards in the wall-panelling vary from two to twenty-five inches in width.

The windows of the first houses had oiled paper to admit light. A colonist wrote back to England to a friend who was soon to follow, " Bring oiled paper for your windows." The minister, Higginson, sent promptly in 1629 for glass for windows. This glass was set in the windows with nails; the sashes were often narrow and oblong, of diamond-shaped panes set in lead, and opening up and down the middle on hinges. Long after the large towns and cities had glass windows, frontier settlements still had heavy wooden shutters. They were a safer

* Frontispiece.

protection against Indian assault, as well as cheaper.
It is asserted that in the province of Kennebec,
which is now the state of Maine, there was not,
even as late as 1745, a house that had a square of
glass in it. Oiled paper was used until this century
in pioneer houses for windows wherever it was difficult to transport glass.

Few of the early houses in New England were
painted, or colored, as it was called, either without
or within. Painters do not appear in any of the
early lists of workmen. A Salem citizen, just previous to the Revolution, had the woodwork of one
of the rooms of his house painted. One of a group
of friends, discussing this extravagance a few days
later, said: "Well! Archer has set us a fine example of expense, — he has laid one of his rooms in
oil." This sentence shows both the wording and
ideas of the times.

There was one external and suggestive adjunct
of the earliest pioneer's home which was found in
nearly all the settlements which were built in the
midst of threatening Indians. Some strong houses
were always surrounded by a stockade, or "palisado," of heavy, well-fitted logs, which thus formed
a garrison, or neighborhood resort, in time of
danger. In the valley of Virginia each settlement
was formed of houses set in a square, connected from

end to end of the outside walls by stockades with
gates ; thus forming a close front.   On the James
River, on Manhattan Island, were stockades.   The
whole town plot of Milford, Connecticut, was
enclosed in 1645, and the Indians taunted the settlers by shouting out, " White men all same like
pigs."   At one time in Massachusetts, twenty
towns proposed an all-surrounding palisade.   The
progress and condition of our settlements can be
traced in our fences.   As Indians disappeared or
succumbed, the solid row of pales gave place to a
log-fence, which served well to keep out depreda-
tory animals.   When dangers from Indians or wild
animals entirely disappeared, boards were still not
over-plenty, and the strength of the owner could
not be over-spent on unnecessary fencing.   Then
came the double-rail fence ; two rails, held in place
one above the other, at each joining, by four
crossed sticks.   It was a boundary, and would
keep in cattle.   It was said that every fence should
be horse-high, bull-proof, and pig-tight.   Then
came stone walls, showing a thorough clearing and
taming of the land.   The succeeding " half-high "
stone wall — a foot or two high, with a single rail
on top — showed that stones were not as plentiful
in the fields as in early days.   The " snake-fence,"
or " Virginia fence," so common in the Southern

states, utilized the second growth of forest trees. The split-rail fence, four or five rails in height, was set at intervals with posts, pierced with holes to hold the ends of the rails. These were used to some extent in the East ; but our Western states were

Pierce Garrison House, Newburyport

fenced throughout with rails split by sturdy pioneer rail-splitters, among them young Abraham Lincoln. Board fences showed the day of the sawmill and its plentiful supply ; the wire fences of to-day equally prove the decrease of our forests and our wood, and the growth of our mineral supplies and manufactures of metals. Thus even our fences might be called historical monuments.

A few of the old block-houses, or garrison houses, the " defensible houses," which were surrounded by these stockades, are still standing. The most interesting are the old Garrison at East Haverhill, Massachusetts, built in 1670; it has walls of solid oak, and brick a foot and a half thick; the Saltonstall House at Ipswich, built in 1633; Cradock Old Fort in Medford, Massachusetts, built in 1634 of brick made on the spot; an old fort at York, Maine; and the Whitefield Garrison House, built in 1639 at Guilford, Connecticut. The one at Newburyport is the most picturesque and beautiful of them all.

As social life in Boston took on a little aspect of court life in the circle gathered around the royal governors, the pride of the wealthy found expression in handsome and stately houses. These were copied and added to by men of wealth and social standing in other towns. The Province House, built in 1679, the Frankland House in 1735, and the Hancock House, all in Boston; the Shirley House in Roxbury, the Wentworth Mansion in New Hampshire, are good examples. They were dignified and simple in form, and have borne the test of centuries, — they wear well. They never erred in over-ornamentation, being scant of interior decoration, save in two or three principal rooms and the hall and staircase. The panelled step ends and soffits, the graceful newels and balusters, of those old staircases hold sway as models to this day.

Knocker, John Hancock House

The same taste which made the staircase the centre of decoration within, made the front door the sole point of ornamentation without; and equal beauty is there focussed. Worthy of study and reproduction, many of the old-time front doors are with their fine panels, graceful, leaded side windows, elaborate and pretty fan-lights, and slight but appropriate carving.   The prettiest leaded windows I ever saw in an American home were in a thereby glorified henhouse.   They had been taken from the discarded front door of a remodelled old Falmouth house. The hens and their owner were not of antiquarian tastes, and relinquished the windows for a machine-made sash more suited to their plebeian tastes and occupations. Many colonial doors had door-latches or knobs of heavy brass ; nearly all had a knocker

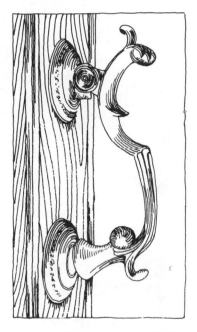

Knocker, Winslow House, Marshfield, Massachusetts

of wrought iron or polished brass, a cheerful ornament that ever seems to resound a welcome to the visitor as well as a notification to the visited.

King-Hooper House, Danvers, Massachusetts

The knocker from the John Hancock House in Boston and that from the Winslow House in Marshfield are here shown ; both are now in the custody of the Bostonian Society, and may be seen at the Old State House in Boston. The latter was given to the society by Dr. Oliver Wendell Holmes.

The " King-Hooper " House, still standing in Danvers, Massachusetts, closely resembled the Hancock House. This house, built by Robert Hooper in 1754, was for a time the refuge of the royal governor of Massachusetts — Governor Gage; and hence is sometimes called General Gage's Headquarters. When the minute-men marched past the house to Lexington on April 18, 1775, they stripped the lead from the gate-posts. " King Hooper" angrily denounced them, and a minuteman fired at him as he entered the house. The bullet passed through the panel of the door, and the rent may still be seen. Hence the house has been often called The House of the Front Door with the Bullet-Hole. The present owner and occupier of the house, Francis Peabody, Esq., has appropriately named it The Lindens, from the stately linden trees that grace its gardens and lawns.

In riding through those portions of our states that were the early settled colonies, it is pleasant to note where any old houses are still standing, or where the sites of early colonial houses are known, the good taste usually shown by the colonists in the places chosen to build their houses. They dearly loved a "sightly location." An old writer said: " My consayte is such; I had rather not to builde a mansyon or a house than to builde one without a good prospect in it, to it, and from it." In Virginia the houses were set on the river slope, where every passing boat might see them. The New England colonists painfully climbed long, tedious hills, that they might have homes from whence could be had a beautiful view, and this was for the double reason, as the old writer said, that in their new homes they might both see and be seen.

CHAPTER II

THE first and most natural way of lighting the houses of the American colonists, both in the North and South, was by the pine-knots of the fat pitch-pine, which, of course, were found everywhere in the greatest plenty in the forests. Governor John Winthrop the younger, in his communication to the English Royal Society in 1662, said this candle-wood was much used for domestic illumination in Virginia, New York, and New England. It was doubtless gathered everywhere in new settlements, as it has been in pioneer homes till our own day. In Maine, New Hampshire, and Vermont it was used till this century. In the Southern states the pine-knots are still burned in humble households for lighting purposes, and a very good light they furnish.

The historian Wood wrote in 1642, in his *New England's Prospect* : —

"Out of these Pines is gotten the Candlewood that is much spoke of, which may serve as a shift among poore folks, but I cannot commend it for singular good, because it droppeth a pitchy kind of substance where it stands."

That pitchy kind of substance was tar, which was one of the most valuable trade products of the colonists. So much tar was made by burning the pines on the banks of the Connecticut, that as early as 1650 the towns had to prohibit the using of candlewood for tar-making if gathered within six miles of the Connecticut River, though it could be gathered by families for illumination and fuel.

Rev. Mr. Higginson, writing in 1633, said of these pine-knots: —

"They are such candles as the Indians commonly use, having no other, and they are nothing else but the wood of the pine tree, cloven in two little slices, something thin, which are so full of the moysture of turpentine and pitch that they burne as cleere as a torch."

To avoid having smoke in the room, and on account of the pitchy droppings, the candle-wood was usually burned in a corner of the fireplace, on a flat stone. The knots were sometimes called pine-torches. One old Massachusetts minister boasted at the end of his life that every sermon of the hundreds he had written, had been copied by the light of these torches. Rev. Mr. Newman, of Rehoboth, is said to have compiled his vast concordance of the

Bible wholly by the dancing light of this candle-
wood.   Lighting was an important item of expense
in any household of so small an income as that of
a Puritan minister; and the single candle was often
frugally extinguished during the long family prayers
each evening.   Every family laid in a good supply
of this light wood for winter use, and it was said
that a prudent New England farmer would as soon
start the winter without hay in his barn as without
candle-wood in his woodshed.

Mr. Higginson wrote in 1630: "Though New
England has no tallow to make candles of, yet by
abundance of fish thereof it can afford oil for lamps."
This oil was apparently wholly neglected, though
there were few, or no domestic animals to furnish
tallow; but when cattle increased, every ounce of
tallow was saved as a precious and useful treasure;
and as they became plentiful it was one of the household riches of New England, which was of value to
our own day.   When Governor Winthrop arrived
in Massachusetts, he promptly wrote over to his
wife to bring candles with her from England when
she came.   And in 1634 he sent over for a large
quantity of wicks and tallow.   Candles cost fourpence apiece, which made them costly luxuries for
the thrifty colonists.

Wicks were made of loosely spun hemp or tow,

or of cotton; from the milkweed which grows so
plentifully in our fields and roads to-day the children gathered in late summer the silver "silk-
down" which was "spun grossly into candle wicke."
Sometimes the wicks were dipped into saltpetre.

Thomas Tusser wrote in England in the sixteenth century in his *Directions to Housewifes:* —

> "Wife, make thine own candle,
>   Spare penny to handle.
> Provide for thy tallow ere frost cometh in,
> And make thine own candle ere winter begin."

Every thrifty housewife in America saved her
penny as in England. The making of the winter's
stock of candles was the special autumnal household duty, and a hard one too, for the great kettles
were tiresome and heavy to handle. An early hour
found the work well under way. A good fire was
started in the kitchen fireplace under two vast
kettles, each two feet, perhaps, in diameter, which
were hung on trammels from the lug-pole or crane,
and half filled with boiling water and melted tallow,
which had had two scaldings and skimmings. At
the end of the kitchen or in an adjoining and cooler
room, sometimes in the lean-to, two long poles were
laid from chair to chair or stool to stool. Across
these poles were placed at regular intervals, like the

rounds of a ladder, smaller sticks about fifteen or
eighteen inches long, called candle-rods. These
poles and rods were kept from year to year, either
in the garret or up on the kitchen beams.

To each candle-rod was attached about six
or eight carefully straightened candle-wicks. The
wicking was twisted strongly one way; then
doubled; then the loop was slipped over the candle-rod, when the two ends, of course, twisted the
other way around each other, making a firm wick.
A rod, with its row of wicks, was dipped in the
melted tallow in the pot, and returned to its place
across the poles. Each row was thus dipped in
regular turn; each had time to cool and harden
between the dips, and thus grew steadily in size.
If allowed to cool fast, they of course grew quickly,
but were brittle, and often cracked. Hence a good
worker dipped slowly, but if the room was fairly
cool, could make two hundred candles for a day's
work. Some could dip two rods at a time. The
tallow was constantly replenished, as the heavy
kettles were used alternately to keep the tallow
constantly melted, and were swung off and on the
fire. Boards or sheets of paper were placed under
the rods to protect the snowy, scoured floors.

Candles were also run in moulds which were
groups of metal cylinders, usually made of tin or

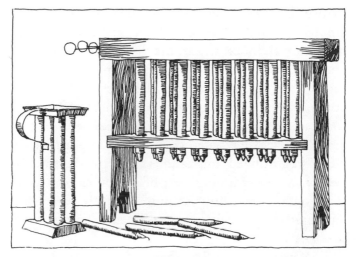

Candle-moulds

pewter. Itinerant candle-makers went from house to house, taking charge of candle-making in the household, and carrying large candle-moulds with them. One of the larger size, making two dozen candles, is here shown; but its companion, the smaller mould, making six candles, is such as were more commonly seen. Each wick was attached to a wire or a nail placed across the open top of the cylinder, and hung down in the centre of each individual mould. The melted tallow was poured in carefully around the wicks.

Wax candles also were made. They were often

shaped by hand, by pressing bits of heated wax around a wick. Farmers kept hives of bees as much for the wax as for the honey, which was of much demand for sweetening, when "loaves" of sugar were so high-priced. Deer suet, moose fat, bear's grease, all were saved in frontier settlements, and carefully tried into tallow for candles. Every particle of grease rescued from pot liquor, or fat from meat, was utilized for candle-making. Rushlights were made by stripping part of the outer bark from common rushes, thus leaving the pith bare, then dipping them in tallow or grease, and letting them harden.

The precious candles thus tediously made were taken good care of. They were carefully packed in

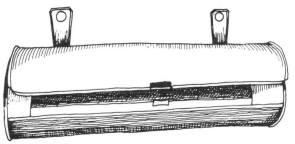

Hanging Candle-box

candle-boxes with compartments ; were covered over, and set in a dark closet, where they would not discolor and turn yellow. A metal candle-box, hung on the edge of the kitchen mantel-shelf, always held two or three candles to replenish those which burnt out in the candlesticks.

A natural, and apparently inexhaustible, material for candles was found in all the colonies in the waxy berries of the bayberry bush, which still grows in large quantities on our coasts. In the year 1748 a Swedish naturalist, Professor Kalm, came to America, and he wrote an account of the bayberry wax which I will quote in full : —

" There is a plant here from the berries of which they make a kind of wax or tallow, and for that reason the Swedes call it the tallow-shrub. The English call the same tree the candle-berry tree or bayberry bush; it grows abundantly in a wet soil, and seems to thrive particularly well in the neighborhood of the sea. The berries look as if flour had been strewed on them. They are gathered late in Autumn, being ripe about that time, and are thrown into a kettle or pot full of boiling water; by this means their fat melts out, floats at the top of the water, and may be skimmed off into a vessel; with the skimming they go on till there is no tallow left. The tallow, as soon as it is congealed, looks like common tallow or wax, but has a dirty green color. By being melted over and refined it acquires a fine and transparent green color. This tallow is dearer than common tallow, but cheaper than wax. Candles of this do not easily bend, nor melt in summer as common candles do; they burn better and slower, nor do they cause any smoke, but yield rather an agreeable smell when they are extinquished.   In Carolina they not only make candles out of the wax of the berries, but likewise sealing-wax."

Beverley, the historian of Virginia, wrote of the smell of burning bayberry tallow : —

" If an accident puts a candle out, it yields a pleasant fragrancy to all that are in the room ; insomuch that nice people often put them out on purpose to have the incense of the expiring snuff."

Bayberry wax was not only a useful home-product, but an article of traffic till this century, and was constantly advertised in the newspapers.   In 1712, in a letter written to John Winthrop, F.R.S., I find : —

" I am now to beg one favour of you, — that you secure for me all the bayberry wax you can possibly put your hands on.   You must take a care they do not put too much tallow among it, being a custom and cheat they have got."

Bayberries were of enough importance to have some laws made about them.   Everywhere on Long Island grew the stunted bushes, and everywhere they were valued.   The town of Brookhaven, in 1687, forbade the gathering of the berries before September 15, under penalty of fifteen shillings' fine.

The pungent and unique scent of the bayberry,

equally strong in leaf and berry, is to me one of
the elements of the purity and sweetness of the air
of our New England coast fields in autumn.   It
grows everywhere, green and cheerful, in sun-with-
ered shore pastures, in poor bits of earth on our
rocky coast, where it has few fellow field-tenants to
crowd the ground.   It is said that the highest
efforts of memory are stimulated through our sense
of smell, by the association of ideas with scents.
That of bayberry, whenever I pass it, seems to
awaken in me an hereditary memory, to recall a life
of two centuries ago.   I recall the autumns of trial
and of promise in our early history, and the bayberry fields are peopled with children in Puritan
garb, industriously gathering the tiny waxen fruit.
Equally full of sentiment is the scent of my burning bayberry candles, which were made last autumn
in an old colony town.

The history of whale-fishing in New England is
the history of one of the most fascinating commercial industries the world has ever known.   It is a
story with every element of intense interest, showing infinite romance, adventure, skill, courage, and
fortitude.   It brought vast wealth to the communities that carried on the fishing, and great independence and comfort to the families of the whalers.
To the whalemen themselves it brought incredible

hardships and dangers, yet they loved the life with a love which is strange to view and hard to understand. In the oil made from these "royal fish" the colonists found a vast and cheap supply for their metal and glass lamps; while the toothed whales had stored in their blunt heads a valuable material which was at once used for making candles; it is termed, in the most ancient reference I have found to it in New England records, Sperma-Coeti.

It was asserted that one of these spermaceti candles gave out more light than three tallow candles, and had four times as big a flame. Soon their manufacture and sale amounted to large numbers, and materially improved domestic illumination.

All candles, whatever their material, were carefully used by the economical colonists to the last bit by a little wire frame of pins and rings called a save-all. Candlesticks of various metals and shapes were found in every house; and often sconces, which were also called candle-arms, or prongs. Candle-beams were rude chandeliers, a metal or wooden hoop with candle-holders. Snuffers were always seen, with which to trim the candles, and snuffers trays. These were sometimes exceedingly richly ornamented, and were often of silver: extinguishers often accompanied the snuffers.

Silver Snuffers and Tray

Though lamps occasionally appear on early inventories and lists of sales, and though there was plenty of whale and fish oil to burn, lamps were not extensively used in America for many years. "Betty-lamps," shaped much like antique Roman lamps, were the earliest form. They were small, shallow receptacles, two or three inches in diameter and about an inch in depth; either rectangular, oval, round, or triangular in shape, with a projecting nose or spout an inch or two long. They usually had a hook and chain by which they could be hung on a nail in the wall, or on the round in the back of a chair; sometimes there was also a smaller hook for cleaning out the nose of the lamp. They were filled with tallow, grease, or oil, while a piece of cotton rag or coarse wick was so placed that, when lighted, the end hung out on the nose. From this wick, dripping dirty grease, rose a dull, smoky, ill-smelling flame.

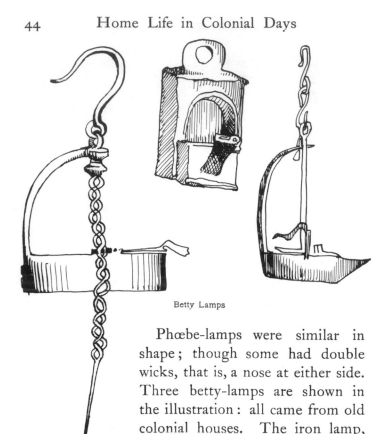

Betty Lamps

Phœbe-lamps were similar in shape; though some had double wicks, that is, a nose at either side. Three betty-lamps are shown in the illustration: all came from old colonial houses.   The iron lamp, solid with the accumulated grease of centuries, was found in a Virginia cabin; the rectangular brass lamp came from a Dutch farmhouse; and the graceful oval brass lamp from a New England homestead.

Pewter was a favorite material for lamps, as it was for all other domestic utensils.   It was specially in favor for the lamps for whale oil and the " Porter's fluid," that preceded our present illuminating medium, petroleum.

A rare form is the pewter lamp here shown. It is in the collection of ancient lamps, lanterns, candlesticks, etc., owned by Mrs. Samuel Bowne Duryea, of Brooklyn. It came from a Salem home, where it was used as a house-lantern. With its clear bull's-eyes of unusually pure glass, it gave what was truly a brilliant light for the century of its use. A group of old pewter lamps, of

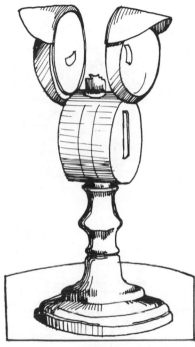

Bull's-Eye Lamp

the shapes commonly used in the homes of our ancestors a century or so ago, is also given ; chosen, not because they were unusual or beautiful, but because they were universal in their use.

The lamps of Count Rumford's invention were doubtless a great luxury, with their clear steady light; but they were too costly to be commonly seen in our grandfathers' homes.   Nor were Argand burners ever universal.   Glass lamps of many simple shapes shared popularity for a long time with the pewter lamps; and as pewter gradually disappeared from household use, these glass lamps

Old Pewter Lamps

monopolized the field.   They were rarely of cut or colored glass, but were pressed glass of common-place form and quality.   A group of them is here

Old Glass Lamps

given which were all used in old New England houses in the early part of this century.

For many years the methods of striking a light were very primitive, just as they were in Europe; many families possessed no adequate means, or very imperfect ones. If by ill fortune the fire in the fireplace became wholly extinguished through

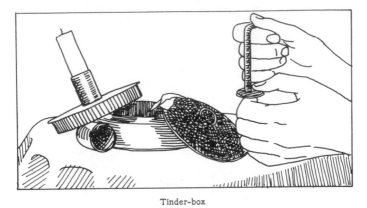

Tinder-box

carelessness at night, some one, usually a small boy, was sent to the house of the nearest neighbor, bearing a shovel or covered pan, or perhaps a broad strip of green bark, on which to bring back coals for relighting the fire.   Nearly all families had some form of a flint and steel, — a method of obtaining fire which has been used from time immemorial by both civilized and uncivilized nations.   This always required a flint, a steel, and a tinder of some vegetable matter to catch the spark struck by the concussion of flint and steel.   This spark was then blown into a flame.   Among the colonists scorched linen was a favorite tinder to catch the spark of fire ; and till this century all the old cambric handkerchiefs, linen underwear, and worn sheets of a household were carefully saved for this purpose.

The flint, steel, and tinder were usually kept together in a circular tinder-box, such as is shown in
the accompanying illustration; it was a shape universal in England and America.   This had an inner
flat cover with a ring, a flint, a horseshoe-shaped
steel, and an upper lid with a place to set a candle-
end in, to carry the newly acquired light.   Though
I have tried hundreds of times with this tinder-box,
I have never yet succeeded in striking a light.   The
sparks fly, but then the operation ceases in modern
hands.   Charles Dickens said if you had good luck,
you could get a light in half an hour.   Soon there

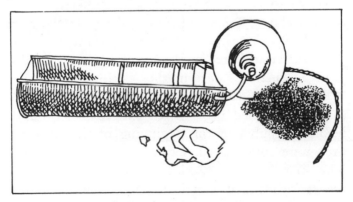

Tinder-wheel, Flint, and Tinder

was an improvement on this tinder-box, by which
sparks were obtained by spinning a steel wheel with
a piece of cord, somewhat like spinning a humming

E

top, and making the wheel strike a flint fixed in the side of a little trough full of tinder. This was an infinite advance in convenience on tinder-box No. 1. This box was called in the South a mill; one is here shown. Then some person invented strips of wood dipped in sulphur and called "spunks." These readily caught fire, and retained it, and were handy to carry light to a candle or pile of chips.

Another way of starting a fire was by flashing a little powder in the pan of an old-fashioned gun; sometimes this fired a twist of tow, which in turn started a heap of shavings.

Down to the time of our grandfathers, and in some country homes of our fathers, lights were started with these crude elements, — flint, steel, tinder, — and transferred by the sulphur splint; for fifty years ago matches were neither cheap nor common.

Though various processes for lighting in which sulphur was used in a match shape, were brought before the public at the beginning of this century, they were complicated, expensive, and rarely seen. The first practical friction matches were "Congreves," made in England in 1827. They were thin strips of wood or cardboard coated with sulphur and tipped with a mixture of mucilage, chlorate of potash, and sulphide of antimony. Eighty-four of them were sold in a box for twenty-five cents, with a piece of "glass-paper" through which the match could be drawn.   There has been a long step this last fifty years between the tinder-box used so patiently for two centuries, and the John Jex Long match-making machine of our times, which turns out seventeen million matches a day.

CHAPTER III

THE kitchen in all the farmhouses of all the colonies was the most cheerful, homelike, and picturesque room in the house; indeed, it was in town houses as well. The walls were often bare, the rafters dingy; the windows were small, the furniture meagre; but the kitchen had a warm, glowing heart that spread light and welcome, and made the poor room a home. In the houses of the first settlers the chimneys and fireplaces were vast in size, sometimes so big that the fore-logs and back-logs for the fire had to be dragged in by a horse and a long chain; or a hand-sled was kept for the purpose. Often there were seats within the chimney on either side. At night children could sit on these seats and there watch the sparks fly upward and join the stars which could plainly be seen up the great chimney-throat.

But as the forests disappeared under the waste of burning for tar, for potash, and through wanton clearing, the fireplaces shrank in size; and Benjamin

Franklin, even in his day, could write of " the fire-places of our fathers."

The inflammable catted chimney of logs and clay, hurriedly and readily built by the first settlers, soon gave place in all houses to vast chimneys of stone, built with projecting inner ledges, on which rested a bar about six or seven or even eight feet from the floor, called a lug-pole (lug meaning to carry) or a back-bar; this was made of green wood, and thus charred slowly — but it charred surely in the generous flames of the great chimney heart. Many annoying, and some fatal accidents came from the collapsing of these wooden back-bars. The destruction of a dinner sometimes was attended with the loss of a life. Later the back-bars were made of iron. On them were hung iron hooks or chains with hooks of various lengths called pothooks, trammels, hakes, pot-hangers, pot-claws, pot-clips, pot-brakes, pot-crooks. Mr. Arnold Talbot, of Providence, Rhode Island, has folding trammels, nine feet long, which were found in an old Narragansett chimney heart. Gib-crokes and recons were local and less frequent names, and the folks who in their dialect called the lug-pole a gallows-balke called the pothooks gallows-crooks. On these hooks pots and kettles could be hung at varying heights over the fire. The iron swinging-crane was a Yankee invention of a century

after the first settlement, and it proved a convenient
and graceful substitute for the back-bar.

Some Dutch houses had an adaptation of a Southern method of housekeeping in the use of a detached
house called a slave-kitchen, where the meals of
the negro house and farm servants were cooked and
served. The slave-kitchen of the old Bergen homestead stood unaltered till within a few years on Third
Avenue in Brooklyn. It still exists in a dismantled
condition. Its picture plainly shows the stone ledges
within the fireplace, the curved iron lug-pole, and
hanging pothooks and trammels. With ample fire
of hickory logs burning on the hearthstone, and the
varied array of primitive cooking-vessels steaming
with savory fare, a circle of laughing, black faces
shining with the glowing firelight and hungry antici-
pation, would make a " Dutch interior " of American
form and shaping as picturesque and artistic as any
of Holland. The fireplace itself sometimes went
by the old English name, clavell-piece, as shown by
the letters of John Wynter, written from Maine in
1634 to his English home. "The Chimney is large,
with an oven at each end of him : he is so large that
wee can place our Cyttle within the Clavell-piece.
Wee can brew and bake and boyl our Cyttle all at
once in him." Often a large plate of iron, called
the fire-back or fire-plate, was set at the back of the

Fireplace of Slave-kitchen

chimney, where the constant and fierce fire crumbled brick and split stone. These iron backs were often cast in a handsome design.

In New York the chimneys and fireplaces were Dutch in shape; the description given by a woman traveller at the end of the seventeenth century ran thus : —

"The chimney-places are very droll-like : they have no jambs nor lintell as we have, but a flat grate, and there projects over it a lum in the form of the cat-and-clay lum, and commonly a muslin or ruffled pawn around it."

The "ruffled pawn" was a calico or linen valance which was hung on the edge of the mantel-shelf, a pretty and cheerful fashion seen in some English as well as Dutch homes.

Another Dutch furnishing, the alcove bedstead, much like a closet, seen in many New York kitchens, was replaced in New England farm-kitchens by the "turn-up" bedstead. This was a strong frame filled with a network of rope which was fastened at the bed-head by hinges to the wall. By night the foot of the bed rested on two heavy legs; by day the frame with its bed furnishings was hooked up to the wall, and covered with homespun curtains or doors. This was the sleeping-place of the master and mistress of the house, chosen because the

kitchen was the warmest room in the house. One
of these "turn-up" bedsteads which was used in
the Sheldon homestead until this century may be
seen in Deerfield Memorial Hall.

Over the fireplace and across the top of the room
were long poles on which hung strings of peppers,
dried apples, and rings of dried pumpkin. And
the favorite resting-place for the old queen's-arm
or fowling-piece was on hooks over the kitchen
fireplace.

On the pothooks and trammels hung what formed
in some households the costliest house-furnishing,
— the pots and kettles. The Indians wished their
brass kettles buried with them as a precious possession, and the settlers equally valued them; often
these kettles were worth three pounds apiece. In
many inventories of the estates of the settlers the
brass-ware formed an important item. Rev. Thomas
Hooker of Hartford had brass-ware which, in the
equalizing of values to-day, would be worth three
or four hundred dollars. The great brass and copper kettles often held fifteen gallons. The vast iron
pot — desired and beloved of every colonist — sometimes weighed forty pounds, and lasted in daily use
for many years. All the vegetables were boiled
together in these great pots, unless some very particular housewife had a wrought-iron potato-boiler

to hold potatoes or any single vegetable in place within the vast general pot.

Iron Potato-boiler

Chafing-dishes and skimmers of brass and copper were also cheerful discs to reflect the kitchen firelight.

Very little tin was seen, either for kitchen or table utensils. Governor Winthrop had a few tin plates, and some Southern planters had tin pans, others " tynnen covers." Tin pails were unknown; and the pails they did own, either of wood, brass, or other sheet metal, had no bails, but were carried by thrusting a stick through little ears on either side of the pail. Latten ware was used instead of tin ; it was a kind of brass. A very good collection of century-old tinware is shown in the illustration.

Old Tinware

By a curious chance this tinware lay unpacked for over ninety years in the attic loft of a country warehouse, in the packing-box, just as it was delivered from an English ship at the close of the Revolution. The pulling down of the warehouse disclosed the box, with its dated labels. The tin utensils are more gayly lacquered than modern ones, otherwise they differ little from the tinware of to-day.

There was one distinct characteristic in the house-furnishing of olden times which is lacking to-day. It was a tendency for the main body of everything to set well up, on legs which were strong enough for adequate support of the weight, yet were slender in appearance. To-day bureaus, bedsteads, cabinets, desks, sideboards, come close to the floor; formerly chests of drawers, Chippendale sideboards, four-post bedsteads, dressing-cases, were set, often a foot high, in a tidy, cleanly fashion; thus they could all be thoroughly swept under. This same peculiarity of form extended to cooking-utensils. Pots and kettles had legs, as shown in those hang-

Iron Skillet, Rabbit Broiler, and Brazier

ing in the slave-kitchen fireplace; gridirons had legs, skillets had legs; and further appliances in the shape of trivets, which were movable frames, took the place of legs. The necessity for the stilting up of cooking-utensils was a very evident one; it was necessary to raise the body of the utensil above the ashes and coals of the open fireplace. If the bed of coals and burning logs were too deep for the skillet or pot-legs, then the utensil must be hung from above by the ever-ready trammel.

Often in the corner of the fireplace there stood a group of trivets, or three-legged

Toasting-forks

stands, of varying heights, through which the exactly desired proximity to the coals could be obtained.

Even toasting-forks, and similar frail utensils of wire or wrought iron, stood on tall, spindling legs, or were carefully shaped to be set up on trivets. They usually had, also, long, adjustable handles, which helped to make endurable the blazing heat of the great logs. All such irons as waffle-irons had far longer handles than are seen on any cooking-utensils in these days of stoves and ranges, where the flames are covered and the housewife shielded.

Gridirons had long handles of wood or iron, which could be fastened to the shorter stationary handles.

Waffle-irons

The two gridirons in the accompanying illustration are a century old. The circular one was the oldest form. The oblong ones, with groove to collect the gravy, did not vary in shape till our own day. Both have indications of fittings for long handles, but the handles have vanished. A long-handled frying-pan is seen hanging by the side of the slave-kitchen fireplace.

An accompaniment of the kitchen fireplace, found, not in farmhouses, but among luxury-loving town-folk, was the plate-warmer. They are seldom named in inventories, and I know of but one of Revolutionary days, and it is here shown. Similar ones are manufactured to-day; the legs, perhaps, are shorter, but the general outline is the same.

An important furnishing of every fireplace was
the andirons.   In kitchen fireplaces these were usually of iron, and the shape known as goose-neck
were common.   Cob irons were the simplest form,
and merely supported the spit ; sometimes they

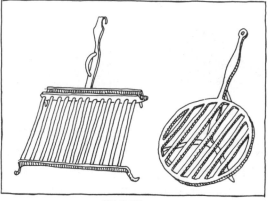

Old Gridirons

had hooks to hold a dripping-pan.   A common
name for the kitchen andirons was fire-dogs ; and
creepers were low, small andirons, usually used with
the tall fire-dogs.   The kitchen andirons were simply for use to help hold the logs and cooking-utensils.   But other fireplaces had handsome fire-dogs
of copper, brass, or cut steel, cast or wrought in
handsome devices.   These were a pride and delight
to the housewife.

A primitive method of roasting a joint of meat or

a fowl was by suspending it in front of the fire by a strong hempen string tied to a peg in the ceiling, while

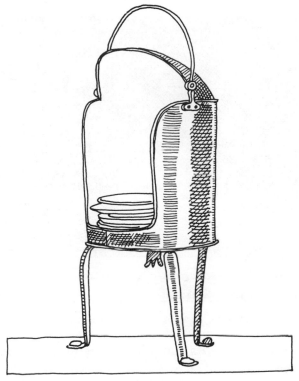

Plate-warmer

some one — usually an unwilling child — occasionally turned the roast around. Sometimes the sole turn-

spit was the housewife, who, every time she basted
the roast, gave the string a good twist, and thereafter
it would untwist, and then twist a little again, and so
on until the vibration ceased, when she again basted

Bake-kettle, Clock-jack, Dutch Oven, and Dye Tub

and started it. As the juices sometimes ran down
in the roast and left the upper part too dry, a
"double string-roaster" was invented, by which the
equilibrium of the joint could be shifted. A jack
was a convenient and magnified edition of the prim-

itive string, being a metal suspensory machine.   A
still further glorification was the addition of a revolving power which ran by clockwork and turned
the roast with regularity; this was known as a
clock-jack.   The one here shown hangs in the fireplace in Deerfield Memorial Hall.   A smoke-jack
was run somewhat irregularly by the pressure of
smoke and the current of hot air in the chimney.
These were noisy and creaking and not regarded
with favor by old-fashioned cooks.

We are apt to think of the turnspit dog as a
creature of European life, but we had them here
in America — little low, bow-legged, patient souls,
trained to run in a revolving cylinder and keep the
roasting joint a-turn before the fire.   Mine host
Clark of the State House Inn in Philadelphia in
the first half of the eighteenth century advertised
in Benjamin Franklin's *Pennsylvania Gazette* that
he had for sale "several dogs and wheels, much
preferable to any jacks for roasting any joints of
meat."   I hope neither he nor any one else had
many of these little canine slaves.

A frequent accompaniment of the kitchen fireplace in the eighteenth century, and a domestic
luxury seen in well-to-do homes, was the various
forms of the "roasting-kitchen," or Dutch oven.
These succeeded the jacks; they were a box-like

arrangement open on one side which when in use
was turned to the fire.   Like other utensils of the
day, they often stood up on legs, to bring the open

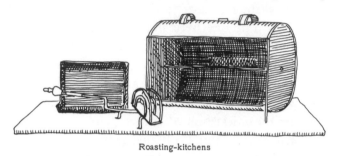

Roasting-kitchens

side before the blaze.   A little door at the back
could be opened for convenience in basting the roast.
These kitchens came in various sizes for roasting
birds or joints, and in them bread was occasionally
baked.   The bake-kettle, which in some communities was also called a Dutch oven, was preferred for
baking bread.   It was a strong kettle, standing,
of course, on stout, stumpy legs, and when in use
was placed among the hot coals and closely covered
with a strong metal, convex cover, on which coals
were also closely heaped.   Such perfect rolls, such
biscuit, such shortcake, as issued from the heaped-
up bake-kettle can never be equalled by other
methods of cooking.

When the great stone chimney was built, there

was usually placed on one side of the kitchen fireplace a brick oven which had a smoke uptake into
the chimney — and an ash-pit below. The great
door was of iron. This oven was usually heated
once a week. A great fire of dry wood, called oven
wood, was kindled within it and kept burning
fiercely for some hours. This thoroughly heated
all the bricks. The coals and ashes were then
swept out, the chimney draught closed, and the
oven filled with brown bread, pies, pots of beans,
etc. Sometimes the bread was baked in pans, sometimes it was baked in a great mass set on cabbage
leaves or oak leaves. In some towns an autumn
harvest of oak leaves was gathered by children to
use throughout the winter. The leaves were
strung on sticks. This gathering was called going
a-leafing.

By the oven side was always a long-handled
shovel known as a peel or slice, which sometimes
had a rack or rest to hold it; this implement was a
necessity in order to place the food well within the
glowing oven. The peel was sprinkled with meal,
great heaps of dough were placed thereon, and by a
dexterous twist they were thrown on the cabbage or
oak leaves. A bread peel was a universal gift to a
bride; it was significant of domestic utility and
plenty, and was held to be luck-bearing. On

Thanksgiving week the great oven had a fire built
in it every morning, and every night it was well
filled and closed till morning.

On one side of the kitchen often stood a dresser,
on which was placed in orderly rows the cheerful
pewter and scant earthenware of the household : —

> " —— the room was bright
> With glimpses of reflected light,
> From plates that on the dresser shone."

In Dutch households plate-racks, spoon-racks,
knife-racks, — all hanging on the wall, — took the
place of the New England dresser.

In the old Phillips farmhouse at Wickford,
Rhode Island, is a splendid chimney over twenty
feet square. So much room does it occupy that
there is no central staircase, but little winding stairs
ascend at three corners of the house. In the vast
fireplace an ox could literally have been roasted.
On each chimney-piece are hooks to hang firearms,
and at one side curious little drawers are set for
pipes and tobacco. In some Dutch houses in New
York these tobacco shelves are in the entry, over
the front door, and a narrow flight of three or four
steps leads up to them. Hanging on a nail alongside the tobacco drawer, or shelf, would usually be
seen a pipe-tongs, or smoking-tongs. They were

slender little tongs, usually of iron or
steel; with them the smoker lifted a
coal from the fireplace to light his pipe.
The tongs owned and used by Captain
Joshua Wingate, of Hampton, New
Hampshire, who lived from 1679 to
1769, are here shown. The handle is
unlike any other I have seen, having
one end elongated, knobbed, and ingeniously bent S-shaped into convenient
form to press down the tobacco into
the bowl of the pipe. Other old-time
pipe tongs were in the form of lazy-
tongs. A companion of the pipe-tongs
on the kitchen mantel was what was
known as a comfortier — a little brazier
of metal in which small coals could be
handed about for pipe-lighting. An
unusual luxury was a comfortier of silver. These were found among the
Dutch settlers.

The Pennsylvania Germans were the
first to use stoves. These were of
various shapes. A curious one, seen
in houses and churches, was of sheet-

Smoking-tongs

metal, box-shaped; three sides were within the
house, and the fourth, with the stove door, outside

the house. Thus what was really the back of the
stove projected into the room, and when the fire
was fed it was necessary for the tender to go
out of doors. These German stoves and hot-air
drums, which heated the second story of the house,
were ever a fresh wonder to travellers of English
birth and descent in Pennsylvania. There is no
doubt that their evident economy and comfort suggested to Benjamin Franklin the " New Pennsylvania Fireplace," which he invented in 1742, in
which both wood and coal could be used, and which
was somewhat like the heating apparatus which we
now call a Franklin stove, or heater.

Thus German settlers had, in respect to heating,
the most comfortable homes of all the colonies.
Among the English settlers the kitchen was, too,
often, the only comfortable room in the house in
winter weather. Indeed, the discomforts and incon-
veniences of a colonial home could scarcely be endured to-day ; of course these culminated in the
winter time, when icy blasts blew fiercely down the
great chimneys, and rattled the loosely fitting windows. Children suffered bitterly in these cold
houses. The rooms were not warm three feet
away from the blaze of the fire. Cotton Mather
and Judge Samuel Sewall both tell, in their diaries,
of the ink freezing in their pens as they wrote within

the chimney-side. One noted that, when a great fire was built on the hearth, the sap forced out of the wood by the flames froze into ice at the end of the logs. The bedrooms were seldom warmed, and had it not been for the deep feather beds and heavy bed-curtains, would have been unendurable. In Dutch and some German houses, with alcove bedsteads, and sleeping on one feather bed, with another for cover, the Dutch settlers could be far warmer than any English settlers, even in four-post bedsteads curtained with woollen.

Water froze immediately if left standing in bed-rooms. One diary, written in Marshfield, Massachu-setts, tells of a basin of water standing on the bed-room hearth, in front of a blazing fire, in which the water froze solid. President John Adams so dreaded the bleak New England winter and the ill-warmed houses that he longed to sleep like a dormouse every year, from autumn to spring. In the South-ern colonies, during the fewer cold days of the win-ter months, the temperature was not so low, but the houses were more open and lightly built than in the North, and were without cellars, and had fewer fireplaces; hence the discomfort from the cold was as great, if not the positive suffering.

The first chilling entrance into the ice-cold bed of a winter bedroom was sometimes mitigated by heating the inner sheets with a warming-pan. This usually hung by the side of the kitchen fire-place, and when used was filled with hot coals, and thrust within the bed, and constantly and rapidly moved back and forth to keep from scorching the bed-linen. The warming-pan was a circular metal pan about a foot in diameter, four or five inches deep, with a long wooden handle and a perforated metal cover, usually of copper or brass, which was kept highly polished, and formed, as it hung on the wall, one of the cheerful kitchen discs to reflect the light of the glowing fire. The warming-pan has been deemed of sufficient decorative capacity to make it eagerly sought after by collectors, and a great room of one of these collectors is hung entirely around the four walls with a frieze of warming-pans.

Warming-pan

Many of our New England poets have given us glimpses in rhyme of the old-time kitchen. Lowell's well-known lines are vivid enough to bear never-dying quotation : —

" A fireplace filled the rooms one side
  With half a cord of wood in —
There warn't no stoves (tell comfort died)
  To bake ye to a puddin'.

" The wa'nut log shot sparkles out
  Towards the pootiest — bless her!
An' little flames danced all about
  The chiny on the dresser.

" Agin the chimbly crooknecks hung,
  An' in amongst 'em rusted
The old queen's-arm that granther Young
  Fetched back from Concord busted."

To me the true essence of the old-time fireside is
found in Whittier's *Snow-bound*. The very chimney,
fireplace, and hearthstone of which his beautiful lines
were written, the kitchen of Whittier's boyhood's
home, at East Haverhill, Massachusetts, is shown
in the accompanying illustration. It shows a swinging crane. His description of the " laying the fire "
can never be equalled by any prose: —

" We piled with care our nightly stack
  Of wood against the chimney back —
The oaken log, green, huge, and thick,
And on its top the stout back-stick;
The knotty fore-stick laid apart,
And filled between with curious art

Kitchen Fireplace of Whittier's Home

The ragged brush; then hovering near,
We watched the first red blaze appear,
Heard the sharp crackle, caught the gleam
On whitewashed wall and sagging beam,
Until the old, rude-furnished room
Burst, flower-like, into rosy bloom."

No greater picture of homely contentment could
be shown than the following lines : —

"Shut in from all the world without,
We sat the clean-winged hearth about,

Content to let the north wind roar
In baffled rage at pane and door,
While the red logs before us beat
The frost-line back with tropic heat;
And ever, when a louder blast
Shook beam and rafter as it passed,
The merrier up its roaring draught
The great throat of the chimney laughed.
The house dog on his paws outspread
Laid to the fire his drowsy head,
The cat's dark silhouette on the wall
A couchant tiger's seemed to fall;
And, for the winter fireside meet,
Between the andirons' straddling feet
The mug of cider simmered slow,
And apples sputtered in a row.
And, close at hand, the basket stood
With nuts from brown October's woods.
What matter how the night behaved!
What matter how the north wind raved!
Blow high, blow low, not all its snow
Could quench our hearth-fire's ruddy glow."

Nor can the passing of years dim the ruddy glow
of that hearth-fire, nor the charm of the poem.
The simplicity of metre, the purity of wording, the
gentle sadness of some of its expressions, make us
read between the lines the deep and affectionate
reminiscence with which it was written.

CHAPTER IV

THE SERVING OF MEALS

PERHAPS no greater difference exists between any mode of the olden times and that of to-day, than can be seen in the manner of serving the meals of the family. In the first place, the very dining-table of the colonists was not like our present ones; it was a long and narrow board, sometimes but three feet wide, with no legs attached to it. It was laid on supports or trestles, shaped usually something like a saw-horse. Thus it was literally a board, and was called a table-board, and the linen cover used at meals was not called a table-cloth, but a board-cloth or board-clothes.

As smoothly sawed and finished boards were not so plentiful at first in the colonies as might naturally be thought when we remember the vast encircling forests, all such boards were carefully treasured, and used many times to avoid sawing others by the tedious and wearying process of pit-sawing. Hence portions of packing-boxes, or chests which had carried stores from England to the colonies, were made

76

into table-boards. One such oaken table-board, still in existence, has on the under side in quaint lettering the name and address of the Boston settler to whom the original packing-box was sent in 1638.

The old-time board-cloth was in no way inferior in quality or whiteness to our present table-linen; for we know how proud colonial wives and daughters were of the linen of their own spinning, weaving, and bleaching. The linen tablecloth was either of holland, huckaback, dowlas, osnaburg, or lockram — all heavy and comparatively coarse materials — or of fine damask, just as to-day; some of the handsome board-cloths were even trimmed with lace.

The colonists had plenty of napkins; more, as a rule, than families of corresponding means and station own to-day. They had need of them, for when America was first settled forks were almost unknown to English people — being used for eating in luxurious Italy alone, where travellers having seen and found them useful and cleanly, afterwards introduced them into England. So hands had to be constantly employed for holding food, instead of the forks we now use, and napkins were therefore as constantly necessary. The first fork brought to America was for Governor John Winthrop, in Boston, in 1633, and it was in a leather case with a knife and a bodkin. If the governor ate with a fork at the table, he was doubtless the only person in the colony who did so. Thirty or forty years later a few two-tined iron and silver forks were brought across the water, and used in New York and Virginia, as well as Massachusetts; and by the end of the century they had come into scant use at the tables of persons of wealth and fashion. The first mention of a fork in Virginia is in an inventory dated 1677; this was of a single fork. The salt-cellar, or saler, as it was first called, was the centrepiece of the table — "Sett in the myddys of the tabull," says an old treatise on laying the table. It was often large and high, of curious device in silver, and was then called a standing salt.

Harvard Standing Salt

Guests of honor were seated "above the salt," that is, near the end of the table where sat the host and hostess side by side; while children and persons who were not of much dignity or account as guests were placed "below the salt," that is, below the middle of the table.

There is owned by Harvard University, and here

shown in an illustration, " a great silver salt " given
to the college in 1644, when the new seat of learning was but eight years old.   At the table it divided
graduates, the faculty, and such, from the under-
graduates.   It was valued at £5 1s. 3d., at five
shillings an ounce, which was equal to a hundred
dollars to-day; a rich gift, which shows to me the
profound affection of the settlers for the new college.   It is inscribed with the name of the giver,
Mr. Richard Harris.   It is of simple English
design well known during that century, and made
in various sizes.   There is no doubt that many of
similar pattern, though not so heavy or so rich,
were seen on the tables of substantial colonists.
They are named in many wills.   Often a small projecting arm was attached to one side, over which a
folded napkin could be thrown to be used as a
cover; for the salt-cellar was usually kept covered,
not only to preserve cleanliness, but in earlier days
to prevent the ready introduction of poison.

There are some very entertaining and curious
old English books which were written in the sixteenth century to teach children and young rustics
correct and elegant manners at the table, and also
helpful ways in which to serve others.   These books
are called *The Babees Boke, The Boke of Nurture,
The Boke of Curteseye,* etc., and with the exception

of variations in the way of serving a dinner, and a few obsolete customs, and in the names and shapes and materials of the different dishes, plates, etc., used at the table, these books are just as instructive and sensible to-day as then. From them we learn that the only kind of table furnishings used at that time were cups to drink out of; spoons and knives to eat with; chafing-dishes to serve hot food; chargers for display and for serving large quantities of food; salt-cellars, and trenchers for use as plates. There were very few other table appointments used on any English table, either humble or great, when the Pilgrims landed at Plymouth.

One of the most important articles for setting the table was the trencher. These were made of wood, and often were only a block of wood, about ten or twelve inches square and three or four deep, hollowed down into a sort of bowl in the middle. In this the food was placed,—porridge, meat, vegetables, etc. Each person did not have even one of these simple dishes; usually two children, or a man and his wife, ate out of one trencher. This was a custom in England for many years; and some very great people, a duke and his wife, not more than a century and a half ago, sat side by side at the table and ate out of one plate to show their unity and affection. It is told of an old Connecticut settler, a deacon, that as he had a wood-turning mill, he thought he would have a trencher apiece for his children. So he turned a sufficient number of round trenchers in his mill. For this his neighbors deemed him deeply extravagant and putting on too many airs, both as to quantity and quality, since square trenchers, one for use by two persons, were good enough for any one, even a deacon. So great a warrior and so prominent a man in the colony as Miles Standish used wooden trenchers at the table, as also did all the early governors. Nor did they disdain to name them in their wills, as valued household possessions. For many years college boys at Harvard ate out of wooden trenchers at the college mess-table.

I have seen a curious old table top, or tableboard, which permitted diners seated at it to dispense with trenchers or plates. It was of heavy oak about six inches thick, and at intervals of about eighteen inches around its edge were scooped out deep, bowl-shaped holes about ten inches in diameter, in which each individual's share of the dinner was placed. After each meal the top was lifted off the trestles, thoroughly washed and dried, and was ready for the next meal.

Poplar-wood is an even, white, and shining wood.

G

Until the middle of this century poplar-wood trenchers and plates were used on the table in Vermont, and were really attractive dishes. From earliest days the Indians made and sold many bowls and trenchers of maple-wood knots. One of these bowls, owned by King Philip, is at the rooms of the Massachusetts Historical Society in Boston. Old wooden trenchers and "Indian bowls" can be seen at the Memorial Hall in Deerfield.

Wooden Trenchers, Spoons, Noggin, Caster, and Dishes

Bottles were made also of wood, and drinking-cups and "noggins," which were a sort of mug with a handle. Wood furnished many articles for the table to the colonist, just as it did in later days on our Western frontiers, where trenchers of wood and plates of birch-bark were seen in every log-cabin.

The word tankard was originally applied to a heavy and large vessel of wood banded with metal, in which to carry water. Smaller wooden drinking tankards were subsequently made and used throughout Europe, and were occasionally brought here by the colonists. The plainly shaped wooden tank-ard, made of staves and hoops and here shown, is from the collection at Deer-field Me-morial Hall. It was found in the house of Rev. Eli Moody. These com-monplace tankards of staves were not so rare as the beautiful carved and hooped tankard which is here pictured, and which is

Wooden Tankard

in the collection of Mrs. Samuel Bowne Duryea, of
Brooklyn.   I have seen a few other quaintly carved
ones, black with age, in American families of Hugue-
not descent; these were apparently Swiss carvings.

Carved Wooden Tankard

The chargers, or large round platters found on
every dining-table, were of pewter.   Some were so
big and heavy that they weighed five or six pounds
apiece.   Pewter is a metal never seen for modern

table furnishing, or domestic use in any form to-
day; but in colonial times what was called a garnish of pewter, that is, a full set of pewter platters,
plates, and dishes, was the pride of every good
housekeeper, and also a favorite wedding gift. It
was kept as bright and shining as silver. One of the
duties of children was to gather a kind of horse-tail
rush which grew in the marshes, and because it was
used to scour pewter, was called scouring-rush.

Pewter bottles of various sizes were sent to the
Massachusetts Bay Colony, in 1629. Governor
Endicott had one, but they were certainly far from
common. Dram cups, wine mugs, and funnels of
pewter were also occasionally seen, but scarcely
formed part of ordinary table furnishings. Metheglin cans and drinking-mugs of pewter were found
on nearly every table. Pewter was used until this
century in the wealthiest homes, both in the North
and South, and was preferred by many who owned
rich china. Among the pewter-lovers was the Revolutionary patriot, John Hancock, who hated the
clatter of the porcelain plates.

Porringers of pewter, and occasionally of silver,
were much used at the table, chiefly for children to
eat from. These were a pretty little shallow circular dish with a flat-pierced handle. Some had a
"fish-tail" handle; these are said to be Dutch.

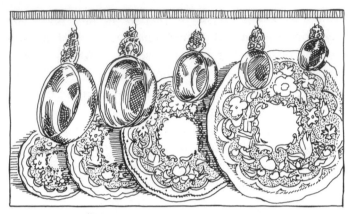

"The porringers that in a row
Hung high and made a glittering show "

These porringers were in many sizes, from tiny little ones two inches in diameter to those eight or nine inches across.   When not in use many house-keepers kept them hanging on hooks on the edge of a shelf, where they formed a pretty and cheerful decoration.   The poet Swift says : —

> "The porringers that in a row
> Hung high and made a glittering show."

It should be stated that the word porringer, as used by English collectors, usually refers to a deep cup with a cover and two handles, while what we call porringers are known to these collectors as bleeding-basins or tasters.   Here we apply the

term taster, or wine-taster, to a small, shallow silver
cup with bosses in the bottom to reflect the light
and show the color and quality of wine.   I have
often seen the item wine-taster in colonial inventories and wills, but never bleeding-basin; while
porringers were almost universal on such lists.
Some families had a dozen.   I have found fifteen
in one old New England farmhouse.   The small
porringers are sometimes called posnets, which is
an old-time word that may originally have referred
to a posset-cup.

"Spoons," says the learned archæologist, La-
borde, "if not as old as the world, are as old as
soup."   All the colonists had spoons, and certainly
all needed them, for at that time much of their food
was in the form of soup and "spoon-meat," such
as had to be eaten with spoons when there were no
forks.   Meat was usually made into hashes or
ragouts; thick stews and soups with chopped vegetables and meats were common, as were hotch pots.
The cereal foods, which formed so large a part of
English fare in the New World, were more frequently
boiled in porridge than baked in loaves.   Many of
the spoons were of pewter.   Worn-out pewter plates
and dishes could be recast into new pewter spoons.
The moulds were of wood or iron.   The spoon
mould of one of the first settlers of Greenfield,

Massachusetts, named Martindale, is here shown with a pewter spoon. In this mould all his spoons and those of his neighbors were cast. It is now in the Deerfield Memorial Hall.

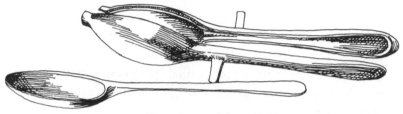

Pewter Spoon and Spoon Mould

A still more universal spoon material was alchymy, also called occamy, alcamy, arkamy, etc., a metal never used now, which was made of a mixture of pan-brass and arsenicum. Wooden spoons, too, were always seen. In Pennsylvania and New York laurel was called spoonwood, because the Indians made pretty white spoons from that wood to sell to the colonists. Horn was an appropriate and available material for spoons. Many Indian tribes excelled as they do to-day in the making of horn spoons. The vulgar affirmation, " By the great horn spoon," has perpetuated their familiar use.

Every family of any considerable possessions or owning good household furnishings had a few silver spoons; nearly every person owned at least one.

At the time America was settled the common form of silver spoon in England had what was known as a baluster stem and a seal head; the assay mark was in the inner part of the bowl.   But the fashion was just changing, and a new and much altered form was introduced which was made in large numbers until the opening reign of George I.   This shape was the very one without doubt in which many of the spoons of the first colonists were made; and wherever such spoons are found, if they are genuine

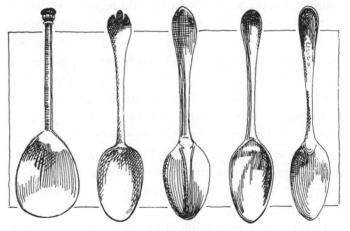

Five Types of Spoons

antiques, they may safely be assigned a date earlier than 1714.   The handle was flat and broad at the end, where it was cleft in three points which

were turned up, that is, not toward the back of the
spoon. This was known as the "hind's-foot
handle." The bowl was a perfectly regular ellipse
and was strengthened by continuing the handle in a
narrow tongue or rat-tail, which ran down the back
of the bowl. The succeeding fashion, in the early
part of the eighteenth century, had a longer elliptical
bowl. The end of the handle was rounded and
turned up at the end, and it had a high sharp ridge
down the middle. This was known as the old
English shape, and was in common use for half a
century. About the period of our Revolutionary
War a shape nearly like the one in ordinary present
use became the mode ; the bowl became egg-shaped,
and the end of the handle was turned down instead
of up. The rat-tail, which extended down the back
of the bowl, was shortened into a drop. Apostle
spoons, and monkey spoons for extraordinary use
were occasionally made, and a few are still preserved ; examples of five types of spoons are shown
from the collection of Edward Holbrook, Esq., of
New York.

Families of consequence had usually a few pieces
of silver besides their spoons and the silver salt.
Some kind of a drinking-cup was the usual form.
Persons of moderate means often owned a silver
cup. I have seen in early inventories and lists the

names of a large variety of silver vessels: tankards, beer-bowls, beakers, flagons, wine cups, wine bowls, wine cans, tasters, caudle-cups, posset-cups, dram-

Dutch Silver Tankard

cups, punch-bowls, tumblers, mugs, dram bottles, two-eared cups, and flasks. Virginians and Marylanders in the seventeenth century had much more silver than New Englanders. Some Dutch mer-

chants had ample amounts.   It was deemed a good
and safe investment for spare money.   Bread-
baskets, salvers, muffineers, chafing-dishes, casters,
milk pitchers, sugar boxes, candlesticks, appear in
inventories at the end of the century.   A tankard
or flagon, even if heavy and handsome, would be
placed on the table for every-day use; the other
pieces were usually set on the cupboard's head for
ornament.

The handsome silver tankard owned by Sarah
Jansen de Rapelje is here shown.   She was the first
child of European parents born in New Netherland.
The tankard was a wedding gift from her husband,
and a Dutch wedding scene is graven on the lid.

There was a great desire for glass, a rare novelty
to many persons at the date of colonization.   The
English were less familiar with its use than settlers
who came from Continental Europe.   The establishment of glass factories was attempted in early days
in several places, chiefly to manufacture sheet-
glass, but with slight success.   Little glass was
owned in the shape of drinking-vessels, none used
generally on the table, I think, during the first few
years.   Glass bottles were certainly a great rarity,
and were bequeathed with special mention in wills,
and they are the only form of glass vessel named.
The earliest glass for table use was greenish in

Colonial Glass Bottles

color, like coarse bottle glass, and poor in quality, sometimes decorated in crude designs in a few colors. Bristol glass, in the shape of mugs and plates, was next seen. It was opaque, a milky white color, and was coarsely decorated with vitrifiable colors in a few lines of red, green, yellow, or black, occasionally with initials, dates, or Scriptural references.

Though shapes were varied, and the number was generally plentiful, there was no attempt made to give separate drinking-cups of any kind to each individual at the table. Blissfully ignorant of the existence or presence of microbes, germs, and bacteria, our sturdy and unsqueamish forbears drank contentedly in succession from a single vessel,

which was passed from hand to hand, and lip
to lip, around the board. Even when tumbler-
shaped glasses were seen in many houses, — flip-
glasses, they were called, — they were of communal
size, — some held a gallon, — and all drank from the
same glass. The great punch-bowl, not a very
handy vessel to handle when filled with punch,
was passed up and down as freely as though it
were a loving-cup, and all drank from its brim.
At college tables, and even at tavern boards, where
table neighbors might be strangers, the flowing bowl

Old Spanish and English Glasses, Iron Loggerheads, and Wooden Toddy Sticks

and foaming tankard was passed serenely from one
to another, and replenished to pass again.

Leather was perhaps the most curious material

used. Pitchers, bottles, and drinking-cups were made of it. Great jugs of heavy black leather, waxed and bound, and tipped with silver, were used to hold metheglin, ale, and beer, and were a very substantial, and at times a very handsome ves-

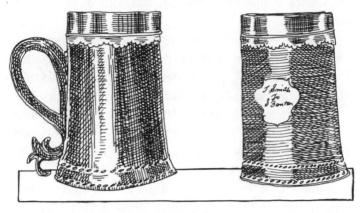

Black Jacks

scl. The finest examples I have ever seen are here represented. The stitches and waxed thread at the base and on the handles can plainly be perceived. They are bound with a rich silver band, and have a silver shield bearing a date of gift to Samuel Brenton in 1778; but they are probably a century older than that date. They are the property by inheritance of Miss Rebecca Shaw, aged ninety-six years, of Wickford, Rhode Island.

The use of these great leather jacks, in a clumsier form than here shown, led to the amusing mistake of a French traveller, that the English drank their ale out of their boots. These leather jugs were commonly called black jacks, and the larger ones were bombards. Giskin was still another and rarer name.

Drinking-cups were sometimes made of horn. A handsome one has been used since colonial days on Long Island for "quince drink," a potent mixture of hot rum, sugar, and quince marmalade, or preserves. It has a base of silver, a rim of silver, and a cover of horn tipped with silver. A stirrup-cup of horn, tipped with silver, was used to "speed the parting guest." Occasionally the whole horn, in true mediæval fashion, was used as a drinking-cup. Often they were carved with considerable skill, as the beautiful ones in the collection of Mr. A. G. Richmond, of Canajoharie, New York.

Gourds were plentiful on the farm, and gathered with care, that the hard-shelled fruit might be shaped into simple drinking-cups. In Elizabeth's time silver cups were made in the shape of these gourds. The ships that brought "lemmons and raysins of the sun" from the tropics to the colonists, also brought cocoanuts. Since the thirteenth century the shells of cocoanuts have been mounted with silver feet and " covercles " in a goblet shape, and been much sought after by Englishmen. Mounted in pewter, and sometimes in silver, or simply shaped with a wooden handle attached, the shell of the cocoanut was a favorite among the English settlers. To this day one of the cocoanut-shell cups, or dippers, is a favorite drinking-cup of many. A handsome cocoanut goblet, richly mounted in silver, is shown in the accompanying

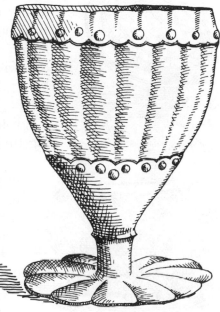

Silver-mounted Cocoanut Drinking-cup

illustration. It was once the property of the Revolutionary patriot, John Hancock, and is now in the custody of the Bostonian Society, at the Old State House, in Boston, Massachusetts.

Popular drinking-mugs of the English, from which specially they drank their mead, metheglin, and ale, were the stoneware jugs which were made in Germany and England, in the sixteenth and seventeenth centuries, in great numbers. An English writer in 1579, spoke of the English custom of drinking from "pots of earth, of sundry colors and moulds, whereof many are garnished with silver, or least-vise with pewter."

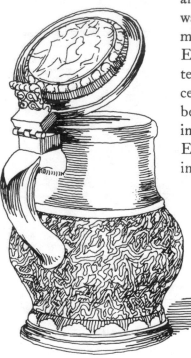

Winthrop Jug

Such a piece of stoneware is the oldest authenticated drinking-jug in this country, which was brought here and used by English colonists. It was the property of Governor John Winthrop, who came to Boston in 1630, and now belongs to the American Antiqua-

rian Society, in Worcester, Massachusetts.   It
stands eight inches in height, is apparently of German Gresware, and is heavily mounted in silver.
The lid is engraved with a quaint design of Adam
and Eve and the tempting serpent in the apple-
tree.   It was a gift to John Winthrop's father
from his sister, Lady Mildmay, in 1607, and was
then, and is still now, labelled, " a stone Pot tipped
and covered with a Silver
Lydd." Many other Bos-
ton colonists had similar
" stone juggs," " fflanders
juggs," "tipt juggs."
What were known
as " Fulham juggs "
were also much
prized. The most
interesting ones are
the Georgius Rex
jugs, those marked
with a crown, the
initials G. R., or a
medallion head of
the first of the Eng-
lish Georges. I

Georgius Rex Jug

know one of these jugs which has a Revolutionary
bullet imbedded in its tough old side, and is not

even cracked.   Many of them had pewter or silver
lids, which are now missing.   Some have the curious hound handle which was so popular with English potters.

There was no china in common use on the table,
and little owned even by persons of wealth throughout the seventeenth century, either in England or
America.   Delft ware was made in several factories
in Holland at the time the Dutch settled in New
Netherland; but even in the towns of its manufacture it was not used for table ware.   The pieces
were usually of large size, what were called state
pieces, for cabinet and decorative purposes.   The
Dutch settlers, however, had " purslin cupps " and
earthen dishes in considerable quantities toward the
end of the century.   The earthen was possibly
Delft ware, and the " Purslin " India china, which
by that time was largely imported to Holland.
Some Portuguese and Spanish pottery was imported,
but was not much desired, as it was ill fired and
perishable.   It was not until Revolutionary times
that china was a common table furnishing; then it
began to crowd out pewter.   The sudden and
enormous growth of East India commerce, and the
vast cargoes of Chinese pottery and porcelain wares
brought to American ports soon gave ample china
to every housewife.   In the Southern colonies

beautiful isolated pieces of porcelain, such as vast
punch-bowls, often were found in the homes of
opulent planters ; but there, as in the North, the
first china for general table use was the handleless
tea-cups, usually of some Canton ware, which crept
with the fragrant herb into every woman's heart —
both welcome Oriental waifs.

It may well be imagined that this long narrow
table — with a high salt-cellar in the middle, with
clumsy wooden trenchers for plates, with round
pewter platters heaped high with the stew of meat
and vegetables, with a great noggin or two of wood,
a can of pewter, or a silver tankard to drink from,
with leather jacks to hold beer or milk, with many
wooden or pewter and some silver spoons, but no
forks, no glass, no china, no covered dishes, no
saucers — did not look much like our dinner tables
to-day.

Even the seats were different; there were seldom
chairs or stools for each person. A long narrow
bench without a back, called a form, was placed on
each side of the table. Children in many households were not allowed to sit, even on these uncomfortable forms, while eating. Many times they had
to stand by the side of the table during the entire
meal ; in old-fashioned families that uncomfortable
and ungracious custom lasted till this century. I

know of children not fifty years ago standing thus
at all meals at the table of one of the Judges of the
Supreme Court. He had a bountiful table, was a
hospitable entertainer and well-known epicure ;
but children sat not at his board. Each stood at
his own place and had to behave with decorum and
eat in entire silence. In some families children
stood behind their parents and other grown persons,
and food was handed back to them from the table —
so we are told. This seems closely akin to throwing food to an animal, and must have been among
people of very low station and social manners.

In other houses they stood at a side-table ; and,
trencher in hand, ran over to the great table to be
helped to more food when their first supply was
eaten.

The chief thought on the behavior of children at
the table, which must be inferred from all the accounts we have of those times is that they were to
eat in silence, as fast as possible (regardless of indi-
gestion), and leave the table as speedily as might be.
In a little book called *A Pretty Little Pocket Book*,
printed in America about the time of the Revolution,
I found a list of rules for the behavior of children
at the table at that date. They were ordered never
to seat themselves at the table until after the bless-
ing had been asked, and their parents told them to

be seated. They were never to ask for anything on the table; never to speak unless spoken to; always to break the bread, not to bite into a whole slice; never to take salt except with a clean knife; not to throw bones under the table. One rule read: "Hold not thy knife upright, but sloping; lay it down at right hand of the plate, with end of blade on the plate." Another, "Look not earnestly at any other person that is eating." When children had eaten all that had been given them, if they were "moderately satisfied," they were told to leave at once the table and room.

When the table-board described herein was set with snowy linen cloth and napkins, and ample fare, it had some compensations for what modern luxuries it lacked, some qualifications for inducing contentment superior even to our beautiful table-settings. There was nothing perishable in its entire furnishing: no frail and costly china or glass, whose injury and destruction by clumsy or heedless servants would make the heart of the housekeeper ache, and her anger nourish the germs of ptomaines within her. There was little of intrinsic value to watch and guard and worry about. There was little to make extra and difficult work, — no glass to wash with anxious care, no elaborate silver to clean, — only a few pieces of pewter to polish occasionally.

It was all so easy and so simple when compared with the complex and varied paraphernalia and accompaniments of serving of meals to-day, that it was like Arcadian simplicity.

In Virginia the table furnishings were similar to those in New England; but there were greater contrasts in table appointments. There was more silver, and richer food; but the negro servants were so squalid, clumsy, and uncouth that the incongruity made the meals very surprising and, at times, repellent.

When dinners of some state were given in the larger towns, the table was not set or served like the formal dinner of to-day, for all the sweets, pastry, vegetables, and meats were placed on the table together, with a grand " conceit" for the ornament in the centre. At one period, when pudding was part of the dinner, it was served first. Thus an old-time saying is explained, which always seemed rather meaningless, " I came early — in pudding-time." There was considerable formality in portioning out the food, especially in carving, which was regarded as much more than a polite accomplishment, even as an art. I have seen a list of sixty or seventy different terms in carving to be applied with exactness to different fish, fowl, and meats. An old author says : —

"How all must regret to hear some Persons, even of quality say, 'pray cut up that Chicken or Hen,' or 'Halve that Plover'; not considering how indiscreetly they talk, when the proper Terms are, 'break that Goose,' 'thrust that Chicken,' 'spoil that Hen,' 'pierce that Plover.' If they are so much out in common Things, how much more would they be with Herons, Cranes, and Peacocks."

It must have required good judgment and constant watchfulness never to say "spoil that Hen," when it was a chicken; or else be thought hopelessly ill-bred.

There were few state dinners, however, served in the American colonies, even in the large cities; there were few dinners, even, of many courses; not always were there many dishes. There were still seen in many homes more primitive forms of serving and eating meals, than were indicated by the lack of individual drinking-cups, the mutual use of a trencher, or even the utilization of the table top as a plate. In some homes an abundant dish, such as a vast bowl of suppawn and milk, a pumpkin stewed whole in its shell, or a savory and mammoth hotchpot was set, often smoking hot, on the table-board; and from this well-filled receptacle each hungry soul, armed with a long-handled pewter or wooden spoon, helped himself, sometimes ladling his great spoonfuls into a trencher or bowl, for more moderate and reserved after-consumption,—just as frequently eating directly from the bountiful dish with a spoon that came and went from dish to mouth without reproach, or thought of ill-manners. The accounts of travellers in all the colonies frequently tell of such repasts; some termed it eating in the fashion of the Dutch. The reports of old settlers often recall the general dish; and some very distinguished persons joined in the circle around it, and were glad to get it. Variety was of little account, compared to quantity and quality. A cheerful hospitality and grateful hearts filled the hollow place of formality and elegance.

By the time that newspapers began to have advertisements in them — about 1750 — we find many more articles for use at the table; but often the names were different from those used to-day. Our sugar bowls were called sugar boxes and sugar pots; milk pitchers were milk jugs, milk ewers, and milk pots. Vegetable dishes were called basins, pudding dishes twifflers, small cups were called sneak cups.

We have still to-day a custom much like one of olden times, when we have the crumbs removed from our tables after a course at dinner. Then a voider was passed around the table near the close of the dinner, and into it the persons at the table placed their trenchers, napkins, and the crumbs from the table. The voider was a deep wicker, wooden, or metal basket. In the *Boke of Nurture*, written in 1577, are these lines : —

> " When meate is taken quyte awaye
> And Voyders in presence,
> Put you your trenchour in the same
> and all your resydence.
> Take you with your napkin & knyfe
> the croms that are fore the,
> In the Voyder your Napkin leave
> for it is a curtesye."

CHAPTER V

FOOD FROM FOREST AND SEA

THOUGH all the early explorers and travellers came to America eager to find precious and useful metals, they did not discover wealth and prosperity underground in mines, but on the top of the earth, in the woods and fields. To the forests they turned for food, and they did not turn in vain. Deer were plentiful everywhere, and venison was offered by the Indians to the first who landed from the ships. Some families lived wholly on venison for nine months of the year. In Virginia were vast numbers of red and fallow deer, the latter like those of England, except in the smaller number of branches of the antlers. They were so devoid of fear as to remain undisturbed by the approach of men; a writer of that day says: "Hard by the Fort two hundred in one herd have been usually observed." They were destroyed ruthlessly by a system of fire-hunting, in which tracts of forests were burned over, by starting a continuous circle of fire miles around, which burnt in toward the centre of the circle; thus the deer were driven into the middle, and hundreds were killed. This miserable, wholesale slaughter was not for venison, but for the sake of the hides, which were very valuable. They were used to make the durable and suitable buckskin breeches and jackets so much worn by the settlers; and they were also exported to Europe in large numbers. A tax was placed on hides for the support of the beloved William and Mary College.

In Georgia, in 1735, the Indians sold a deer for sixpence. Deer were just as abundant in the more Northern colonies. At Albany a stag was sold readily by the Indians for a jack-knife or a few iron nails. The deer in winter came and fed from the hog-pens of Albany swine. Even in 1695, a quarter of venison could be bought in New York City for ninepence. At the first Massachusetts Thanksgiving, in 1621, the Indians brought in five deer to the colonists for their feast. That year there was also "great store of wild turkies." These beautiful birds of gold and purple bronze were at first plentiful everywhere, and were of great weight, far larger than our domestic turkeys to-day. They came in flocks of a hundred, Evelyn says of three hundred on the Chesapeake, and they weighed thirty or forty pounds

each : Josselyn says he saw one weighing sixty
pounds. William Penn wrote that turkeys weighing thirty pounds apiece sold in his day and colony
for a shilling only. They were shy creatures and
fled inland from the white man, and by 1690 were
rarely shot near the coast of New England, though
in Georgia, in 1733, they were plentiful enough and
cheap enough to sell for fourpence apiece. Flights
of pigeons darkened the sky, and broke down the
limbs of trees on which they lighted. From Maine
to Virginia these vast flocks were seen. Some years
pigeons were so plentiful that they were sold for a
penny a dozen in Boston. Pheasant, partridge,
woodcock, and quail abounded, plover, snipe, and
curlew were in the marsh-woods; in fact, in Virginia
every bird familiar to Englishmen at home was
found save peacock and domestic fowl.

Wild hare and squirrels were so many that they
became pests, and so much grain was eaten by them
that bounties were paid in many towns for the heads
of squirrels. County treasuries were exhausted by
these premiums. The Swedish traveller, Kalm,
said that in Pennsylvania in one year, 1749, £8000
was paid out for heads of black and gray squirrels,
at threepence a head, which would show that over
six hundred thousand were killed.

From the woods came a sweet food-store, one

specially grateful when sugar was so scarce and so high-priced, — wild honey, which the colonists eagerly gathered everywhere from hollow tree-trunks. Curiously enough, the traveller, Kalm, insisted that bees were not native in America, but were brought over by the English; that the Indians had no name for them and called them English flies.

Governor Berkeley of Virginia, writing in 1706, called the maple the sugar-tree; he said: —

"The Sugar-Tree yields a kind of Sap or Juice which by boiling is made into Sugar. This Juice is drawn out, by wounding the Trunk of the Tree, and placing a Receiver under the Wound. It is said that the Indians make one Pound of Sugar out of eight Pounds of the Liquor. It is bright and moist with a full large Grain, the Sweetness of it being like that of good Muscovada."

The sugar-making season was ever hailed with delight by the boys of the household in colonial days, who found in this work in the woods a wonderful outlet for the love of wild life which was strong in them. It had in truth a touch of going a-gypsying, if any work as hard as sugaring-off could have anything common with gypsy life. The maple-trees were tapped as soon as the sap began to run in the trunk and showed at the end of the twigs; this was in late winter if mild, or in the earliest spring. A notch was cut in the trunk of the tree at a convenient height from the ground, usually four or five feet, and the running sap was guided by setting in the notch a semicircular basswood spout cut and set with a special tool called a tapping-gauge. In earlier days the trees were " boxed," that is, a great gash cut across the side and scooped out and down to gather the sap. This often proved fatal to the trees, and was abandoned. A trough, usually made of a butternut log about three feet long, was dug out, Indian fashion, and placed under the end of the spout. These troughs were made deep enough to hold about ten quarts. In later years a hole was bored in the tree with an augur; and sap-buckets were used instead of troughs.

Sometimes these troughs were left in distant sugar-camps from year to year, turned bottom side up, through the summer and winter. It was more thrifty and tidy, however, to carry them home and store them. When this was done, the men and boys began work by drawing the troughs and spouts and provisions to the woods on hand-sleds. Sometimes a mighty man took in a load on his back. It is told of John Alexander of Brattleboro, Vermont, that he once went into camp *upon snow-shoes* carrying for three miles one five-pail iron kettle, two sap-buckets, an axe and trappings, a knapsack, four days' provisions, and a gun and ammunition.

The master of ceremonies — the owner of the camp — selected the trees and drove the spouts, while the boys placed the troughs. Then the snow had to be shovelled away on a level spot about eighteen or twenty feet square, in which strong forked sticks were set twelve feet apart. Or the ground was chosen so that two small low-spreading and strong trees could be trimmed and used as forks. A heavy green stick was placed across from fork to fork, and the sugaring-off kettles, sometimes five in number, hung on it. Then dry wood had to be gathered for the fires; hard work it was to keep them constantly supplied. It was often cut a year in advance. As the sap collected in the troughs it was gathered in pails or buckets which, hung on a sap-yoke across the neck, were brought to the kettles and the sap set a-boiling down. When there was a "good run of sap," it was usually necessary to stay in the camp over night. Many times the campers stayed several nights. As the "good run" meant milder weather, a night or two was not a bitter experience; indeed, I have never heard any one speak nor seen any account of a night spent in a sugar-camp except with keen expressions of delight. If possible, the time was chosen during a term of

i

moonlight; the snow still covered the fields and its pure shining white light could be seen through the trees.

> "God makes sech nights, so white and still
> Fer's you can look and listen.
> Moonlight an' snow, on field and hill,
> All silence and all glisten."

The great silence, broken only by steady dropping of the sap, the crackle of blazing brush, and the occasional hooting of startled owls; the stars seen singly overhead through the openings of the trees, shining down the dark tunnel as bright as though there were no moon; above all, the clearness and sweetness of the first atmosphere of spring, — gave an exaltation of the senses and spirit which the country boy felt without understanding, and indeed without any formulated consciousness.

If the camp were near enough to any group of farmhouses to have visitors, the last afternoon and evening in camp was made a country frolic. Great sled-loads of girls came out to taste the new sugar, to drop it into the snow to candy, and to have an evening of fun.

Long ere the full riches of the forests were tested the colonists turned to another food-supply, — the treasures of the sea.

The early voyagers and colonists came to the

coasts of the New World to find gold and furs. The gold was not found by them nor their children's children in the land which is now the United States, till over two centuries had passed from the time of the settlement, and the gold-mines of California were opened. The furs were at first found and profitably gathered, but the timid fur-bearing animals were soon exterminated near the settlements. There was, however, a vast wealth ready for the colonists on the coast of the New World which was greater than gold, greater than furs; a wealth ever-obtainable, ever-replenished, ever-useful, ever-salable; it was *fish*. The sea, the rivers, the lakes, teemed with fish. Not only was there food for the settlers, but for the whole world, and all Europe desired fish to eat. The ships of the early discoverer, Gosnold, in 1602, were "pestered with cod." Captain John Smith, the acute explorer, famous in history as befriended by Pocahontas, went to New England, in 1614, to seek for whale, and instead he fished for cod. He secured sixty thousand in one month; and he wrote to his countrymen, "Let not the meanness of the word *fish* distaste you, for it will afford as good gold as the mines of Guiana or Potosi, with less hazard and charge, and more certainty and facility." This promise of wealth has proved true a thousandfold. Smith wrote home to

England full accounts of the fisheries, of the proper
equipment of a fishing-vessel, of the methods of
fishing, the profits, all in a most enticing and familiar style.   He said in his *Description of New England* : —

"What pleasure can be more than to recreate themselves before their owne doores in their owne boates, upon
the Sea, where man, woman, and childe, with a small hooke
and line by angling, may take diverse sorts of excellent fish,
at their pleasure ?   And is it not pretty sport to pull up
twopence, sixpence, or twelvepence, as fast as you can hale
and veare a line ?   If a man worke but three days in seaven
hee may get more than hee can spend unless hee will be
excessive.

"Young boyes and girles, salvages, or any other, be they
never such idlers may turne, carry, and returne fish without
shame or either great pain: hee is very idle that is past
twelve years of age and cannot doe so much: and shee is
very old that cannot spin a thread to catch them."

His accounts and similar ones were so much read
in England that when the Puritans asked King
James of England for permission to come to America, and the king asked what profit would be found
by their emigration, he was at once answered, " Fishing."   Whereupon he said in turn, " In truth 'tis
an honest trade; 'twas the apostles' own calling."
Yet in spite of their intent to fish, the first English

ships came but poorly provided for fishing, and the settlers had little success at first even in getting fish for their own food.   Elder Brewster of Plymouth, who had been a courtier in Queen Elizabeth's time, and had seen and eaten many rich feasts, had nothing to eat at one time but clams.   Yet he could give thanks to God that he was " permitted to suck of the abundance of the seas and the treasures hid in the sand."   The Indian Squanto showed the Pilgrims many practical methods of fishing, among them one of treading out eels from the brook with his feet and catching them with his hands.   And every ship brought in either cod-hooks and lines, mackerel-hooks and lines, herring-nets, seines, shark-hooks, bass-nets, squid-lines, eel-pots, coils of rope and cable, " drails, barbels, pens, gaffs," or mussel-hooks.

Josselyn, in his *New England's Rarities*, written in 1672, enumerated over two hundred kinds of fish that were caught in New England waters.

Lobsters certainly were plentiful enough to prevent starvation.   The minister Higginson, writing of lobsters at Salem, said that many of them weighed twenty-five pounds apiece, and that " the least boy in the plantation may catch and eat what he will of them."   In 1623, when the ship *Anne* arrived from England, bringing many of the wives and children of the Pilgrims who had come in the first ships, the only feast of welcome that the poor husbands had to offer the newcomers was "a lobster or a piece of fish without bread or anything else but a cup of spring water."

Patriarchal lobsters five and six feet long were caught in New York Bay. The traveller, Van der Donck, says "those a foot long are better for serving at table." Truly a lobster six feet long would seem a little awkward to serve on a dinner table. Eddis, in his *Letters from America,* written in 1792, says these vast lobsters were caught in New York waters until Revolutionary days, when "since the incessant cannonading, they have entirely forsaken the coast; not one having been taken or seen since the commencement of hostilities." Beside these great shell-fish the giant lobster confined in our New York Aquarium in 1897 seems but a dwarf. In Virginia waters lobsters were caught, and vast crabs, often a foot in length and six inches broad, with a long tail and many legs. One of these crabs furnished a sufficient meal for four men.

From the gossiping pages of the Labadist missionaries who came to America in 1697 we find hints of good fare in oysters in Brooklyn.

"Then was thrown upon the fire, to be roasted, a pail full of Gowanes oysters which are the best in the country. They are fully as good as those of England, better than those we eat at Falmouth. I had to try some of them raw. They are large and full, some of them not less than a foot long. Others are young and small. In consequence of the great quantities of them everybody keeps the shells for the burning of lime. They pickle the oysters in small casks and send them to Barbados."

Van der Donck corroborates the foot-long oysters seen by the Labadist travellers. He says the "large oysters roasted or stewed make a good bite," —a very good bite, it would seem to us.

Strachey, in his *Historie of Travaile into Virginia,* says he saw oysters in Virginia that were thirteen inches long. Fortunately for the starving Virginians, oyster banks rose above the surface at ebb-tide at the mouth of the Elizabeth River, and in 1609 a large number of these famished Virginia colonists found in these oyster banks a means of preservation of life.

As might be expected of any country so intersected with arms of the sea and fresh-water streams, Virginia at the time of settlement teemed with fish. The Indians killed them in the brooks by striking them with sticks, and it is said the colonists scooped them up in frying-pans. Horses ridden into the

rivers stepped on the fish and killed them.   In one
cast of a seine the governor, Sir Thomas Dale,
caught five thousand sturgeon as large as cod.
Some sturgeon were twelve feet long.   The works
of Captain John Smith, Rolfe's *Relation*, and other
books of early travellers, all tell of the enormous
amount of fish in Virginia.

The New York rivers were also full of fish, and
the bays; their plenty in New Netherland inspired
the first poet of that colony to rhyming enumera-
tion of the various kinds of fish found there; among
them were sturgeon — beloved of the Indians and
despised of Christians; and terrapin — not despised
by any one.   "Some persons," wrote the Dutch
traveller, Van der Donck, in 1656, "prepare delicious dishes from the water terrapin, which is luscious food."   The Middle and Southern states paid
equally warm but more tardy tribute to the terrapin's reputation as luscious food.

While other fish were used everywhere for food,
cod was the great staple of the fishing industry.
By the year 1633 Dorchester and Marblehead had
started in the fisheries for trading purposes.   Sturgeon also was caught at a little later date, and bass
and alewives.

Morton, in his *New England Canaan*, written in
1636, says, "I myself at the turning of the tyde have

seen such multitudes of sea bass that it seemed to
me that one might goe over their backs dri-shod."

The regulation of fish-weirs soon became an
important matter in all towns where streams let alewives up from the sea. The New England ministers took a hand in promoting and encouraging
the fisheries, as they did all positive social movements and commercial benefits. Rev. Hugh Peter
in Salem gave the fisheries a specially good turn.
Fishermen were excused from military training,
and portions of the common stock of corn were
assigned to them. The General Court of Massachusetts exempted " vessels and stock " from
" country charges " (which were taxes) for seven
years. Seashore towns assigned free lands to each
boat to be used for stays and flakes for drying. As
early as 1640 three hundred thousand dried codfish were sent to market from New England.

Codfish consisted of three sorts, " marchantable,
middling, and refuse." The first grade was sold
chiefly to Roman Catholic Europe, to supply the
constant demands of the fast-days of that religion,
and also those of the Church of England; the
second was consumed at home or in the merchant
vessels of New England; the third went to the
negroes of the West Indies, and was often called
Jamaica fish. The dun-fish or dumb-fish, as the

word was sometimes written, were the best; so
called from the dun-color. Fish was always eaten
in New England for a Saturday dinner; and Mr.
Palfrey, the historian, says that until this century
no New England dinner on Saturday, even a formal dinner party, was complete without dun-fish
being served.

Of course the first fishing-vessels had to be built
and sent from England. Some carried fifty men.
They arrived on the coast in early spring, and by
midsummer sailed home. The crew had for wages
one-third share of the fish and oil; another third
paid for the men's food, the salt, nets, hooks, lines,
etc.; the other third went to the ship's owners for
profit.

This system was not carried out in New England. There, each fisherman worked on " his own
hook " — and it was literally his own hook; for a
tally was kept of the fish caught by each man, and
the proceeds of the trip were divided in proportion
to the number of fish each caught. When there
was a big run of fish, the men never stopped to eat
or sleep, but when food was held to them gnawed
it off while their hands were employed with the fish-
lines. With every fishing-vessel that left Gloucester and Marblehead, the chief centres of the fishing
industries, went a boy of ten or twelve to learn to be

a skilled fisherman.   He was called a " cut-tail,"
for he cut a wedge-shaped bit from the tail of every
fish he caught, and when the fish were sorted out
the cut-tails showed the boy's share of the profit.

For centuries, fish was plentiful and cheap in
New England.   The traveller Bennet wrote of
Boston, in 1740 : —

"Fish is exceedingly cheap.   They sell a fine cod, will
weigh a dozen pounds or more, just taken out of the sea
for about twopence sterling.   They have smelts, too,
which they sell as cheap as sprats in London.   Salmon,
too, they have in great plenty, and these they sell for about
a shilling apiece which will weigh fourteen or fifteen
pounds."

Two kinds of delicious fish, beloved, perhaps,
above all others to-day, — salmon and shad, — seem
to have been lightly regarded in colonial days.
The price of salmon — less than a penny a pound
— shows the low estimation in which it was held in
the early years of the eighteenth century.   It is told
that farm-laborers in the vicinity of the Connecticut
River when engaged to work stipulated that they
should have salmon for dinner but once a week.

Shad were profoundly despised ; it was even held
to be somewhat disreputable to eat them ; and the
story is told of a family in Hadley, Massachusetts,
who were about to dine on shad, that, hearing a knock

at the door, they would not open it till the platter holding the obnoxious shad had been hidden.   At first they were fed chiefly to hogs.   Two shad for a penny was the ignoble price in 1733, and it was never much higher until after the Revolution. After shad and salmon acquired a better reputation as food, the falls of various rivers became great resorts for American fishermen as they had been for the Indians.   Both kinds of fish were caught in scoop-nets and seines below the falls.   Men came from a distance and loaded horses and carts with the fish to carry home.   Every farmhouse near was filled with visitors.   It was estimated that at the falls at South Hadley there were fifteen hundred horses in one day.

Salted fish was as carefully prepared and amiably regarded for home use in New England and New York as in England and Holland at the same date. The ling and herring of the old countries of Europe gave place in America to cod, shad, and mackerel. The greatest pains was taken in preparing, drying, and salting the plentiful fish.   It is said that in New York towns, such as New York and Brooklyn, after shad became a popular fish, great heaps were left when purchased at each door, and that the necessary cleaning and preparation of the shad was done on the street.   As all housewives purchased shad and salted and packed at about the same time, those public scavengers, the domestic hogs who roamed the town streets unchecked (and ever welcomed), must have been specially useful at shad-time.

Not in the waters, but of it, were the magnificent tribes of marine fowl that, undiminished by the feeble weapons and few numbers of the Indians, had peopled for centuries the waters of the New World. The Chesapeake and its tributaries furnished each autumn vast feeding-grounds of wild celery and other aquatic plants to millions of those creatures. The firearms of Captain John Smith and his two companions were poor things compared with the fowling-pieces of to-day, but with their three shots they killed a hundred and forty-eight ducks at one firing. The splendid wild swan wheeled and trumpeted in the clear autumn air; the wild geese flew there in their beautiful V-shaped flight; duck in all the varieties known to modern sportsmen — canvas-back, mallard, widgeon, redhead, oxeye, dottrel — rested on the Chesapeake waters in vast flocks a mile wide and seven miles long. Governor Berkeley named also brant, shell drake, teal, and blewings. The sound of their wings was said to be "like a great storm coming over the water." For centuries these ducks have been killed by the white man, and still they return each autumn to their old feeding-places.

CHAPTER VI

A GREAT field of tall Indian corn waving its stately and luxuriant green blades, its graceful spindles, and glossy silk under the hot August sun, should be not only a beautiful sight to every American, but a suggestive one; one to set us thinking of all that Indian corn means to us in our history. It was a native of American soil at the settlement of this country, and under full and thoroughly intelligent cultivation by the Indians, who were also native sons of the New World. Its abundance, adaptability, and nourishing qualities not only saved the colonists' lives, but altered many of their methods of living, especially their manner of cooking and their tastes in food.

One of the first things that every settler in a new land has to learn is that he must find food in that land; that he cannot trust long to any supplies of food which he has brought with him, or to any fresh supplies which he has ordered to be sent after him. He must turn at once to hunting, fishing, planting, to furnish him with food grown and found in the very place where he is.

This was quickly learned by the colonists in America, except in Virginia, where they had sad starving-times before all were convinced that corn was a better crop for settlers than silk or any of the many hoped-for productions which might be valuable in one sense but which could not be eaten. Powhatan, the father of the Indian princess Pocahontas, was one of the first to " send some of his People that they may teach the English how to sow the Grain of his Country." Captain John Smith, ever quick to learn of every one and ever practical, got two Indians, in the year 1608, to show him how to break up and plant forty acres of corn, which yielded him a good crop. A succeeding governor of Virginia, Sir Thomas Dale, equally practical, intelligent, and determined, assigned small farms to each colonist, and encouraged and enforced the growing of corn. Soon many thousand bushels were raised. There was a terrible Indian massacre in 1622, for the careless colonists, in order to be free to give their time to the raising of that new and exceedingly alluring and high-priced crop, tobacco, had given the Indians firearms to go hunting game for them; and the lesson of easy killing with powder and shot, when once learned, was turned with havoc

upon the white men.   The following year comparatively little corn was planted, as the luxuriant foliage made a perfect ambush for the close approach
of the savages to the settlements.   There was, of
course, scarcity and famine as the result; and a
bushel of corn-meal became worth twenty to thirty
shillings, which sum had a value equal to twenty to
thirty dollars to-day.   The planters were each com-
pelled by the magistrates the following year to raise
an ample amount of corn to supply all the families;
and to save a certain amount for seed as well.   There
has been no lack of corn since that time in Virginia.

The French colonists in Louisiana, perhaps because they were accustomed to more dainty food
than the English, fiercely hated corn, as have the
Irish in our own day.   A band of French women
settlers fairly raised a " petticoat rebellion " in revolt
against its daily use.   A despatch of the governor
of Louisiana says of these rebels: —

" The men in the colony begin through habit to use
corn as an article of food; but the women, who are mostly
Parisians, have for this food a dogged aversion, which has
not been subdued.   They inveigh bitterly against His
Grace, the Bishop of Quebec, who, they say, has enticed
them away from home under pretext of sending them to
enjoy the milk and honey of the land of promise."

This hatred of corn was shared by other races. An old writer says : —

"Peter Martyr could magnifie the Spaniards, of whom he reports they led a miserable life for three days together, with parched grain of maize onlie " —

which, when compared with the diet of New England settlers for weeks at a time, seems such a bagatelle as to be scarce worth the mention of Peter Martyr. By tradition, still commemorated at Forefathers' Dinners, the ration of Indian corn supplied to each person in the colony in time of famine was but five kernels.

The stores brought over by the Pilgrims were poor and inadequate enough ; the beef and pork were tainted, the fish rotten, the butter and cheese corrupted. European wheat and seeds did not mature well. Soon, as Bradford says in his now famous *Log-Book*, in his picturesque and forcible English, "the grim and grizzled face of starvation stared" at them. The readiest supply to replenish the scanty larder was fish, but the English made surprisingly bungling work over fishing, and soon the most unfailing and valuable supply was the native Indian corn, or " Guinny wheat," or " Turkie wheat," as it was called by the colonists.

Famine and pestilence had left eastern Massachu-

K

setts comparatively bare of inhabitants at the time
of the settlement of Plymouth ; and the vacant corn-
fields of the dead Indian cultivators were taken and
planted by the weak and emaciated Plymouth men,
who never could have cleared new fields.   From the
teeming sea, in the April run of fish, was found the
needed fertilizer.   Says Governor Bradford : —

"In April of the first year they began to plant their
corne, in which service Squanto stood them in great stead,
showing them both ye manner how to set it, and after, how
to dress and tend it."

From this planting sprang not only the most useful
food, but the first and most pregnant industry of the
colonists.

The first fields and crops were communal, and
the result was disastrous.   The third year, at the
sight of the paralyzed settlement, Governor Bradford wisely decided, as did Governor Dale of Virginia, that "they should set corne every man for his
owne particuler, furnishing a portion for public officers, fishermen, etc., who could not work, and in that
regard trust to themselves."   Thus personal energy
succeeded to communal inertia ; Bradford wrote
that women and children cheerfully worked in the
fields to raise corn which should be their very own.

A field of corn on the coast of Massachusetts or

Narragansett or by the rivers of Virginia, growing long before any white man had ever been seen on these shores, was precisely like the same field planted three hundred years later by our American farmers. There was the same planting in hills, the same number of stalks in the hill, with pumpkin-vines running among the hills, and beans climbing the stalks. The hills of the Indians were a trifle nearer together than those of our own day are usually set, for the native soil was more fertile.

The Indians taught the colonists much more than the planting and raising of corn ; they showed also how to grind the corn and cook it in many palatable ways. The various foods which we use to-day made from Indian corn are all cooked just as the Indians cooked them at the time of the settlement of the country ; and they are still called with Indian names, such as hominy, pone, suppawn, samp, succotash.

The Indian method of preparing maize or corn was to steep or parboil it in hot water for twelve hours, then to pound the grain in a mortar or a hollowed stone in the field, till it was a coarse meal. It was then sifted in a rather closely woven basket, and the large grains which did not pass through the sieve were again pounded and sifted.

Samp was often pounded in olden times in a

primitive and picturesque Indian mortar made of a hollowed block of wood or a stump of a tree, which had been cut off about three feet from the ground. The pestle was a heavy block of wood shaped like the inside of the mortar, and fitted with a handle attached to one side. This block was fastened to the top of a young and slender tree, a growing sapling, which was bent over and thus gave a sort of spring which pulled the pestle up after being pounded down on the corn. This was called a sweep and mortar mill.

They could be heard at a long distance. Two New Hampshire pioneers made clearings about a quarter of a mile apart and built houses. There was an impenetrable gully and thick woods between the cabins; and the blazed path was a long distance around, so the wives of the settlers seldom saw each other or any other woman. It was a source of great comfort and companionship to them both that they could signal to each other every day by pounding on their mortars. And they had an ingenious system of communication which one spring morning summoned one to the home of the other, where she arrived in time to be the first to welcome fine twin babies.

After these simple stump and sapling mortars were abandoned elsewhere they were used on Long

Island, and it was jestingly told that sailors in a fog
could always know on what shore they were, when
they could hear the pounding of the samp-mortars
on Long Island.

Rude hand-mills next were used, which were
called quernes, or quarnes. Some are still in existence and known as samp-mills. Windmills followed, of which the Indians were much afraid,
dreading "their long arms and great teeth biting
the corn in pieces"; and thinking some evil spirit
turned the arms. As soon as maize was plentiful,
English mills for grinding meal were started in
many towns. There was a windmill at Watertown,
Massachusetts, in 1631. In 1633 the first water-
mill, at Dorchester, was built, and in Ipswich a grist-
mill was built in 1635. The mill built by Governor
John Winthrop in New London is still standing.

The first windmill erected in America was one
built and set up by Governor Yeardley in Virginia
in 1621. By 1649 there were five water-mills, four
windmills, and a great number of horse and hand
mills in Virginia. Millers had one-sixth of the
meal they ground for toll.

Suppawn was another favorite of the settlers, and
was an Indian dish made from Indian corn; it was
a thick corn-meal and milk porridge. It was soon
seen on every Dutch table, for the Dutch were very

fond of all foods made from all kinds of grain ; and it is spoken of by all travellers in early New York, and in the Southern colonies.

Samp and samp porridge were soon abundant dishes.   Samp is Indian corn pounded to a coarsely ground powder.   Roger Williams wrote of it : —

" Nawsamp is a kind of meal pottage unparched.   From this the English call their samp, which is the Indian corn beaten and boiled and eaten hot or cold with milk and butter, and is a diet exceedingly wholesome for English bodies."

The Swedish scientist, Professor Kalm, told that the Indians gave him " fresh maize-bread, baked in an oblong shape, mixed with dried huckleberries, which lay as close in it as raisins in a plum pudding."

Roger Williams said that sukquttahhash was "corn seethed like beans."   Our word "succotash " we now apply to corn cooked with beans.   Pones were the red men's appones.

The love of the Indians for " roasting ears " was quickly shared by the white man.   In Virginia a series of plantings of corn were made from the first of April to the last of June, to afford a three months' succession of roasting ears.

The traveller, Strachey, writing of the Indians in

1618, said: "They lap their corn in rowles within the leaves of the corne and so boyle yt for a dayntie." This method of cooking we have also retained to the present day.

It seemed to me very curious to read in Governor Winthrop's journal, written in Boston about 1630, that when corn was "parched," as he called it, it turned inside out and was "white and floury within"; and to think that then little English children were at that time learning what pop-corn was, and how it looked when it was parched, or popped.

Hasty pudding had been made in England of wheat-flour or oatmeal and milk, and the name was given to boiled puddings of corn-meal and water. It was not a very suitable name, for corn-meal should never be cooked hastily, but requires long boiling or baking. The hard Indian pudding slightly sweetened and boiled in a bag was everywhere made. It was told that many New England families had three hundred and sixty-five such puddings in a year.

The virtues of "jonny-cake" have been loudly sung in the interesting pages of *Shepherd Tom*. The way the corn should be carried to the mill, the manner in which it should be ground, the way in which the stones should revolve, and the kind of stones, receive minute description, as does the mixing and the baking, to the latter of which the middle board of red oak from the head of a flour-barrel is indispensable as a bakeboard, while the fire to bake with must be of walnut logs. Hasty pudding, corn dumplings, and corn-meal porridge, so eminently good that it was ever mentioned with respect in the plural, as "them porridge," all are described with the exuberant joyousness of a happy, healthful old age in remembrance of a happy, high-spirited, and healthful youth.

The harvesting of the corn afforded one of the few scenes of gayety in the lives of the colonists. A diary of one Ames, of Dedham, Massachusetts, in the year 1767, thus describes a corn-husking, and most ungallantly says naught of the red ear and attendant osculation : —

"Made a husking Entertainm't. Possibly this leafe may last a Century and fall into the hands of some inquisitive Person for whose Entertainm't I will inform him that now there is a Custom amongst us of making an Entertainm't at husking of Indian Corn whereto all the neighboring Swains are invited and after the Corn is finished they like the Hottentots give three Cheers or huzza's but cannot carry in the husks without a Rhum bottle; they feign great Exertion but do nothing till Rhum enlivens them, when all is done in a trice, then after a hearty Meal about 10 at Night they go to their pastimes."

There was one way of eating corn which was spoken of by all the early writers and travellers which we should not be very well satisfied with now, but it shows us how useful and necessary corn was at that time, and how much all depended on it. This preparation of corn was called nocake or nookick. An old writer named Wood thus defined it : —

"It is Indian corn parched in the hot ashes, the ashes being sifted from it; it is afterwards beaten to powder and put into a long leatherne bag trussed at the Indian's backe like a knapsacke, out of which they take three spoonsful a day."

It was held to be the most nourishing food known, and in the smallest and most condensed form. Both Indians and white men usually carried it in a pouch when they went on long journeys, and mixed it with snow in the winter and water in summer. Gookin says it was sweet, toothsome, and hearty. With only this nourishment the Indians could carry loads "fitter for elephants than men." Roger Williams says a spoonful of this meal and water made him many a good meal. When we read this we are not surprised that the Pilgrims could keep alive on what is said was at one time of famine their food for a day, — five kernels of corn apiece. The apostle

Eliot, in his Indian Bible, always used the word
nookick for the English words flour or meal.

We ought to think of the value of food in those
days; and we may be sure the governor and his
council thought corn of value when they took it
for taxes and made it a legal currency just like
gold and silver, and forbade any one to feed it to
pigs. If you happen to see the price of corn
during those years down to Revolutionary times,
you will, perhaps, be surprised to see how much the
price varied. From ten shillings a bushel in 1631,
to two shillings in 1672, to twenty in 1747, to two
in 1751, and one hundred shillings at the opening
of the Revolution. In these prices of corn, as in
the price of all other articles at this time, the difference was in the money, which had a constantly
changing value, not in the article itself or its usefulness. The corn had a steady value, it always
furnished just so much food; and really was a
standard itself rather than measured and valued
by the poor and shifting money.

There are many other interesting facts connected
with the early culture of corn: of the finding hidden
in caves or "caches" in the ground the Indian's
corn which he had stored for seed; of the sacred
"corn-dances" of the Indians; that the first patent
granted in England to an American was to a Phila-

delphia woman for a mill to grind a kind of hominy; of the great profit to the colonists in corn-raising, for the careless and greedy Indians always ate up all their corn as soon as possible, then had to go out and trap beavers in the woods to sell the skins to the colonists for corn to keep them from starving. One colonist planted about eight bushels of seed-corn. He raised from this eight hundred and sixty-four bushels of corn, which he sold to the Indians for beaver skins which gave him a profit of £327.

Many games were played with the aid of kernels of corn : fox and geese, checkers, " hull gull, how many," and games in which the corn served as counters.

The ears of corn were often piled into the attic until the floor was a foot deep with them. I once entered an ell bedroom in a Massachusetts farm-house where the walls, rafters, and four-post bedstead were hung solid with ears of yellow corn, which truly " made a sunshine in a shady place."

Some of the preparation of corn fell upon the boys ; it was their regular work all winter in the evening firelight to shell corn from the ears by scraping them on the iron edge of the wooden shovel or on the fire-peel. My father told me that even in his childhood in the first quarter of this century many families of moderate means fastened the long-

handled frying-pan across a tub and drew the corn
ears across the sharp edge of the handle of the pan.
I note in Peter Parley's reminiscences of his child-

Old Corn-sheller

hood a similar use of a frying-pan handle in his
home. Other farmers set the edge of a knife blade
in a piece of wood and scraped on the back of the
blade. In some households the corn was pounded

into hominy in wooden mortars. An old corn-sheller used in western Massachusetts is here shown.

When the corn was shelled, the cobs were not carelessly discarded or disregarded. They were stored often in a lean-to or loft in the kitchen ell; from thence they were brought down in skepes or boxes about a bushel at a time; and after being used by the children as playthings to build "cob-houses," were employed as light wood for the fire. They had a special use in many households for smoking hams; and their smoke was deemed to impart a specially delightful flavor to hams and bacon.

One special use of corn should be noted. By order of the government of Massachusetts Bay in 1623, it was used as ballots in public voting. At annual elections of the governors' assistants in each town, a kernel of corn was deposited to signify a favorable vote upon the nominee, while a bean signi-fied a negative vote; "and if any free-man shall put in more than one Indian corn or bean he shall forfeit for every such offence Ten Pounds."

The choice of a national flower or plant is much talked about to-day. Aside from the beauty of maize when growing and its wonderful adaptability in every part for decoration, would not the noble and useful part played by Indian corn in our early his-tory entitle it to be our first choice?

CHAPTER VII

MEAT AND DRINK

THE food brought in ships from Europe to the colonists was naturally limited by the imperfect methods of transportation which then existed. Nothing like refrigerators were known; no tinned foods were even thought of; ways of packing were very crude and careless; so the kinds of provisions which would stand the long voyage on a slow sailing-vessel were very few. The settlers turned at once, as all settlers in a new land should, to the food-supplies found in the new home; of these the three most important ones were corn, fish, and game. I have told of their plenty, their value, and their use. There were many other bountiful and good foods, among them pumpkins or pompions, as they were at first called.

The pumpkin has sturdily kept its own place on the New England farm, varying in popularity and use, but always of value as easy of growth, easy of cooking, and easy to keep in a dried form. Yet the colonists did not welcome the pumpkin with eagerness, even in times of great want. They were justly rebuked for their indifference and dislike by Johnson in his *Wonder-working Providence,* who called the pumpkin "a fruit which the Lord fed his people with till corn and cattle increased"; and another pumpkin-lover referred to "the times wherein old Pompion was a saint." One colonial poet gives the golden vegetable this tribute: —

"We have pumpkins at morning and pumpkins at noon,
    If it were not for pumpkins we should be undone."

I am very sure were I living on dried corn and scant shell-fish, as the Pilgrims were forced to do, I should have turned with delight to "pompion-sause" as a change of diet. Stewed pumpkins and pumpkin bread were coarse ways of using the fruit for food. Pumpkin bread — made of half Indian meal — was not very pleasing in appearance. A traveller in 1704 called it an "awkward food." It is eaten in Connecticut to this day. The Indians dried pumpkins and strung them for winter use, and the colonists followed the Indian custom.

In Virginia pumpkins were equally plentiful and useful. Ralph Hamor, in his *True Discourse,* says they grew in such abundance that a hundred were often observed to spring from one seed. The Virginia Indians boiled beans, peas, corn, and pumpkins together, and the colonists liked the dish. In the trying times at " James-Citty," the plentiful pump-kins played a great part in providing food-supplies for the starving Virginians.

Squashes were also native vegetables. The name is Indian. To show the wonderful and varied way in which the English spelt Indian names let me tell you that Roger Williams called them askuta-squashes; the Puritan minister Higginson, squanter-squashes; the traveller Josselyn, squontorsquashes, and the historian Wood, isquoukersquashes.

Potatoes were known to New Englanders, but were rare and when referred to were probably sweet pota-toes. It was a long time before they were much liked. A farmer at Hadley, Massachusetts, had what he thought a very large crop in 1763 — it was eight bushels. It was believed by many persons that if a man ate them every day, he could not live seven years. In the spring all that were left on hand were carefully burned, for many believed that if cattle or horses ate these potatoes they would die. They were first called, when carried to England, Virginia potatoes; then they became much liked and grown in Ireland; then the Irish settlers in New Hampshire brought them back to this conti-nent, and now they are called, very senselessly, Irish potatoes. Many persons fancied the balls were what should be eaten, and said they " did not much desire them." A fashionable way of cooking them was with butter, sugar, and grape-juice; this was mixed with dates, lemons, and mace; seasoned with cinnamon, nutmeg, and pepper; then covered with a frosting of sugar — and you had to hunt well to find the potato among all these other things.

In the Carolinas the change in English diet was effected by the sweet potato. This root was cooked in various ways : it was roasted in the ashes, boiled, made into puddings, used as a substitute for bread, made into pancakes which a foreigner said tasted as though composed of sweet almonds; and in every way it was liked and was so plentiful that even the slaves fed upon it.

Beans were abundant, and were baked by the Indians in earthen pots just as we bake them to-day. The settlers planted peas, parsnips, turnips, and carrots, which grew and thrived. Huckleberries, blackberries, strawberries, and grapes grew wild. Apple-trees were planted at once, and grew well in New England and the Middle states. Twenty years after the Roman Catholic settlement of Maryland the fruitful orchards were conspicuously flourishing.

Johnson, writing in 1634, said that all then in New England could have apple, pear, and quince

L

tarts instead of pumpkin-pies. They made apple-slump, apple-mose, apple-crowdy, apple-tarts, mess apple-pies, and puff apple-pies. The Swedish parson, Dr. Acrelius, writing home in 1758 an account of the settlement of Delaware, said : —

"Apple-pie is used through the whole year, and when fresh apples are no longer to be had, dried ones are used. It is the evening meal of children. House-pie, in country places, is made of apples neither peeled nor freed from their cores, and its crust is not broken if a wagon wheel goes over it."

The making of a portion of the autumn's crop of apples into dried apples, apple-sauce, and apple-butter for winter was preceded in many country homes by an apple-paring. The cheerful kitchen of a farmhouse was set with an array of empty pans, tubs, and baskets ; of sharp knives and heaped-up barrels of apples. A circle of laughing faces completed the scene, and the barrels of apples were quickly emptied by the many skilful hands. The apples intended for drying were strung on linen thread and hung on the kitchen and attic rafters. The following day the stout crane in the open fireplace was hung with brass kettles which were filled with the pared apples, sweet and sour in proper proportions, the sour at the bottom since they required more time to cook. If quinces could be had, they were added to give flavor, and molasses, or boiled-down pungent " apple-molasses," was added for sweetening. As there was danger that the sauce would burn over the roaring logs, many housewives placed clean straw at the bottom of the kettle to keep the apples from the fiercest heat. Days were spent in preparing the winter's stock of apple-sauce, but when done and placed in barrels in the cellar, it was always ready for use, and when slightly frozen was a keen relish. Apple-butter was made of the pared apples boiled down with cider.

Wheat did not at first ripen well, so white bread was for a time rarely eaten. Rye grew better, so bread made of " rye-an'-injun," which was half rye-meal, half corn-meal, was used instead. Bake-shops were so many in number in all the towns that it is evident that housewives in towns and villages did not make bread in every home as to-day, but bought it at the baker's.

At the time when America was settled, no European peoples drank water as we do to-day, for a constant beverage. The English drank ale, the Dutch beer, the French and Spanish light wines, for every-day use. Hence it seemed to the colonists a great trial and even a very dangerous experiment to drink water in the New World. They were forced

to do it, however, in many cases; and to their surprise found that it agreed with them very well, and
that their health improved. Governor Winthrop
of Massachusetts, who was a most sensible and
thoughtful man, soon had water used as a constant
drink by all in his household.

As cows increased in number and were cared for,
milk of course was added to the every-day fare.
Rev. Mr. Higginson wrote in 1630 that milk cost in
Salem but a penny a quart; while another minister,
John Cotton, said that milk and ministers were the
only things cheap in New England. At that time
milk cost but a penny and a quarter a quart in old
England.

Milk became a very important part of the food
of families in the eighteenth century. In 1728 a
discussion took place in the Boston newspapers as
to the expense of keeping a family " of middling
figure." These writers all named only bread and
milk for breakfast and supper. Ten years later
a minister, calculating the expenses of his family,
set down bread and milk for both breakfast and
supper. Milk and hasty pudding, milk and stewed
pumpkin, milk and baked apples, milk and berries, were variations. In winter, when milk was
scarce, sweetened cider diluted with water was used
instead. Sometimes bread was soaked with this

mixture. It is said that children were usually very
fond of it.

As comparatively few New England families in
the seventeenth century owned churns, I cannot
think that many made
butter; of course
families of wealth ate
it, but it was not com-
mon as to-day. In
the inventories of the
property of the early
settlers of Maine
there is but one churn
named. Butter was
worth from three-
pence to sixpence a
pound. As cattle in-
creased the duties of
the dairy grew, and
soon were never-ceas-

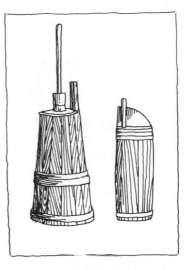

Upright Churns

ing and ever-tiring. The care of cream and making
of butter was in the eighteenth century the duty of
every good wife and dame in the country, and usually in the town.

Though the shape and ease of action of churns
varied, still butter-making itself varied little from
the same work to-day. Several old-time churns

are shown, the revolving one being the most
unusual.

Cheese was plentiful and good in all the Northern
colonies. It was also an unending care from the
time the milk was set over the fire to warm and then
to curdle ; through the breaking of the curds in the

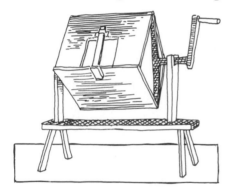

cheese-basket;
through shaping
into cheeses and
pressing in the
cheese-press, plac-
ing them on the
cheese-ladders,
and   constantly
turning and rub-
bing them.   An
old cheese-press,
cheese-ladder,

Revolving Churn

and cheese-basket from Deerfield Memorial Hall
are shown in the illustration.

In all households, even in those of great wealth
and many servants, assistance was given in all house-
wifery by the daughters of the household. In the
South it was chiefly by superintendence and teaching through actual exposition the negro slaves ; in
the North it was by the careful performance of the
work.

Cheese-basket, Cheese-ladder, Cheese-press

The manuscript cooking receipt-book of many an ancient dame shows the great care they took in family cooking. English methods of cooking at the time of the settlement of this country were very complicated and very laborious.

It was a day of hashes, ragouts, soups, hotchpots, etc. There were no great joints served until the time of Charles the First. In almost every six-teenth-century receipt for cooking meat, appear some such directions as these: " Y-mynce it, smyte them on gobbets, hew them on gobbets, chop on gob-bets, hew small, dyce them, skern them to dyce, kerf it to dyce, grind all to dust, smyte on peces, parcel-hem ; hew small on morselyen, hack them small, cut them on culpons." Great amounts of spices were used, even perfumes ; and as there was no preservation of meat by ice, perhaps the spices and perfumes were necessary.

Of course the colonists were forced to adopt simpler ways of cooking, but as towns and commerce increased there were many kitchen duties which made much tedious work. Many pickles, spiced fruits, preserves, candied fruits and flowers, and marmalades were made.

Preserving was a very different art from canning fruit to-day. There were no hermetically sealed jars, no chemical methods, no quick work about it. Vast jars were filled with preserves so rich that there was no need of keeping the air from them ; they could be opened, that is, the paper cover taken off, and used as desired ; there was no fear of fermentation, souring, or moulding.

The housewives pickled samphire, fennel, purple cabbage, nasturtium-buds, green walnuts, lemons, radish-pods, barberries, elder-buds, parsley, mushrooms, asparagus, and many kinds of fish and fruit. They candied fruits and nuts, made many marmalades and quiddonies, and a vast number of fruit wines and cordials. Even their cakes, pies, and puddings were most complicated, and humble households were lavish in the various kinds they manufactured and ate.

They collared and potted many kinds of fish and game, and they salted and soused. Salted meat was eaten, and very little fresh meat; for there were no means of keeping meat after it was killed. Every well-to-do family had a " powdering-tub," in which meat was " powdered," that is, salted and pickled. Many families had a smoke-house, in which beef, ham, and bacon were smoked.

Perhaps the busiest month of the year was November, — called " killing time." When the chosen day arrived, oxen, cows, and swine which had been fattened for the

Sausage-gun (open)

winter's stock were slaughtered early in the morning, that the meat might be hard and cold before

being put in the pickle.   Sausages, rolliches, and
headcheese were made, lard tried out, and tallow
saved.

A curious and quaint domestic implement or
utensil found hanging on the walls of some kitchens was what was known
as a sausage-gun.   One
here is shown with the
piston detached, and also
ready for use.   The sau-
sage-meat was forced out
through the nozzle into
the sausage-cases.   A
simpler form of sausage-
stuffer has also been
seen, much like a tube-
and-piston garden-
syringe; though I must
add a suspicion which has
always lingered in my
mind that the latter utensil was really a syringe-
gun, such as once was
used to disable humming-birds by squirting water
upon them.

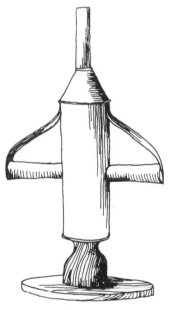

Sausage-gun (closed)

Sausage-meat was thus prepared in New York
farmhouses.   The meat was cut coarsely into half-

inch pieces and thrown into wooden boxes about
three feet long and ten inches deep.   Then its first
chopping was by men using spades which had been
ground to a sharp edge.

There were many families that found all their
supply of sweetening in maple sugar and honey ;
but housewives of dignity and elegance desired to
have some supply of sugar, certainly to offer visitors
for their dish of tea.   This sugar was always loaf-
sugar, and truly loaf-sugar ; for it was purchased
ever in great loaves or cones which averaged in
weight about nine to ten pounds apiece.   One cone
would last thrifty folk for a year.   This pure clear
sugar-cone always came wrapped in a deep blue-purple
paper, of such unusual and beautiful tint and so
color-laden that in country homes it was carefully
saved and soaked, to supply a dye for a small amount
of the finest wool, which was used when spun and
dyed for some specially choice purpose.   The cutting of this cone of sugar into lumps of equal size
and regular shape was distinctly the work of the
mistress and daughters of the house.   It was too
exact and too dainty a piece of work to be in-
trusted to clumsy or wasteful servants.   Various
simply shaped sugar-shears or sugar-cutters were
used.   An ordinary form is shown in the illustration.   I well recall the only family in which I ever

saw this solemn function of sugar-cutting take place
-- it was about thirty years ago.   An old Boston
East India merchant, one of the last to cling to a
residence in what is known now as the " Burnt Dis-
trict," always desired (and his desire was law) to use

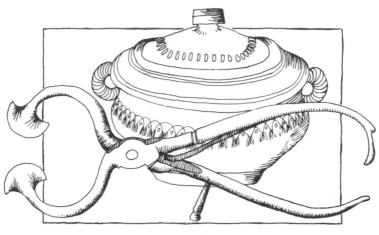

Sugar-cutters

these loaves of sugar in his household. I don't
know where he got them so long after every one else
had apparently ceased buying them — he may have
specially imported them ; at any rate he had them,
and to the end of her life it was the morning duty
of his wife " to cut the sugar."   I can see my old
cousin still in what she termed her breakfast room,
dressed very handsomely, standing before a bare

mahogany table on which a maid placed the considerable array of a silver salver without legs, which was set on a folded cloth and held the sugar-loaf and the sugar-cutter; and another salver with legs that bore various bowls and one beautiful silver sugar-box which was kept filled high for her husband's toddy. It seemed an interminably tedious work to me and a senseless one, as I chafingly waited for the delightful morning drive in delightful Boston. It was in this household that I encountered the sweetest thing of my whole life; I have written elsewhere its praises in full; a barrel, a small one, to be sure, but

Spice-mortars and Spice-mills

still a whole teak-wood barrel full of long strings of glistening rock-candy. I had my fill of it at will, though it was not kept as a sweetmeat, but was a

kitchen store having a special use in the manufacture of rich brandy sauces for plum puddings, and of
a kind of marchepane ornamentation for desserts.

All the spices used in the household were also
ground at home, in spice-mortars and spice-mills.
These were of various sizes, including the pepper-
mills, which were set on the table at meal-times, and
the tiny ornamental graters which were carried in
the pocket.

The entire food of a household was the possible
production of a farm.   In a paper published in the
American Museum in 1787 an old farmer says: —

" At this time my farm gave me and my whole family a
good living on the produce of it, and left me one year with
another one hundred and fifty silver dollars, for I never
spent more than ten dollars a year which was for salt, nails,
and the like.   Nothing to eat, drink or wear was bought, as
my farm provided all."

The farm food was not varied, it is true, as to-
day ; for articles of luxury came by importation.
The products of tropical countries, such as sugar,
molasses, tea, coffee, spices, found poor substitutes
in home food-products.   Dried pumpkin was a poor
sweetening instead of molasses ; maple sugar and
honey were not esteemed as was sugar ; tea was ill-
replaced by raspberry leaves, loosestrife, hardhack,

goldenrod, dittany, blackberry leaves, yeopon, sage, and a score of other herbs ; coffee was better than parched rye and chestnuts ; spices could not be compensated for or remotely imitated by any substitutes.

So though there was ample quantity of food, the quality, save in the town, was not such as English housewives had been accustomed to ; there were many deprivations in their kitchens which tried them sorely.   The better cooks they were, the more trying were the limitations.   Every woman with a love for her fellow-woman must feel a thrill of keen sympathy for the goodwife of Newport, New Hampshire, who had to make her Thanksgiving mince-pies with a filling of bear's meat and dried pumpkins, sweetened with maple sugar, and her crust of corn-meal.   Her husband loyally recorded that they were the best mince-pies he ever ate.

As years passed on and great wealth came to individuals, the tables of the opulent, especially in the Middle colonies, rivalled the luxury of English and French houses of wealth.   It is surprising to read in Dr. Cutler's diary that when he dined with Colonel Duer in New York in 1787, there were fifteen kinds of wine served besides cider, beer, and porter.

John Adams probably lived as well as any New Englander of similar position and means.   A Sunday dinner at his house was thus described by a visitor : the first course was a pudding of Indian meal, molasses, and butter; then came a course of veal and bacon, neck of mutton, and vegetables. When the New Englander went to Philadelphia, his eyes opened wide at the luxury and extravagance of fare. He has given in his diary some accounts of the lavishness of the Philadelphia larder. Such entries as these are found : —

(Of the home of Miers Fisher, a young Quaker lawyer.) "This plain Friend, with his plain but pretty wife with her Thees and Thous, had provided us a costly entertainment; ducks, hams, chickens, beef, pig, tarts, creams, custards, jellies, fools, trifles, floating islands, beer, porter, punch, wine and a long, etc."

(At the home of Chief Justice Chew.) "About four o'clock we were called to dinner. Turtle and every other thing, flummery, jellies, sweetmeats of twenty sorts, trifles, whipped sillabubs, floating islands, fools, etc., with a dessert of fruits, raisins, almonds, pears, peaches."

"A most sinful feast again! everything which could delight the eye or allure the taste; curds and creams, jellies, sweetmeats of various sorts, twenty kinds of tarts, fools, trifles, floating islands, whipped sillabubs, etc. Parmesan cheese, punch, wine, porter, beer."

By which lists may plainly be seen that our second President had somewhat of a sweet tooth.

The Dutch were great beer-drinkers and quickly established breweries at Albany and New York. But before the century had ended New Englanders had abandoned the constant drinking of ale and beer for cider. Cider was very cheap; but a few shillings a barrel. It was supplied in large amounts to students at college, and even very little children drank it. President John Adams was an early and earnest wisher for temperance reform; but to the end of his life he drank a large tankard of hard cider every morning when he first got up. It was free in every farmhouse to all travellers and tramps.

A cider-mill was usually built on a hillside so the building could be one story high in front and two in the back. Thus carts could easily unload the apples on the upper level and take away the barrels of cider on the lower. Standing below on the lower floor you could see two upright wooden cylinders, set a little way apart, with knobs, or nuts as they were called, on one cylinder which fitted loosely into holes on the other. The cylinders worked in opposite directions and drew in and crushed the apples poured down between them. The nuts and holes frequently clogged with the pomace. Then the mill was stopped and a boy scraped out with a stick or hook the crushed apples. A horse walking in a small circle moved a

M

lever which turned the motor wheel. It was slow
work; it took three hours to grind a cart-load of
apples; but the machinery was efficient and simple.
The pomace fell into a large shallow vat or tank,
and if it could lie in the vat overnight it was a
benefit. Then the pomace was put in a press.
This was simple in construction. At the bottom was
a platform grooved in channels; a sheaf of clean
straw was spread on the platform, and with wooden
shovels the pomace was spread thick over it. Then a
layer of straw was laid at right angles with the first,
and more pomace, and so on till the form was about
three feet high; the top board was put on as a
cover; the screw turned and blocks pressed down,
usually with a long wooden hand-lever, very slowly
at first, then harder, until the mass was solid and
every drop of juice had trickled into the channels
of the platform and thence to the pan below.
Within the last two or three years I have seen
those cider-mills at work in the country back of old
Plymouth and in Narragansett, sending afar their
sourly fruity odors. And though apple orchards
are running out, and few new trees are planted, and
the apple crop in those districts is growing smaller
and smaller, yet is the sweet cider of country cider-
mills as free and plentiful a gift to any passer-by
as the water from the well or the air we breathe.

Perry was made from pears, as cider is from apples, and peachy from peaches. Metheglin and mead, drinks of the old Druids in England, were made from honey, yeast, and water, and were popular everywhere. In Virginia whole plantations of the honey-locust furnished locust beans for making metheglin. From persimmons, elderberries, juniper berries, pumpkins, corn-stalks, hickory nuts, sassafras bark, birch bark, and many other leaves, roots, and barks, various light drinks were made. An old song boasted : —

> " Oh, we can make liquor to sweeten our lips
> Of pumpkins, of parsnips, of walnut-tree chips."

Many other stronger and more intoxicating liquors were made in large quantities, among them enormous amounts of rum, which was called often " kill-devil." The making of rum aided and almost supported the slave-trade in this country. The poor negroes were bought on the coast of Africa by New England sea-captains and merchants and paid for with barrels of New England rum. These slaves were then carried on slave-ships to the West Indies, and sold at a large profit to planters and slave-dealers for a cargo of molasses. This was brought to New England, distilled into rum, and sent off to Africa. Thus the circle of molasses, rum, and slaves was completed.   Many slaves were also landed in New England, but there was no crop there that needed negroes to raise it.   So slavery never was as common in New England as in the South, where the tropical tobacco and rice fields needed negro labor.   But New England's share in promoting negro slavery in America was just as great as was Virginia's.

Besides all the rum that was sent to Africa, much was drunk by Americans at home.   At weddings, funerals, christenings, at all public meetings and private feasts, New England rum was ever present. In nothing is more contrast shown between our present day and colonial times than in the habits of liquor-drinking.   We cannot be grateful enough for the temperance reform, which began at the early part of this century, and was so sadly needed.

For many years the colonists had no tea, chocolate, or coffee to drink; for those were not in use in England when America was settled.   In 1690 two dealers were licensed to sell tea "in publique" in Boston.   Green and bohea teas were sold at the Boston apothecaries' in 1712.   For many years tea was also sold like medicine in England at the apothecaries' and not at the grocers'.

Many queer mistakes were made through ignorance of its proper use.   Many colonists put the tea into water, boiled it for a time, threw the liquid away, and ate the tea-leaves. In Salem they did not find the leaves very attractive, so they put butter and salt on them.

In 1670 a Boston woman was licensed to sell coffee and chocolate, and soon coffee-houses were established there. Some did not know how to cook coffee any more than tea, but boiled the whole coffee-beans in water, ate them, and drank the liquid; and naturally this was not very good either to eat or drink.

At the time of the Stamp Act, when patriotic Americans threw the tea into Boston harbor, Americans were just as great tea-drinkers as the English. Now it is not so. The English drink much more tea than we do; and the habit of coffee-drinking, first acquired in the Revolution, has descended from generation to generation, and we now drink more coffee than tea. This is one of the differences in our daily life caused by the Revolution.

Many home-grown substitutes were used in Revolutionary times for tea: ribwort was a favorite one; strawberry and currant leaves, sage, thoroughwort, and "Liberty Tea," made from the four-leaved loosestrife. "Hyperion tea" was raspberry leaves, and was said by good patriots to be "very delicate and most excellent."

CHAPTER VIII

IN recounting the various influences which assisted the Americans to success in the War for Independence, such as the courage and integrity of the American generals, the generosity of the American people, the skill of Americans in marksmanship, their powers of endurance, their acclimatization, their confidence and faith, etc., we must never forget to add their independence in their own homes of any outside help to give them every necessity of life. No farmer or his wife need fear any king when on every home farm was found food, drink, medicine, fuel, lighting, clothing, shelter. Home-made was an adjective that might be applied to nearly every article in the house. Such would not be the case under similar stress to-day. In the matter of clothing alone we could not now be independent. Few farmers raise flax to make linen; few women can spin either wool or flax, or weave cloth; many cannot knit. In early days every farmer and his sons raised wool and flax; his wife and daughters spun them into thread and yarn, knit these into stockings and mittens, or wove them into linen and cloth, and then made them into clothing. Even in large cities nearly all women spun yarn and thread, all could knit, and many had hand-looms to weave cloth at home. These home occupations in the production of clothing have been very happily termed the "homespun industries."

Nearly every one has seen one of the pretty foot-wheels for spinning flax thread for linen, which may yet be found in the attics of many of our farm-houses, as well as in some of our parlors, where, with a bunch of flax wound around and tied to the spindle, they have within a few years been placed as a relic of the olden times.

If one of these flax-wheels could speak to-day, it would sing a tale of the patient industry, of the tiring work of our grandmothers, even when they were little children, which ought never to be forgotten.

As soon as the colonists had cleared their farms from stones and stumps, they planted a field, or "patch" of flax, and usually one of hemp. The seed was sown broadcast like grass-seed in May. Flax is a graceful plant with pretty drooping blue flowers; hemp has but a sad-colored blossom.

Thomas Tusser says in his *Book of House-wifery* : —

> " Good flax and good hemp to have of her own,
> In May a good huswife will see it be sown.
> And afterwards trim it to serve in a need ;
> The fimble to spin, the card for her seed."

When the flax plants were three or four inches high, they were weeded by young women or children who had to work barefoot, as the stalks were very tender. If the land had a growth of thistles, the weeders could wear three or four pairs of woollen stockings. The children had to step facing the wind, so if any plants were trodden down the wind would help to blow them back into place. When the flax was ripe, in the last of June or in July, it was pulled up by the roots and laid out carefully to dry for a day or two, and turned several times in the sun,; this work was called pulling and spreading, and was usually done by men and boys. It then was " rippled." A coarse wooden or heavy iron wire comb with great teeth, named a ripple-comb, was fastened on a plank ; the stalks of flax were drawn through it with a quick stroke to break off the seed-bolles or " bobs," which fell on a sheet spread to catch them ; these were saved for seed for the next crop, or for sale.

Rippling was done in the field.   The stalks were
then tied in bundles called beats or bates and
stacked.   They were tied only at the seed end, and
the base of the stalks was spread out forming a
tent-shaped stack, called a stook.   When dry, the
stalks were watered to rot the leaves and softer
fibres.   Hemp was watered without rippling.   This
was done preferably in running water, as the rotting
flax poisoned fish.   Stakes were set in the water in
the form of a square, called a steep-pool, and the
bates of flax or hemp were piled in solidly, each
alternate layer at right angles with the one beneath
it.   A cover of boards and heavy stones was
piled on top.   In four or five days the bates were
taken up and the rotted leaves removed.   A slower
process was termed dew-retting; an old author
calls it "a vile and naughty way," but it was the
way chiefly employed in America.

When the flax was cleaned, it was once more
dried and tied in bundles.   Then came work for
strong men, to break it on the ponderous flax-brake,
to separate the fibres and get out from the centre
the hard woody "hexe" or "bun."   Hemp was
also broken.

A flax-brake is an implement which is almost
impossible to describe.   It was a heavy log of wood
about five feet long, either large enough so the flat

top was about three feet from the ground, or set on heavy logs to bring it to that height. A portion of the top was cut down leaving a block at each end,

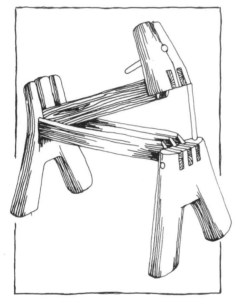

Flax-brake

and several long slats were set in lengthwise and held firm at each end with edges up, by being set into the end blocks. Then a similar set of slats, put in a heavy frame, was made with the slats set far enough apart to go into the spaces of the lower slats. The flax was laid on the lower slats, the frame and upper slats placed on it, and then pounded down with a heavy wooden mallet weighing many pounds. Sometimes the upper frame of slats, or knives as they were called, were hinged to the big under log at one end, and heavily weighted at the other, and thus the blow was given by the fall of the weight, not by the force of the farmer's muscle. The tenacity of the flax can be seen when it would stand this violent beating; and the cruel blow can be imagined, which the farmer's fingers sometimes got when he carelessly thrust his hand with the flax too far under the descending jaw — a shark's maw was equally gentle.

Flax was usually broken twice, once with an "open - tooth brake," once with a "close or strait brake," that is, one where the long, sharp-edge strips of wood were set closely together. Then it was scutched or swingled with a swingling block and knife, to take out any small particles of bark that might adhere. A man could

Swingling Block and Swingling Knives

swingle forty pounds of flax a day, but it was hard work.   All this had to be done in clear sunny weather when the flax was as dry as tinder.

The clean fibres were then made into bundles called strikes. The strikes were swingled again, and from the refuse called swingle-tree hurds, coarse bagging could be spun and woven. After being thoroughly cleaned the rolls or strikes were sometimes beetled, that is, pounded in a wooden trough with a great pestle-shaped beetle over and over again until soft.

Then came the hackling or hetcheling, and the fineness of the flax depended upon the number of hacklings, the fineness of the various hackles or hetchels or combs, and the dexterity of the operator. In the hands of a poor hackler the best of flax would be converted into tow. The flax was slightly wetted, taken hold of at one end of the bunch, and drawn through the hackle-teeth towards the hetcheller, and thus fibres were pulled and laid into continuous threads, while the short fibres were combed out.   It was dusty, dirty work. The threefold process had to be all done at once; the fibres had to be divided to their fine filaments, the long threads laid in untangled line, and the tow separated and removed. After the first hackle, called a ruffler, six other finer hackles were often used.   It

Flax, Flax Basket, Flax Hetchels

was one of the surprises of flax preparation to see
how little good fibre would be left after all this
hackling, even from a large mass of raw material,
but it was equally surprising to see how much linen
thread could be made from this small amount of
fine flax.   The fibres were sorted according to fineness ; this was called spreading and drawing.   So
then after over twenty dexterous manipulations the

flax was ready for the wheel, for spinning, — the most dexterous process of all, — and was wrapped round the spindle.

Seated at the small flax-wheel, the spinner placed

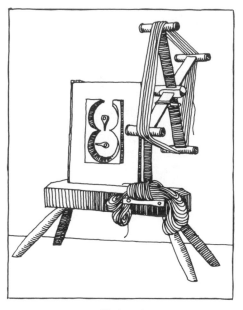

Clock-reel

her foot on the treadle, and spun the fibre into a long, even thread. Hung on the wheel was a small bone, wood, or earthenware cup, or a gourd-shell, filled with water, in which the spinner moistened her fingers as she held the twisting flax, which by the movement of the wheel was wound on bobbins. When all were filled, the thread was wound off in knots and skeins on a reel. A machine called a clock-reel counted the exact number of strands in a knot, usually forty, and ticked when the requisite

number had been wound.   Then the spinner would
stop and tie the knot.   A quaint old ballad has the
refrain : —

" And he kissed Mistress Polly when the clock-reel ticked."

That is, the lover seized the rare and propitious
moments of Mistress Polly's comparative leisure
to kiss her.

Usually the knots or lays were of forty threads,
and twenty lays made a skein or slipping.   The
number varied, however, with locality.   To spin
two skeins of linen thread was a good day's work ;
for it a spinner was paid eight cents a day and " her
keep."

These skeins of thread had to be bleached.   They
were laid in warm water for four days, the water
being frequently changed, and the skeins constantly
wrung out.   Then they were washed in the brook
till the water came from them clear and pure.   Then
they were " bucked," that is, bleached with ashes
and hot water, in a bucking-tub, over and over
again, then laid in clear water for a week, and
afterwards came a grand seething, rinsing, beating,
washing, drying, and winding on bobbins for the
loom.   Sometimes the bleaching was done with
slaked lime or with buttermilk.

These were not the only bleaching operations the

flax went through; others will be detailed in the chapter on hand-weaving.

One lucrative product of flax should be mentioned — flaxseed. Flax was pulled for spinning when the base of the stalk began to turn yellow, which was usually the first of July. An old saying was, " June brings the flax." For seed it stood till it was all yellow. The flaxseed was used for making oil. Usually the upper chambers of country stores were filled a foot deep with flaxseed in the autumn, waiting for good sleighing to convey the seed to town.

In New Hampshire in early days, a wheelwright was not a man who made wagon-wheels (as such he would have had scant occupation), but one who made spinning-wheels. Often he carried them around the country on horseback selling them, thus adding another to the many interesting itineracies of colonial days. Spinning-wheels would seem clumsy for horse-carriage, but they were not set up, and several could be compactly carried when taken apart; far more ticklish articles went on pack-horses, — large barrels, glazed window-sashes, etc. Nor would it seem very difficult for a man to carry spinning-wheels on horseback, when frequently a woman would jump on horseback in the early morning, and with a baby on one arm and a flax-wheel tied behind, would ride several miles to a neighbor's to spend the day spinning in cheerful companionship. A century ago one of these wheelwrights sold a fine spinning-wheel for a dollar, a clock-reel for two dollars, and a wool-wheel for two dollars.

Few persons are now living who have ever seen carried on in a country home in America any of these old-time processes which have been recounted. As an old antiquary wrote : —

"Few have ever seen a woman hatchel flax or card tow, or heard the buzzing of the foot-wheel, or seen bunches of flaxen yarn hanging in the kitchen, or linen cloth whitening on the grass. The flax-dresser with the shives, fibres, and dirt of flax covering his garments, and his face begrimed with flax-dirt has disappeared; the noise of his brake and swingling knife has ended, and the boys no longer make bonfires of his swingling tow. The sound of the spinning-wheel, the song of the spinster, and the snapping of the clock-reel all have ceased; the warping bars and quill wheel are gone, and the thwack of the loom is heard only in the factory. The spinning woman of King Lemuel cannot be found."

Frequent references are made to flax in the Bible, notably in the Book of Proverbs ; and the methods of growing and preparing flax by the ancient Egyptians were precisely the same as those of the American colonist a hundred years ago, of the Finn, Lapp,

N

Norwegian, and Belgian flax-growers to-day.   This
ancient skill was not confined to flax-working.
Rosselini, the eminent hierologist, says that every
modern craftsman may see on Egyptian monuments
four thousand years old, representations of the
process of his craft just as it is carried on to-day.
The paintings in the Grotto of El Kab, shown in
Hamilton's *Ægyptica*, show the pulling, stocking,
tying, and rippling of flax going on just as it is
done in Egypt now.   The four-tooth ripple of the
Egyptian is improved upon, but it is the same
implement.   Pliny gives an account of the mode
of preparing flax : plucking it up by the roots, tying
it in bundles, drying, watering, beating, and hackling
it, or, as he says, " combing it with iron hooks."
Until the Christian era linen was almost the only
kind of clothing used in Egypt, and the teeming
banks of the Nile furnished flax in abundance.   The
quality of the linen can be seen in the bands preserved on mummies.   It was not, however, spun on
a wheel, but on a hand-distaff, called sometimes a
rock, on which the women in India still spin the
very fine thread which is employed in making India
muslins.   The distaff was used in our colonies ; it
was ordered that children and others tending sheep
or cattle in the fields should also " be set to some
other employment withal, such as spinning upon

the rock, knitting, weaving tape, etc." I heard recently a distinguished historian refer in a lecture to this colonial statute, and he spoke of the children *sitting upon a rock* while knitting or spinning, etc., evidently knowing naught of the proper significa- tion of the word.

The homespun industries have ever been held to have a beneficent and peace-bringing influence on women. Wordsworth voiced this sentiment when he wrote his series of sonnets beginning : —

> " Grief! thou hast lost an ever-ready friend
> Now that the cottage spinning-wheel is mute."

Chaucer more cynically says, through the *Wife of Bath* : —

> " Deceite, weepynge, spynnynge God hath give
> To wymmen kyndely that they may live."

Spinning doubtless was an ever-ready refuge in the monotonous life of the early colonist. She soon had plenty of material to work with. Everywhere, even in the earliest days, the culture of flax was encouraged. By 1640 the Court of Massachusetts passed two orders directing the growth of flax, ascer- taining what colonists were skilful in breaking, spin- ning, weaving, ordering that boys and girls be taught to spin, and offering a bounty for linen

grown, spun, and woven in the colony. Connecticut passed similar measures.   Soon spinning-classes
were formed, and every family ordered to spin so
many pounds of flax a year, or to pay a fine.   The
industry received a fresh impulse through the immigration of about one hundred Irish families from
Londonderry.   They settled in New Hampshire on
the Merrimac about 1719, and spun and wove
with far more skill than prevailed among those
English settlers who had already become Americans.
They established a manufactory according to Irish
methods, and attempts at a similar establishment
were made in Boston.

There was much public excitement over spinning,
and prizes were offered for quantity and quality.
Women, rich as well as poor, appeared on Boston
Common with their wheels, thus making spinning a
popular holiday recreation.   A brick building was
erected as a spinning-school costing £15,000, and
a tax was placed on carriages and coaches in 1757
to support it.   At the fourth anniversary in 1749 of
the " Boston Society for promoting Industry and
Frugality," three hundred " young spinsters " spun
on their wheels on Boston Common.   And a pretty
sight it must have been : the fair young girls in the
quaint and pretty dress of the times, shown to us in
Hogarth's prints, spinning on the green grass under

the great trees.   In 1754, on a like occasion, a
minister preached to the " spinsters," and a collection of £453 was taken up.   This was in currency
of depreciated value.   At the same time premiums
were offered in Pennsylvania for weaving linen and
spinning thread.   Benjamin Franklin wrote in his
Poor Richard's Almanac : —

> " Many estates are spent in the getting,
>   Since women for tea forsook spinning and knitting."

But the German colonists long before this had been
famous flax-raisers.   A Pennsylvania poet in 1692
descanted on the flax-workers of Germantown : —

> " Where live High German people and Low Dutch
>   Whose trade in weaving linen cloth is much,
>   There grows the flax as also you may know,
>   That from the same they do divide the tow."

Father Pastorius, their leader, forever commemorated his interest in his colony and in the textile
arts by his choice for a device for a seal.   Whittier
thus describes it in his *Pennsylvania Pilgrim* : —

> " Still on the town-seal his device is found,
>   Grapes, flax, and thread-spool on a three-foil ground
>   With *Vinum, Linum, et Textrinum* wound."

Virginia was earlier even in awakening interest in
manufacturing flax than Massachusetts, for wild flax

grew there in profusion, ready for gathering. In
1646 two houses were ordered to be erected at
Jamestown as spinning-schools. These were to be
well built and well heated. Each county was to
send to these schools two poor children, seven or
eight years old, to be taught carding, spinning, and
knitting. Each child was to be supplied by the
county authorities on admission to the school with
six barrels of Indian corn, a pig, two hens, clothing,
shoes, a bed, rug, blanket, two coverlets, a wooden
tray, and two pewter dishes or cups. This plan was
not wholly carried out. Prizes in tobacco (which
was the current money of Virginia in which everything was paid) were given, however, for every
pound of flax, every skein of yarn, every yard of
linen of Virginia production, and soon flax-wheels
and spinners were plentiful.

Intelligent attempts were made to start these
industries in the South. Governor Lucas wrote to
his daughter, Mrs. Pinckney, in Charleston, South
Carolina, in 1745 : —

" I send by this Sloop two Irish servants, viz. : a Weaver
and a Spinner. I am informed Mr. Cattle hath produced
both Flax and Hemp. I pray you will purchase some, and
order a loom and spinning-wheel to be made for them, and
set them to work. I shall order Flax sent from Philadelphia with seed, that they may not be idle. I pray you will

also purchase Wool and sett them to making Negroes clothing which may be sufficient for my own People.

"As I am afraid one Spinner can't keep a Loom at work,
I pray you will order a Sensible Negroe woman or two to
learn to spin, and wheels to be made for them; the man
Servant will direct the Carpenter in making the loom and
the woman will direct the Wheel."

The following year Madam Pinckney wrote to
her father that the woman had spun all the material
they could get, so was idle ; that the loom had been
made, but had no tackling ; that she would make
the harness for it, if two pounds of shoemaker's
thread were sent her. The sensible negro woman
and hundreds of others learned well to spin, and
excellent cloth has been always woven in the low
country of Carolina, as well as in the upper districts,
till our own time.

In the revolt of feeling caused by the Stamp Act,
there was a constant social pressure to encourage
the manufacture and wearing of goods of American
manufacture. As one evidence of this movement
the president and first graduating class of Rhode
Island College — now Brown University — were
clothed in fabrics made in New England. From
Massachusetts to South Carolina the women of the
colonies banded together in patriotic societies called
Daughters of Liberty, agreeing to wear only gar-

ments of homespun manufacture, and to drink no
tea.   In many New England towns they gathered
together to spin, each bringing her own wheel.   At
one meeting seventy linen-wheels were employed.
In Rowley, Massachusetts, the meeting of the
Daughters is thus described : —

" A number of thirty-three respectable ladies of the town
met at sunrise with their wheels to spend the day at the
house of the Rev'd Jedediah Jewell, in the laudable design
of a spinning match.   At an hour before sunset, the ladies
there appearing neatly dressed, principally in homespun, a
polite and generous repast of American production was set
for their entertainment.   After which being present many
spectators of both sexes, Mr. Jewell delivered a profitable
discourse from Romans xii. 2 : " Not slothful in business,
fervent in spirit, serving the Lord."

Matters of church and patriotism were never far
apart in New England ; so whenever the spinners
gathered at New London, Newbury, Ipswich, or
Beverly, they always had an appropriate sermon.
A favorite text was Exodus xxxv. 25 :   " And all
the women that were wise-hearted did spin with
their hands."   When the Northboro women met,
they presented the results of their day's work to
their minister.   There were forty-four women and
they spun 2223 knots of linen and tow, and wove
one linen sheet and two towels.

By Revolutionary times General Howe thought
" Linen and Woollen Goods much wanted by the
Rebels"; hence when he prepared to evacuate Boston
he ordered all such goods carried away with him.
But he little knew the domestic industrial resources
of the Americans.   Women were then most proficient in spinning.   In 1777 Miss Eleanor Fry of
East Greenwich, Rhode Island, spun seven skeins one
knot linen yarn in one day, an extraordinary amount.
This was enough to weave twelve linen handkerchiefs.   At this time when there were about five or
six skeins to a pound of flax, the pay for spinning
was sixpence a skein.   The Abbé Robin wondered
at the deftness of New England spinners.

In 1789 an outcry was raised against the luxury
said to be eating away the substance of the new
country.   The poor financial administration of the
government seemed deranging everything; and again
a social movement was instituted in New England
to promote " Occonomy and Household Industries."   " The Rich and Great strive by example to
convince the Populace of their error by Growing
their own Flax and Wool, having some one in the
Family to dress it, and all the Females spin, several
weave and bleach the linen."   The old spinning-
matches were revived.   Again the ministers preached
to the faithful women " Oeconomists," who thus

combined religion, patriotism, and industry. Truly it was, as a contemporary writer said, "a pleasing Sight: some spinning, some reeling, some carding cotton, some combing flax," as they were preached to.

Within a few years attempts have been made in England and Ireland to encourage flax-growing, as before it is spun it gives employment to twenty different classes of laborers, many parts of which work can be done by young and unskilled children. In Courtrai, where hand spinning and weaving of flax still flourish, the average earnings of a family are three pounds a week. In Finland homespun linen still is made in every household. The British Spinning and Weaving School in New Bond Street is an attempt to revive the vanished industry in England. In our own country it is pleasant to record that the National Association of Cotton Manufacturers is planning to start on a large scale the culture and manufacture of flax in our Eastern states; this is not, however, with any thought of reviving either the preparation, spinning, or weaving of flax by old-time hand processes.

Flax-spinning

CHAPTER IX

WOOL CULTURE AND SPINNING

With a Postscript on Cotton

THE art of spinning was an honorable occupation for women as early as the ninth century; and it was so universal that it furnished a legal title by which an unmarried woman is known to this day. Spinster is the only one of all her various womanly titles that survives; webster, shepster, litster, brewster, and baxter are obsolete. The occupations are also obsolete save those indicated by shepster and baxter — that is, the cutting out of cloth and baking of bread; these are the only duties among them all that she still performs.

The wool industry dates back to prehistoric man. The patience, care, and skill involved in its manufacture have ever exercised a potent influence on civilization. It is, therefore, interesting and gratifying to note the intelligent eagerness of our first colonists for wool culture. It was quickly and proudly noted of towns and of individuals as a proof of their rapid and substantial progress that they could carry on any of the steps of the cloth industry. Good Judge Sewall piously exulted when Brother Moody started a successful fulling-mill in Boston. Johnson in his *Wonder-working Providence* tells with pride that by 1654 New Eng-landers " have a fulling-mill and caused their little ones to be very dilligent in spinning cotton-woole, many of them having been clothiers in England." This has ever seemed to me one of the fortunate conditions that tended to the marked success of the Massachusetts Bay Colony, that so many had been "clothiers" or cloth-workers in England; or had come from shires in England where wool was raised and cloth made, and hence knew the importance of the industry as well as its practical workings.

As early as 1643 the author of *New England's First Fruits* wrote: " They are making linens, fustians, dimities, and look immediately to woollens from their own sheep." Johnson estimated the number of sheep in the colony of Massachusetts, about 1644, as three thousand. Soon the great wheel was whir-ring in every New England house. The raising of sheep was encouraged in every way. They were permitted to graze on the commons; it was for-bidden to send them from the colony; no sheep under two years old could be killed to sell; if a dog killed a sheep, the dog's owner must hang him and pay double the cost of the sheep. All persons who were not employed in other ways, as single women, girls, and boys, were required to spin. Each family must contain one spinner. These spinners were formed into divisions or "squadrons" of ten persons; each division had a director. There were no drones in this hive; neither the wealth nor high station of parents excused children from this work. Thus all were levelled to one kind of labor, and by this levelling all were also elevated to independence. When the open expression of revolt came, the homespun industries seemed a firm rock for the foundation of liberty. People joined in agreements to eat no lamb or mutton, that thus sheep might be preserved, and to wear no imported woollen cloth. They gave prizes for spinning and weaving.

Great encouragement was given in Virginia in early days to the raising and manufacture of wool. The Assembly estimated that five children not over thirteen years of age could by their work readily spin and weave enough to keep thirty persons clothed. Six pounds of tobacco was paid to any one bringing to the county court-house where he resided a yard of homespun woollen cloth, made wholly in his family; twelve pounds of tobacco were offered for reward for a dozen pair of wool-

len hose knitted at home.   Slaves were taught to
spin; and wool-wheels and wool-cards are found
by the eighteenth century on every inventory of
planters' house furnishings.

The Pennsylvania settlers were early in the encouragement of wool manufacture.   The present
industry of hosiery and knit goods long known as
Germantown goods began with the earliest settlers
of that Pennsylvania town.   Stocking-weavers were
there certainly as early as 1723; and it is asserted
there were knitting-machines.   At any rate, one
Mack, the son of the founder of the Dunkers, made
"leg stockings" and gloves.   Rev. Andrew Bur-
naby, who was in Germantown in 1759, told of a
great manufacture of stockings at that date.   In
1777 it was said that a hundred Germantown stocking-weavers were out of employment through the
war.   Still it was not till 1850 that patents for
knitting-machines were taken out there.

Among the manufactures of the province of
Pennsylvania in 1698 were druggets, serges, and
coverlets; and among the registered tradesmen were
dyers, fullers, comb-makers, card-makers, weavers,
and spinners.   The Swedish colony as early as 1673
had the wives and daughters "employing themselves in spinning wool and flax and many in weaving."   The fairs instituted by William Penn for

the encouragement of domestic manufactures and trade in general, which were fostered by Franklin and continued till 1775, briskly stimulated wool and flax manufacture.

In 1765 and in 1775 rebellious Philadelphians banded together with promises not to eat or suffer to be eaten in their families any lamb or "meat of the mutton kind"; in this the Philadelphia butchers, patriotic and self-sacrificing, all joined. A wool-factory was built and fitted up and an appeal made to the women to save the state. In a month four hundred wool-spinners were at work. But the war cut off the supply of raw material, and the manufacture languished. In 1790, after the war, fifteen hundred sets of irons for spinning-wheels were sold from one shop, and mechanics everywhere were making looms.

New Yorkers were not behindhand in industry. Lord Cornbury wrote home to England, in 1705, that he "had seen serge made upon Long Island that any man might wear; they make very good linen for common use; as for Woollen I think they have brought that to too great perfection."

In Cornbury's phrase, "too great perfection," may be found the key for all the extraordinary and apparently stupid prohibitions and restrictions placed by the mother-country on colonial wool manufacture.   The growth of the woollen industry in any colony was regarded at once by England with jealous eyes.   Wool was the pet industry and principal staple of Great Britain; and well it might be, for until the reign of Henry VIII. English garments from head to foot were wholly of wool, even the shoes.   Wool was also received in England as currency.   Thomas Fuller said, " The wealth of our nation is folded up in broadcloth."   Therefore, the Crown, aided by the governors of the provinces, sought to maintain England's monopoly by regulating and reducing the culture of wool in America through prohibiting the exportation to England of any American wool or woollen materials.   In 1699 all vessels sailing to England from the colonies were prohibited taking on board any " Wool, Woolfells, Shortlings, Moslings, Wool Flocks, Worsteds, Bays, Bay or Woollen Yarn, Cloath, Serge, Kersey, Says, Frizes, Druggets, Shalloons, etc." ; and an arbitrary law was passed prohibiting the transportation of home-made woollens from one American province to another.   These laws were never fully observed and never checked the culture and manufacture of wool in this country.   Hence our colonies were spared the cruel fate by which England's same policy paralyzed and obliterated in a few years the glorious wool industry of Ireland.   Luckily for us, it is further across the Atlantic Ocean than across St. George's Channel.

The " all-wool goods a yard wide," which we so easily purchase to-day, meant to the colonial dame or daughter the work of many weeks and months, from the time when the fleeces were first given to her deft hands. Fleeces had to be opened with care, and have all pitched or tarred locks, dag-locks, brands, and feltings cut out. These cut-tings were not wasted, but were spun into coarse yarn. The white locks were carefully tossed and separated and tied into net bags with tallies to be dyed. Another homely saying, " dyed in the wool," showed a process of much skill. Blue, in all shades, was the favorite color, and was dyed with indigo. So great was the demand for this dye-stuff that indigo-pedlers travelled over the country selling it.

Madder, cochineal, and logwood dyed beautiful reds. The bark of red oak or hickory made very pretty shades of brown and yellow. Various flowers growing on the farm could be used for dyes. The flower of the goldenrod, when pressed of its juice, mixed with indigo, and added to alum, made a beautiful green. The juice of the pokeberry boiled with alum made crimson dye, and a violet juice from the petals of the iris, or " flower-de-luce,"

o

that blossomed in June meadows, gave a delicate light purple tinge to white wool.

The bark of the sassafras was used for dyeing yellow or orange color, and the flowers and leaves of the balsam also. Fustic and copperas gave yellow dyes. A good black was obtained by boiling woollen cloth with a quantity of the leaves of the common field-sorrel, then boiling again with logwood and copperas.

In the South there were scores of flowers and leaves that could be used for dyes. During the Revolutionary War one enterprising South Carolinian got a guinea a pound for a yellow dye he made from the sweet-leaf or horse-laurel. The leaves and berries of gall-berry bush made a good black much used by hatters and weavers. The root of the barberry gave wool a beautiful yellow, as did the leaves of the devil's-bit. The petals of Jerusalem artichoke and St.-John's-wort dyed yellow. Yellow root is a significant name and reveals its use: oak, walnut, or maple bark dyed brown. Often the woven cloth was dyed, not the wool.

The next process was carding; the wool was first greased with rape oil or "melted swine's grease," which had to be thoroughly worked in; about three pounds of grease were put into ten pounds of wool. Wool-cards were rectangular pieces of thin board,

with a simple handle on the back or at the side; to
this board was fastened a smaller rectangle of strong
leather, set thick with slightly bent wire teeth, like
a coarse brush.   The carder took one card with her

Carding Wool

left hand, and resting it on her knee, drew a tuft of
wool across it several times, until a sufficient quantity
of fibre had been caught upon the wire teeth.   She
then drew the second wool-card, which had to be
warmed, across the first several times, until the

fibres were brushed parallel by all these "tummings." Then by a deft and catchy motion the
wool was rolled or carded into small fleecy rolls
which were then ready for spinning.

Wool-combs were shaped like the letter T, with
about thirty long steel teeth from ten to eighteen
inches long set at right angles with the top of the T.
The wool was carefully placed on one comb, and
with careful strokes the other comb laid the long
staple smooth for hard-twisted spinning. It was
tedious and slow work, and a more skilful operation than carding; and the combs had to be kept
constantly heated; but no machine-combing ever
equalled hand-combing. There was a good deal
of waste in this combing, that is, large clumps of
tangled wool called noil were combed out. They
were not really wasted, we may be sure, by our
frugal ancestors, but were spun into coarse yarn.

An old author says: "The action of spinning
must be learned by practice, not by relation." Sung
by the poets, the grace and beauty of the occupation
has ever shared praise with its utility.

Wool-spinning was truly one of the most flexible
and alert series of movements in the world, and
to its varied and graceful poises our grandmothers
may owe part of the dignity of carriage that was so
characteristic of them. The spinner stood slightly

Wool-spinning

leaning forward, lightly poised on the ball of the
left foot; with her left hand she picked up from
the platform of the wheel a long slender roll of the
soft carded wool about as large round as the little
finger, and deftly wound the end of the fibres on
the point of the spindle.   She then gave a gentle

motion to the wheel with a wooden peg held in her right hand, and seized with the left the roll at exactly the right distance from the spindle to allow for one "drawing." Then the hum of the wheel rose to a sound like the echo of wind; she stepped backward quickly, one, two, three steps, holding high the long yarn as it twisted and quivered. Suddenly she glided forward with even, graceful stride and let the yarn wind on the swift spindle. Another pinch of the wool-roll, a new turn of the wheel, and *da capo*.

The wooden peg held by the spinner deserves a short description; it served the purpose of an elongated finger, and was called a driver, wheel-peg, etc. It was about nine inches long, an inch or so in diameter; and at about an inch from the end was slightly grooved in order that it might surely catch the spoke and thus propel the wheel.

It was a good day's work for a quick, active spinner to spin six skeins of yarn a day. It was estimated that to do that with her quick backward and forward steps she walked over *twenty miles*.

The yarn might be wound directly upon the wooden spindle as it was spun, or at the end of the spindle might be placed a spool or broach which twisted with the revolving spindle, and held the new-spun yarn. This broach was usually simply a

stiff roll of paper, a corn-cob, or a roll of corn-husk.
When the ball of yarn was as large as the broach

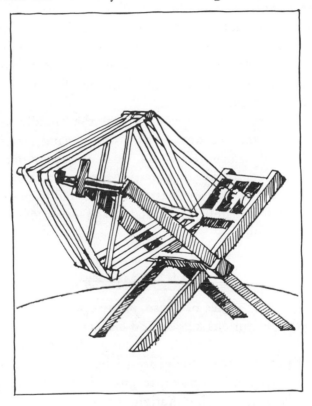

Triple Reel

would hold, the spinner placed wooden pegs in
certain holes in the spokes of her spinning-wheel

and tied the end of the yarn to one peg.   Then she took off the belt of her wheel and whirred the big wheel swiftly round, thus winding the yarn on the pegs into hanks or clews two yards in circumference, which were afterwards tied with a loop of yarn into knots of forty threads; while seven of these knots made a skein.   The clock-reel was used for winding yarn, also a triple reel.

The yarn might be wound from the spindle into skeins in another way, — by using a hand-reel, an implement which really did exist in every farm-house, though the dictionaries are ignorant of it, as they are of its universal folk-name, niddy-noddy. This is fortunately preserved in an every-day domestic riddle : —

> "Niddy-noddy, niddy-noddy,
> Two heads and one body."

The three pieces of these niddy-noddys were set together at curious angles, and are here shown rather than described in words.   Holding the reel in the left hand by seizing the central " body " or rod, the yarn was wound from end to end of the reel, by an odd, waving, wobbling motion, into knots and skeins of the same size as by the first process described. One of these niddy-noddys was owned by Nabby Marshall of Deerfield, who lived to be one hundred

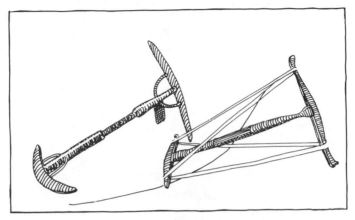

" Niddy-noddy, two heads and one body "

and four years old. The other was brought from Ireland in 1733 by Hugh Maxwell, father of the Revolutionary patriot Colonel Maxwell. As it was at a time of English prohibitions and restrictions of American manufactures, this niddy-noddy, as an accessory and promoter of colonial wool manufacture, was smuggled into the country.

Sometimes the woollen yarn was spun twice; especially if a close, hard-twisted thread was desired, to be woven into a stiff, wiry cloth. When there were two, the first spinning was called a roving. The single spinning was usually deemed sufficient to furnish yarn for knitting, where softness and warmth were the desired requisites.

It was the pride of a good spinster to spin the finest yarn, and one Mistress Mary Prigge spun a pound of wool into fifty hanks of eighty-four thousand yards; in all, nearly forty-eight miles. If the yarn was to be knitted, it had to be washed and cleansed. The wife of Colonel John May, a prominent man in Boston, wrote in her diary for one day : —

"A large kettle of yarn to attend upon. Lucretia and self rinse, scour through many waters, get out, dry, attend to, bring in, do up and sort 110 score of yarn; this with baking and ironing. Then went to hackling flax."

It should be remembered that all those bleaching processes, the wringing out and rinsing in various waters, were far more wearisome then than they would be to-day, for the water had to be carried laboriously in pails and buckets, and drawn with pumps and well-sweeps; there were no pipes and conduits. Happy the household that had a running brook near the kitchen door.

Of course all these operations and manipulations usually occupied many weeks and months, but they could be accomplished in a much shorter time. When President Nott of Union College, and his brother Samuel, the famous preacher, were boys on a stony farm in Connecticut, one of the brothers needed a new suit of clothes, and as the father was sick there was neither money nor wool in the house. The mother sheared some half-grown fleece from her sheep, and in less than a week the boy wore it as clothing. The shivering and generous sheep were protected by wrappings of braided straw. During the Revolution, it is said that in a day and a night a mother and her daughters in Townsend, Massachusetts, sheared a black and a white sheep, carded from the fleece a gray wool, spun, wove, cut and made a suit of clothes for a boy to wear off to fight for liberty.

The wool industry easily furnished home occupation to an entire family. Often by the bright firelight in the early evening every member of the household might be seen at work on the various stages of wool manufacture or some of its necessary adjuncts, and varied and cheerful industrial sounds fill the room. The old grandmother, at light and easy work, is carding the wool into fleecy rolls, seated next the fire; for, as the ballad says, " she was old and saw right dimly." The mother, stepping as lightly as one of her girls, spins the rolls into woollen yarn on the great wheel. The oldest daughter sits at the clock-reel, whose continuous buzz and occasional click mingles with the humming rise and fall of the wool-wheel, and the irritating

scratch, scratch, of the cards.   A little girl at a small
wheel is filling quills with woollen yarn for the loom,
not a skilled work; the irregular sound shows her
intermittent industry.   The father is setting fresh
teeth in a wool-card, while the boys are whittling
hand-reels and loom-spools.

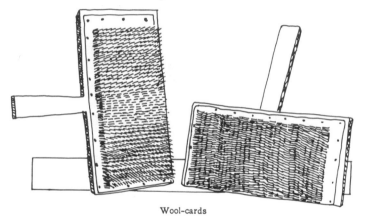

Wool-cards

One of the household implements used in wool
manufacture, the wool-card, deserves a short special
history as well as a description.   In early days the
leather back of the wool-card was pierced with an
awl by hand; the wire teeth were cut off from a
length of wire, were slightly bent, and set and
clinched one by one.   These cards were laboriously
made by many persons at home, for their household
use.   As early as 1667 wire was made in Massachu-

setts; and its chief use was for wool-cards.   By Revolutionary times it was realized that the use of wool-cards was almost the mainspring of the wool industry, and £100 bounty was offered by Massachusetts for card-wire made in the state from iron mined in what they called then the " United American States."   In 1784 a machine was invented by an American which would cut and bend thirty-six thousand wire teeth an hour.   Another machine pierced the leather backs.   This gave a new employment to women and children at home and some spending-money.   They would get boxes of the bent wire teeth and bundles of the leather backs from the factories and would set the teeth in the backs while sitting around the open fire in the evening.   They did this work, too, while visiting — spending an afternoon ; and it was an unconscious and diverting work like knitting; scholars set wool-cards while studying, and schoolmistresses while teaching.   This method of manufacture was superseded fifteen years later by a machine invented by Amos Whittemore, which held, cut, and pierced the leather, drew the wire from a reel, cut and bent a looped tooth, set it, bent it, fastened the leather on the back, and speedily turned out a fully made card. John Randolph said this machine had everything but an immortal soul.   By this time spinning and weav-

ing machinery began to crowd out home work, and
the machine-made cards were needed to keep up with
the increased demand.   At last machines crowded
into every department of cloth manufacture; and
after carding-machines were invented in England
— great rollers set with card-teeth — they were set
up in many mills throughout the United States.

Families soon sent all their wool to these mills
to be carded even when it was spun and woven at
home.   It was sent rolled up in a homespun sheet
or blanket pinned with thorns; and the carded rolls
ready for spinning were brought home in the same
way, and made a still bigger bundle which was light
in weight for its size.   Sometimes a red-cheeked
farmer's lass would be seen riding home from the
carding-mill, through New England woods or along
New England lanes, with a bundle of carded wool
towering up behind her bigger than her horse.

Of the use and manufacture of cotton I will
speak very shortly.   Our greatest, cheapest, most
indispensable fibre is also our latest one.   It never
formed one of the homespun industries of the colonies; in fact, it was never an article of extended
domestic manufacture.

A little cotton was always used in early days for
stuffing bedquilts, petticoats, warriors' armor, and
similar purposes.   It was bought by the pound,

East India cotton, in small quantities; the seeds
were picked out one by one, by hand; it was carded
on wool-cards, and spun into a rather intractable yarn
which was used as warp for linsey-woolsey and rag
carpets.   Even in England no cotton weft, no all-
cotton fabrics, were made till after 1760, till Har-
greave's time.   Sometimes a twisted yarn was made
of one thread of cotton and one of wool which was
knit into durable stockings.   Cotton sewing-thread
was unknown in England.   Pawtucket women
named Wilkinson made the first cotton thread on
their home spinning-wheels in 1792.

Cotton was planted in America, Bancroft says, in
1621, but MacMaster asserts it was never seen
growing here till after the Revolution save as a
garden ornament with garden flowers.   This asser-
tion seems oversweeping when Jefferson could write
in a letter in 1786 : —

" The four southermost States make a great deal of
cotton.   Their poor are almost entirely clothed with it in
winter and summer.   In winter they wear shirts of it and
outer clothing of cotton and wool mixed.   In summer
their shirts are linen, but the outer clothing cotton.   The
dress of the women is almost entirely of cotton, manufactured by themselves, except the richer class, and even
many of these wear a great deal of homespun cotton.   It
is as well manufactured as the calicoes of Europe."

Still cotton was certainly not a staple of consequence. We were the last to enter the list of cotton-
producing countries and we have surpassed them all.

The difficulty of removing the seeds from the
staple practically thrust cotton out of common use.
In India a primitive and cumbersome set of rollers
called a churka partially cleaned India cotton. A
Yankee schoolmaster, Eli Whitney, set King Cotton on a throne by his invention of the cotton-gin
in 1792. This comparatively simple but inesti-
mable invention completely revolutionized cloth
manufacture in England and America. It also
changed general commerce, industrial development,
and the social and economic order of things, for it
gave new occupations and offered new modes of life
to hundreds of thousands of persons. It entirely
changed and cheapened our dress, and altered rural
life both in the North and South.

A man could, by hand-picking, clean only about
a pound of cotton a day. The cotton-gin cleaned
as much in a day as had taken the hand-picker a
year to accomplish. Cotton was at once planted
in vast amounts ; but it certainly was not plentiful
till then. Whitney had never seen cotton nor
cotton seed when he began to plan his invention ;
nor did he, even in Savannah, find cotton to experiment with until after considerable search.

After the universal manufacture and use of the cotton-gin, negro women wove cotton in Southern houses, sometimes spinning their own cotton thread ; more frequently buying it mill-spun.   But, after all, this was in too small amounts to be of importance ; it needed the spinning-jennies and power-looms of vast mills to use up the profuse supply afforded by the gin.

A very interesting account of the domestic manufacture of cotton in Tennessee about the year 1850 was written for me by Mrs. James Stuart Pilcher, State Regent of the Daughters of the American Revolution in Tennessee.   A portion of her pleasant story reads : —

"There were two looms in the loom-room, and two negro women were kept busy all the time weaving; there were eight or ten others who did nothing but spin cotton and woollen thread; others spooled and reeled it into hanks. The spinning was all done on the large wheel, from the raw cotton; a corn-shuck was wrapped tightly around the steel spindle, then the thread was run and spun on this shuck until it was full; then these were reeled off into hanks of thread, then spooled on to corn-cobs with holes burned through them.   These were placed in an upright frame, with long slender rods of hickory wood something like a ramrod run through them.   The frame held about one hundred of these cob-spools; the end of the cotton

P

thread from each spool was gathered up by an experienced warper who carried all the threads back and forth on the large warping-bars; this was a difficult task; only the brightest negro women were warpers. The thread had been dyed before spooling and the vari-colored cob-spools could be arranged to make stripes lengthwise of the cloth; and the hanks had also been dipped in a boiling-hot sizing made of meal and water. The warp-threads were carefully taken from the bars and rolled upon the wooden beam of the loom, the ends passed through the sley and tied. The weaver then began her work. The thread for the filling (called the woof by the negroes) was reeled from the hank on the winding-blades, upon small canes about four inches long which, when full, were placed in the wooden shuttles. These women spun and wove all the clothing worn by the negroes on the plantation; cotton cloth for women and men in the summer time; and jeans for the men; linsey-woolsey for the women and children for winter. All were well clothed. The women taught us to spin, but the weavers were cross and would not let us touch the loom, for they said we broke the threads in the warp. My grandmother never interfered with them when they were careful in their work. We would say, ' Please make Aunt Rhody let me weave!' She answered, ' No, she is managing the loom; if she is willing, very well; if not, you must not worry her.' We thought it great fun to try to weave, but generally had to pay Aunt Rhody for our meddling by giving her cake, ribbons, or candy."

The colonists were constantly trying to find new materials for spinning, and also used many make-shifts. Parkman, in his *Old Régime*, tells that in the year 1704, when a ship was lost that was to bring cloth and wool to Quebec, a Madame de Rèpentigny, one of the aristocrats of the French-Canadian colony, spun and wove coarse blankets of nettle and linden bark. Similar experiments were made by the English colonists. Coarse thread was spun out of nettle-fibre by pioneers in western New York. Levi Beardsley, in his *Reminiscences*, tells of his mother at the close of the last century, in her frontier home at Richfield Springs, weaving bags and coarse garments from the nettles which grew so rankly everywhere in that vicinity. Deer hair and even cow's hair was collected from the tanners, spun with some wool, and woven into a sort of felted blanket.

Silk-grass, a much-vaunted product, was sent back to England on the first ships and was every-where being experimented with. Coarse wicking was spun from the down of the milkweed — an airy, feathery material that always looks as if it ought to be put to many uses, yet never has seemed of much account in any trial that has been made of it.

CHAPTER X

HAND-WEAVING

ANY one who passed through a New England village on a week day a century ago, or rode up to the door of a Pennsylvania or Virginia house, would probably be greeted with a heavy thwack-thwack from within doors, a regular sound which would readily be recognized by every one at that time as proceeding from weaving on a hand-loom. The presence of these looms was, perhaps, not so universal in every house as that of their homespun companions, the great and little wheels, for they required more room; but they were found in every house of any considerable size, and in many also where they seemed to fill half the building. Many households had a loom-room, usually in an ell part of the house; others used an attic or a shed-loft as a weaving-room. Every farmer's daughter knew how to weave as well as to spin, yet it was not recognized as wholly woman's work as was spinning; for there was a trade of hand-weaving for men, to which they were apprenticed. Every

town had professional weavers. They were a universally respected class, and became the ancestors of
many of the wealthiest and most influential citizens
to-day. They took in yarn and thread to weave on
their looms at their own homes at so much a yard;
wove their own yarn into stuffs to sell; had appren-
tices to their trade; and also went out working by
the day at their neighbors' houses, sometimes carrying their looms many miles with them.

Weavers were a universally popular element of
the community. The travelling weaver was, like
all other itinerant tradesmen of the day, a welcome
newsmonger; and the weaver who took in weaving
was often a stationary gossip, and gathered inquiring
groups in his loom-room; even children loved to
go to his door to beg for bits of colored yarn —
thrums — which they used in their play, and also
tightly braided to wear as shoestrings, hair-laces, etc.

The hand-loom used in the colonies, and occasionally still run in country towns to-day, is an historic
machine, one of great antiquity and dignity. It is,
perhaps, the most absolute bequest of past centuries
which we have had, unchanged, in domestic use till
the present time. You may see a loom like the Yankee one shown here in Giotto's famous fresco in the
Campanile, painted in 1335; another, still the same,
in Hogarth's *Idle Apprentice*, painted just four hun-

dred years later. Many tribes and nations have
hand-looms resembling our own ; but these are
exactly like it. Hundreds of thousands of men and
women of the generations of these seven centuries
since Giotto's day have woven on just such looms
as our grandparents had in their homes.

This loom consists of a frame of four square timber posts, about seven feet high, set about as far
apart as the posts of a tall four-post bedstead, and
connected at top and bottom by portions of a frame.
From post to post across one end, which may be
called the back part of the loom, is the yarn-beam,
about six inches in diameter. Upon it are wound
the warp-threads, which stretch in close parallels
from it to the cloth-beam at the front of the loom.
The cloth-beam is about ten inches in diameter, and
the cloth is wound as the weaving proceeds.

The yarn-beam or yarn-roll or warp-beam was
ever a very important part of the loom. It should
be made of close-grained, well-seasoned wood. The
iron axle should be driven in before the beam is
turned. If the beam is ill-turned and irregular in
shape, no even, perfect woof can come from it. The
slightest variation in its dimensions makes the warp
run off unevenly, and the web never "sets" well,
but has some loose threads.

We have seen the homespun yarn, whether linen

or woollen, left in carefully knotted skeins after being spun and cleaned, bleached, or dyed.   To prepare

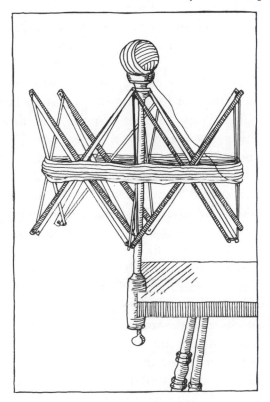

Swifts

it for use on the loom a skein is placed on the swift, an ingenious machine, a revolving cylindrical frame made of strips of wood arranged on the principle of the lazy-tongs so the size can be increased or diminished at pleasure, and thus take on and hold firmly any sized skein of yarn. This cylinder is supported on a centre shaft that revolves in a socket, and may be set in a heavy block on the floor or fastened to a table or chair. A lightly made, carved swift was a frequent lover's gift. I have a beautiful one of whale-ivory, mother-of-pearl, and fine white bone which was made on a three years' whaling voyage by a Nantucket sea-captain as a gift to his waiting bride; it has over two hundred strips of fine white carved bone. Both quills for the weft and spools for the warp may be wound from the swift by a quilling-wheel, small wheels of various shapes, some being like a flax-wheel, but more simple in construction. The quill or bobbin is a small reed or quill, pierced from end to end, and when wound is set in the recess of the shuttle.

When the piece is to be set, a large number of shuttles and spools are filled in advance. The full spools are then placed in a row one above the other in a spool-holder, sometimes called a skarne or scarne. As I have not found this word in any dictionary, ancient or modern, its correct spelling is unknown. Sylvester Judd, in his *Margaret*, spells it skan. Skean and skayn have also been seen.

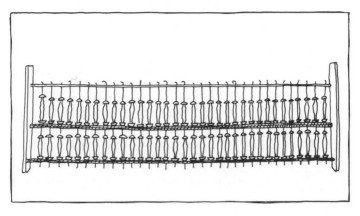

Skarne with Loom Spools

Though ignored by lexicographers, it was an article and word in established and universal use in the colonies. I have seen it in newspaper advertisements of weavers' materials, and in inventories of weavers' estates, spelled *ad libitum;* and elderly country folk, both in the North and South, who remember old-time weaving, know it to-day.

It seems to me impossible to explain clearly in words, though it is simple enough in execution, the laying of the piece, the orderly placing the warp on the warp-beam. The warping-bars are entirely detached from the loom, are an accessory, not a part of it. They are two upright bars of wood, each holding a number of wooden pins set at right angles to the bars, and held together by crosspieces. Let forty full spools be placed in the skarne, one above the other. The free ends of threads from the spools are gathered in the hand, and fastened to a pin at the top of the warping-bars. The group of threads then are carried from side to side of the bars, passing around a pin on one bar, then around a pin on the opposite bar, to the extreme end; then back again in the same way, the spools revolving on wires and freely playing out the warp-threads, till a sufficient length of threads are stretched on the bars. Weavers of olden days could calculate exactly and skilfully the length of the threads thus wound. You take off twenty yards of threads if you want to weave twenty yards of cloth. Forty warp-threads make what was called a bout or section. A warp of two hundred threads was designated as a warp of five bouts, and the bars had to be filled five times to set it unless a larger skarne with more spools was used. From the warping-bars these bouts are carefully wound on the warp-beam.

Without attempting to explain farther, let us consider the yarn-beam neatly wound with these warp-threads and set in the loom — that the "warping" and "beaming" are finished. The "drawing" or "entering" comes next; the end of each warp-thread in regular order is "thumbed" or drawn in with a warping-needle through the eye or "mail" of the harness, or heddle.

The heddle is a row of twines, cords, or wires called leashes, which are stretched vertically between two horizontal bars or rods, placed about a foot apart. One rod is suspended by a pulley at the top of the loom; and to the lower rod is hitched the foot-treadle. In the middle of each length of twine or wire is the loop or eye, through which a warp-thread is passed. In ordinary weaving there are two heddles, each fastened to a foot-treadle.

There is a removable loom attachment which when first shown to me was called a raddle. It is not necessary in weaving, but a convenience and help in preparing to weave. It is a wooden bar with a row of closely set, fine, wooden pegs. This is placed in the loom, and used only during the setting of the warp to keep the warp of proper width; the pegs keep the bouts or sections of the warp disentangled during the "thumbing in" of the threads through the heddle-eyes. This attachment is also called a ravel or raivel; and folk-names for it (not in the dictionary) were wrathe and rake; the latter a very good descriptive title.

The warp-threads next are drawn through the interspaces between two dents or strips of the sley or reed. This is done with a wire hook called a

sley-hook or reed-hook. Two warp-
threads are drawn in each space.

The sley or reed is composed of a row
of short and very thin parallel strips of
cane or metal, somewhat like comb-teeth,
called dents, fixed at both ends closely in
two long, strong, parallel bars of wood set
two or three or even four inches apart.
There may be fifty or sixty of these dents
to one inch, for weaving very fine linen;
usually there are about twenty, which
gives a "bier" — a counting out of forty
warp-threads to each inch. Sleys were
numbered according to the number of biers
they held. The number of dents to an
inch determined the "set of the web," the
fineness of the piece. This reed is placed
in a groove on the lower edge of a heavy
batten (or lay or lathe). This batten
hangs by two swords or side bars and
swings from an axle or "rocking tree" at
the top of the loom. As the heavy batten
swings on its axle, the reed forces with a
sharp blow every newly placed thread of
the weft into its proper place close to the
previously woven part of the texture.
This is the heavy thwacking sound heard
in hand-weaving.

On the accurate poise of the batten depends largely the evenness of the completed woof. If the material is heavy, the batten should be swung high, thus having a good sweep and much force in its blow. The batten should be so poised as to swing back itself into place after each blow.

The weaver, with foot on treadle, sits on a narrow, high bench, which is fastened from post to post of the loom. James Maxwell, the weaver-poet, wrote under his portrait in his *Weaver's Meditations*, printed in 1756: —

"Lo! here 'twixt Heaven and Earth I swing,
  And whilst the Shuttle swiftly flies,
With cheerful heart I work and sing
  And envy none beneath the skies."

There are three motions in hand-weaving. First: by the action of one foot-treadle one harness or heddle, holding every alternate warp-thread, is depressed from the level of the entire expanse of warp-threads.

The separation of the warp-threads by this depression of one harness is called a shed. Some elaborate patterns have six harnesses. In such a piece there are ten different sheds, or combinations of openings of the warp-threads. In a four-harness piece there are six different sheds.

Room is made by this shed for the shuttle, which, by the second motion, is thrown from one side of the loom to the other by the weaver's hand, and thus goes over every alternate thread. The revolving quill within the shuttle lets the weft-thread play out during this side-to-side motion of the shuttle. The shuttle must not be thrown too sharply else it will rebound and make a slack thread in the weft. By the third motion the batten crowds this weft-thread into place. Then the motion of the other foot-treadle forces down the other warp-threads which pass through the second set of harnesses, the shuttle is thrown back through this shed, and so on.

In order to show the amount of work, the number of separate motions in a day's work in weaving of close woollen cloth like broadcloth (which was only about three yards), we must remember that the shuttle was thrown over three thousand times, and the treadles pressed down and batten swung the same number of times.

A simple but clear description of the process of weaving is given in Ovid's *Metamorphoses*, thus Englished in 1724: —

" The piece prepare
And order every slender thread with care;
The web enwraps the beam, the reed divides

While through the widening space the shuttle glides,
Which their swift hands receive, then poised with lead
The swinging weight strikes close the inserted thread."

A loom attachment which I puzzled over was a tomble or tumble, the word being seen in eighteenth-century lists, etc., yet absolutely untraceable. I at last inferred, and a weaver confirmed my inference, that it was a corruption of temple, an attachment made of flat, narrow strips of wood as long as the

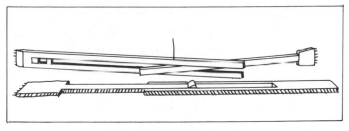

Loom Temples

web is wide, with hooks or pins at the end to catch into the selvage of the cloth, and keep the cloth stretched firmly an even width while the reed beats the weft-thread into place.

There were many other simple yet effective attachments to the loom. Their names have been upon the lips of scores of thousands of English-speaking people, and the words are used in all treatises on weaving; yet our dictionaries are dumb and ignorant of their existence.   There was the pace-weight, which kept the warp even ; and the bore staff, which tightened the warp.   When a sufficient length of woof had been woven (it was usually a few inches), the weaver proceeded to do what was called drawing a bore or a sink.   He shifted the temple forward ; rolled up the cloth on the cloth bar, which had a crank-handle and ratchets ; unwound the warp a few inches, shifted back the rods and heddles, and started afresh.

Looms and their appurtenances were usually made by local carpenters ; and it can plainly be seen that thus constant work was furnished to many classes of workmen in every community,—wood-turners, beam-makers, timber-sawyers, and others.   The various parts of the looms were in unceasing demand, though apparently they never wore out.   The sley was the most delicate part of the mechanism.   Good sley-makers could always command high prices for their sleys.   I have seen one whole and good, which has been in general use for weaving rag carpets ever since the War of 1812, for which a silver dollar was paid. Spools were turned and marked with the maker's in-itials.   There were choice and inexplicable lines in the shape of a shuttle as there are in a boat's hull. When a shuttle was carefully shaped, scraped, hol-lowed out, tipped with steel, and had the maker's initials burnt in it, it was a proper piece of work, of which any craftsman might be proud.   Apple-wood and boxwood were the choice for shuttles.

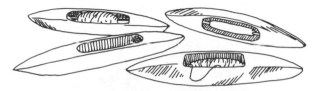

Loom Shuttles

Smaller looms, called tape-looms, braid-looms, belt-looms, garter-looms, or "gallus-frames," were seen in many American homes, and useful they were in days when linen, cotton, woollen, or silk tapes, bobbins, and webbings or ribbons were not common and cheap as to-day.   Narrow bands such as tapes, none-so-pretty's, ribbons, caddises, ferretings, inkles, were woven on these looms for use for garters, points, glove-ties, hair-laces, shoestrings, belts, hat-bands, stay-laces, breeches-suspenders, etc.

These tape-looms are a truly ancient form of appliance for the hand-weaving of narrow bands, — a heddle-frame.   They are rudely primitive in shape, but besides serving well the colonists in all our original states, are still in use among the Indian tribes in New Mexico and in Lapland, Italy, and northern Germany.   They are scarcely more than a slightly shaped board so cut in slits that the centre of the board is a row of narrow slats. These slats are pierced in a row by means of a heated wire

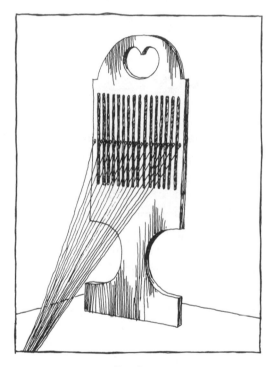

Tape-loom

and the warp-threads are passed through the holes.

A common form of braid-loom was one that was laid upon a table. A still simpler form was held upright on the lap, the knees being firmly pressed into semicircular indentations cut for the purpose on either side of the board which formed the lower part of the loom. The top of the loom was steadied by being tied with a band to the top of a chair, or a hook in the wall. It was such light and pretty work that it seemed merely an industrial amusement, and girls carried their tape-looms to a neighbor's house for an afternoon's work, just as they did their knitting-needles and ball of yarn. A fringe-loom might also be occasionally found, for weaving decorative fringes; these were more common in the Hudson River valley than elsewhere.

I have purposely given minute, but I trust not tiresome, details of the operation of weaving on a hand-loom, because a few years more will see the last of those who know the operation and the terms used. The fact that so many terms are now obsolete proves how quickly disuse brings oblivion. When in a country crowded full of weavers, as was England until about 1845, the knowledge has so suddenly disappeared, need we hope for much greater memory or longer life here? When what is termed the Westmoreland Revival of domestic industries was begun eight or ten years ago, the greatest difficulty was found in obtaining a hand-loom. No one knew how to set it up, and it was a long time before a weaver could be found to run it and teach others its use.

The first half of this century witnessed a vital struggle in England, and to an extent in America, between hand and power machinery, and an interesting race between spinning and weaving. Under old-time conditions it was calculated that it took the work of four spinners, who spun swiftly and constantly, to supply one weaver. As spinning was ever what was known as a by-industry, — that is, one that chiefly was done by being caught up at odd moments, — the supply both in England and America did not equal the weavers' demands, and ten spinners had to be calculated to supply yarn for one weaver. Hence weavers never had to work very hard; as a rule, they could have one holiday in the week. What with Sundays, wakes, and fairs, Irish weavers worked only two hundred days in the year. In England the weaver often had to spend one day out of the six hunting around the country for yarn for weft. So inventive wits were set at work to enlarge the supply of yarn, and spinning machinery was the result. Thereafter the looms and weavers were pushed hard and had to turn to invention. The shuttle had always simply been passed from one hand to the other of the weaver on either side of the web. The fly-shuttle was now invented, which by a simple piece of machinery, worked by one hand, threw the shuttle swiftly backward and forward, and the loom was ahead in the race. Then came the spinning-jenny, which spun yarn

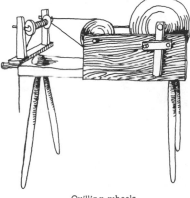

Quilling-wheels

with a hundred spindles on each machine. But this was for weft yarns, and did not make strong warps. Finally Arkwright supplied this lack in water-twist or " throstle-spun " yarn. All these inventions again overcrowded the weavers; all attempts at hand-spinning of cotton had become quickly extinct. Wool-spinning lingered longer.   Five Tomlinson sisters, — the youngest forty years old, — with two pair of wool-cards and five hand-wheels, paid the rent of their farm, kept three cows, one horse, had a ploughed field, and made prime butter and eggs.   One sister clung to her spinning till 1822.   Power-looms were invented to try to use up the jenny's supply of yarn, but these did not crowd out hand-looms.   Weavers never had so good wages.   It was the Golden Age of Cotton.   Some families earned six pounds a week ; good clothes, even to the extent of ruffled shirts, good furniture, even to silver spoons, good food, plentiful ale and beer, entered every English cottage with the weaving of cotton and wool.   A far more revolutionary and more hated machine than the power-loom was the combing-machine called Big Ben.

" Come all ye Master Combers, and hear of our Big Ben.
    He'll comb more wool than fifty of your men
    With their hand-combs, and comb-pots, and such old-
        fashioned way."

Flax-spinning and linen-weaving by power machinery were slower in being established.   Englishmen were halting in perfecting these machines. Napoleon offered in 1810 a million francs for a flax-spinning machine.   A clever Frenchman claimed to have invented one in response in a single day, but similar clumsy machines had then been running in England for twenty years. By 1850 men, women, and children — combers, spinners, and weavers — were no longer individual workers; they had become part of that great monster, the mill-machinery. Riots and misery were the first result of the passing of hand weaving and spinning.

In the *Vision of Piers Ploughman* (1360) are these lines : —

> " Cloth that cometh fro the wevyng
> Is nought comly to were
> Till it be fulled under foot
> Or in fullyng stokkes
> Wasshen wel with water
> And with taseles cracched,
> Y-touked and y-tented
> And under taillours hande."

Just so in the colonies four centuries later, cloth that came from the weaving was not comely to wear till it was fulled under foot or in fulling-stocks, washed well in water, scratched and dressed with teazels, dyed and tented, and put in the tailor's hands. Nor did the roll of centuries bring a change in the manner of proceeding. If grease had been put on the wool when it was carded, or sizing in the warp for the weaving, it was washed out by good rinsing from the woven cloth. This became now somewhat uneven and irregular in appearance, and full of knots and fuzzes which were picked out with hand-tweezers by burlers before it was fulled or milled, as it was sometimes called. The fulling-stocks were a trough in which an enormous oaken hammer was made to pound up and down, while the cloth was kept thoroughly wet with warm soap and water, or fullers' earth and water. Naturally this thickened the web much and reduced it in length. It was then teazelled; that is, a nap or rough surface was raised all over it by scratching it with weavers' teazels or thistles. Many wire brushes and metal substitutes have been tried to take the place of nature's gift to the cloth-worker, the teazel, but nothing has been invented to replace with full satisfaction that wonderful scratcher. For the slender recurved bracts of the teazel heads are stiff and prickly enough to roughen thoroughly the nap of the cloth, yet they yield at precisely the right point to keep from injuring the fabric.

If the cloth were to be "y-touked," that is, dyed, it was done at this period, and it was then "y-tented," spread on the tenter-field and caught on tenter-hooks, to shrink and dry.

Nowadays, we sometimes cut or crop the nap

with long shears, and boil the web to give it a lus-
tre, and ink it to color any ill-dyed fibres, and press
it between hot plates before it goes to the tailor's

Loom Basket and Bobbins

hands; but these injurious processes were omitted in
olden times. Worsted stuffs were not fulled, but
were woven of hand-combed wool.

Linen webs after they were woven had even more manipulations to come to them than woollen stuffs. In spite of all the bleaching of the linen thread, it still was light brown in color, and it had to go through at least twoscore other processes, of bucking, possing, rinsing, drying, and bleaching on the grass. Sometimes it was stretched out on pegs with loops sewed on the selvage edge. This bleaching was called crofting in England, and grassing in America. Often it was thus spread on the grass for weeks, and was slightly wetted several times a day; but not too wet, else it would mildew. In all, over forty bleaching operations were employed upon "light linens." Sometimes they were "soured" in buttermilk to make them purely white. Thus at least sixteen months had passed since the flaxseed had been sown, in which, truly, the spinster had not eaten the bread of idleness. In the winter months the fine, white, strong linen was made into "board cloths" or tablecloths, sheets, pillow-biers, aprons, shifts, shirts, petticoats, short gowns, gloves, cut from the spinner's own glove pattern, and a score of articles for household use. These were carefully marked, and sometimes embroidered with home-dyed crewels, as were also splendid sets of bed-hangings, valances, and testers for four-post bedsteads.

The homespun linens that were thus spun and woven and bleached were one of the most beautiful expressions and types of old-time home life. Firm, close-woven, and pure, their designs were not greatly varied, nor was their woof as symmetrical and perfect as modern linens — but thus were the lives of those who made them; firm, close-woven in neighborly kindness, with the simplicity both of innocence and ignorance; their days had little variety, and life was not altogether easy, and, like the web they wove, it was sometimes narrow. I am always touched when handling these homespun linens with a consciousness of nearness to the makers; with a sense of the energy and strength of those enduring women who were so full of vitality, of unceasing action, that it does not seem to me they can be dead.

The strong, firm linen woven in many struggling country homes was too valuable and too readily exchangeable and salable to be kept wholly for farm use, especially when there were so few salable articles produced on the farm. It was sold or more frequently exchanged at the village store for any desired commodity, such as calico, salt, sugar, spices, or tea. It readily sold for forty-two cents a yard. Therefore the boys and .even the fathers did not always have linen shirts to wear. From the tow

which had been hatchelled out from harl a coarse
thread was spun and cloth was woven which
was made chiefly into shirts and smocks and tow
"tongs" or "skilts," which were loose flapping
summer trousers which ended almost half-way from
the knee to the ankle. This tow stuff was never
free from prickling spines, and it proved, so tradition states, an absolute instrument of torture to the
wearer, until frequent washings had worn it out and
thus subdued its knots and spines.

A universal stuff woven in New Hampshire by
the Scotch-Irish linen-weavers who settled there,
and who influenced husbandry and domestic manufactures and customs all around them, was what was
known as striped frocking. It was worn also to a
considerable extent in Connecticut and Massachusetts. The warp was strong white cotton or tow
thread, the weft of blue and white stripes made by
weaving alternately a shuttleful of indigo-dyed
homespun yarn and one of white wool or tow.
Many boys grew to manhood never wearing, except
on Sundays, any kind of coat save a long, loose,
shapeless jacket or smock of this striped frocking,
known everywhere as a long-short. The history
of the old town of Charmingfare tells of the farmers
in that vicinity tying tight the two corners of this
long-short at the waist and thus making a sort of

loose bag in which various articles could be carried.
Sylvester Judd, in his *Margaret*, the classic of old
New England life, has his country women dressed
also in long-shorts, and tells of the same fabric.

Another material which was universal in country
districts had a flax or tow warp, and a coarser slack-
twisted cotton or tow filling. This cloth was dyed
and pressed and was called fustian. It was worth a
shilling a yard in 1640. It was named in the earliest
colonial accounts, and was in truth the ancient fustian, worn throughout Europe in the Middle Ages
for monks' robes and laborers' dress, not the stuff
to-day called fustian. We read in *The Squier of
Low Degree*, "Your blanketts shall be of fustayne."

Another coarse cloth made in New England,
Pennsylvania, Virginia, and the Carolinas was crocus. The stuff is obsolete and the name is forgotten
save in a folk-saying which lingers in Virginia —
"as coarse as crocus." Homespun stuff for the
wear of negroes was known and sold as "Virginia
cloth." Vast quantities of homespun cloth was
made on Virginian plantations, thousands of yards
annually at Mount Vernon for slave-wear, and for
the house-mistress as well.

It is told of Martha Washington that she always
carefully dyed all her worn silk gowns and silk
scraps to a desired shade, ravelled them with care,

wound them on bobbins, and had them woven into chair and cushion covers. Sometimes she changed the order of things. To a group of visitors she at one time displayed a dress of red and white striped material of which the white stripes were cotton, and the red, ravelled chair covers and silk from the General's worn-out stockings.

Checked linen, with bars of red or blue, was much used for bedticks, pillow-cases, towelling, aprons, and even shirts and summer trousers. In all the Dutch communities in New York it was woven till this century. When Benjamin Tappan first attended meeting in Northampton, Massachusetts, in 1769, he was surprised to find that all the men in the church but four or five wore checked shirts. Worcester County men always wore white shirts, and deemed a checked shirt the mark of a Connecticut River man.

It is impossible to overestimate the durability of homespun materials. I have "flannel sheets" a hundred years old, the lightest, most healthful, and agreeable summer covering for children's beds that ever any one was blessed with. Cradle sheets of this thin, closely woven, white worsted stuff are not slimsy like thin flannel, yet are softer than flannel. Years of use with many generations of children have left them firm and white.

Weaving Rag Carpet

Grain-bags have been seen that have been in constant and hard use for seventy years, homespun from coarse flax and hemp. I have several delightful bags about four feet long and two feet wide, of rather closely woven pure white homespun linen, not as heavy, however, as crash. They have the date of their manufacture, 1789, and the initials of the weaver, and have linen tapes woven in at each side. They are used every spring — packed with furs and blankets and placed in cedar chests, and with such usage will easily round out another century.

The product of these hand-looms which has lingered longest in country use, especially in the Northern states, and which is the sole product of all the hand-looms that I know to be set up and in use in New England (except one notable example to which I will refer hereafter), is the rag carpet. It is still in constant demand and esteem on farms and in small villages and towns, and is an economical and thrifty, and may be a comely floor-covering. The accompanying illustration of a woman weaving rag carpet on an old hand-loom is from a fine photograph taken by Mrs. Arthur Sewall of Bath, Maine, and gives an excellent presentment of the machine and the process.

The warp of these carpets was, in olden times, a strong, heavy flaxen thread. To-day it is a heavy

cotton twine bought machine-spun in balls or
hanks. The weft or filling is narrow strips of all
the clean and varicolored rags that accumulate in
a household.

The preparing of this filling requires considerable
judgment. Heavy woollen cloth should be cut in
strips about half an inch wide. If there were
sewn with these strips of light cotton stuff of equal

Hand Stamps for Calico Printing

width, the carpet would prove a poor thing, heavy
in spots and slimsy in others. Hence lighter stuffs
should be cut in wider strips, as they can then be
crowded down by the batten of the loom to the
same width and substance as the heavy wools.
Calicoes, cottons, all-wool delaines, and lining cam-
brics should be cut in strips at least an inch wide.
These strips, of whatever length they chance to be,

are sewn into one continuous strip, which is rolled into a hard ball weighing about a pound and a quarter. It is calculated that one of these balls will weave about a yard of carpeting. The joining must be strongly and neatly done and should not be bunchy. An aged weaver who had woven many thousand yards of carpeting assured me the prettiest carpets were always those in which every alternate strip was white or very light in color. Another thrifty way of using old material is the cutting into inch-wide strips of woven ingrain or three-ply carpet. This, through the cotton warp, makes a really artistic monochrome floor-covering.

In one of the most romantic and beautiful spots in old Narragansett lives the last of the old-time weavers; not a weaver who desultorily weaves a run of rag carpeting to earn a little money in the intervals of other work, or to please some importunate woman-neighbor who has saved up her rags; but a weaver whose lifelong occupation, whose only means of livelihood, has always been, and is still, hand-weaving. I have told his story at some length in my book, *Old Narragansett,*— of his kin, his life, his work. His home is at the cross-roads where three townships meet, a cross-roads where has often taken place that curious and senseless survival of old-time tradition and superstition —

R

shift marriages.   A widow, a cousin of the Weaver
Rose's father, was the last to undergo this ordeal;
clad only in her shift, she thrice crossed the King's
Highway and was thus married to avoid payment
of her first husband's debts.   It is not far from the
old Church Foundation of St. Paul's of Narragansett, and the tumble-down house of Sexton Martin
Read, the prince of Narragansett weavers in ante-
Revolutionary days.   Weaver Rose learned to
weave from his grandfather, who was an apprentice
of Weaver Read.

In the loom-room of Weaver Rose a veritable
atmosphere of the past still lingers.   Everything
appertaining to the manufacture of homespun
materials may there be found.   Wheels, skarnes,
sleys, warping-bars, clock-reels, swifts, quilling-
wheels, vast bales of yarns and thread — for he no
longer spins his thread and yarn.   There are piles
of old and new bed coverlets woven in those fanciful geometric designs, which are just as the ancient
Gauls wove them in the Bronze Age, and which
formed a favorite bed-covering of our ancestors,
and of country folk to-day.   These coverlets the
weaver calls by the good old English name of
hap-harlot, a name now obsolete in England, which
I have never seen used in text of later date than
Holinshead's *Survey of London*, written four hundred

years ago. His manuscript pattern-book is over a hundred years old, and has the rules for setting the harnesses. They bear many pretty and odd names, such as " Rosy Walk," " Baltimore Beauty,"

"Orange Peel," "Blazing Star," "Chariot Wheels and Church Windows,"
"Bachelor's Fancy"

"Girl's Love," "Queen's Fancy," "Devil's Fancy," "Everybody's Beauty," "Four Snow Balls," "Five Snow Balls," "Bricks and Blocks," "Gardener's Note," "Green Vails," "Rose in Bloom," "Pansies and Roses in the Wilderness," "Flag-Work," "Royal Beauty," "Indian March," "Troy's Beauty," "Primrose and Diamonds," "Crown and Diamonds," "Jay's Fancy," "In Summer and Winter," "Boston Beauty," and "Indian War." One named "Bony Part's March" was very pretty, as was "Orange Peel," and "Orange Trees"; "Dog Tracks" was even checkerwork, "Blazing Star," a herring-bone design. "Perry's Victory" and "Lady Washington's Delight" show probably the date of their invention, and were handsome designs, while the "Whig Rose from Georgia," which had been given to the weaver by an old lady a hundred years old, had proved a poor and ugly thing. "Kapa's Diaper" was a complicated design which took "five harnesses" to make. "Rattlesnake's Trail," "Wheels of Fancy," "Chariot Wheels and Church Windows," and "Bachelor's Fancy" were all exceptionally fine designs.

Sometimes extremely elaborate patterns were woven in earlier days. An exquisitely woven coverlet as fine as linen sheeting, a corner of which is here shown, has an elaborate border of patriotic and

Hand-woven Bed Coverlet

Masonic emblems, patriotic inscriptions, and the name of the maker, a Red Hook, Hudson valley, dame of a century ago, who wove this beautiful bedspread as the crowning treasure of her bridal outfit. The "setting-up" of such a design as this is entirely beyond my skill as a weaver to explain or even comprehend. But it is evident that the border must have been woven by taking up a single warp-thread at a time, with a wire needle, not by passing a shuttle, as it is far too complicated and varied for any treadle-harness to be able to make a shed for a shuttle.

Hand-weaving in Weaver Rose's loom-room to-day is much simplified in many of its preparatory details by the employment of machine-made materials. The shuttles and spools are made by machinery; and more important still, both warp and weft is purchased ready-spun from mills. The warp is simply a stout cotton twine or coarse thread bought in balls or hanks; while various cheap mill-yarns or what is known as worsteds or coarse crewels are used as filling. These, of course, are cheap, but alas! are dyed with fleeting or garish aniline dyes. No new blue yarn can equal either in color or durability the old indigo-dyed, homespun, hard-twisted yarn made on a spinning-wheel. Germantown, early in the field in American wool manufacture, still supplies nearly all the yarn for his hand-looms.

The transition half a century or more ago from what Horace Bushnell called " mother and daughter power to water and steam power," was a complete revolution in domestic life, and indeed of social manners as well. When a people spin and weave and make their own dress, you have in this very fact the assurance that they are home-bred, home-living, home-loving people. You are sure, also, that the lives of the women are home-centred. The chief cause for women's intercourse with any of the outside world except neighborly acquaint-tance, her chief knowledge of trade and exchange, is in shopping, dressmaking, etc. These causes scarcely existed in country communities a century ago. The daughters who in our days of factories leave the farm for the cotton-mill, where they perform but one of the many operations in cloth manufacture, can never be as good home-makers or as helpful mates as the homespun girls of our grand-mothers' days; nor can they be such co-workers in great public movements.

In the summer of 1775, when all the preparations for the War of the Revolution were in a most unsettled and depressing condition, especially the supplies for the Continental army, the Provincial Congress made a demand on the people for thirteen thousand warm coats to be ready for the soldiers by cold weather. There were no great contractors then as now to supply the cloth and make the garments, but by hundreds of hearthstones throughout the country wool-wheels and hand-looms were started eagerly at work, and the order was filled by the handiwork of patriotic American women. In

the record book of some New England towns may
still be found the lists of the coat-makers.   In the
inside of each coat was sewed the name of the town
and the maker.   Every soldier volunteering for
eight months' service was given one of these homespun, home-made, all-wool coats as a bounty.   So
highly were these " Bounty Coats " prized, that the
heirs of soldiers who were killed at Bunker Hill
before receiving their coats were given a sum of
money instead.   The list of names of soldiers who
then enlisted is known to this day as the " Coat
Roll," and the names of the women who made
the coats might form another roll of honor.   The
English sneeringly called Washington's army the
" Homespuns."   It was a truthful nickname, but
there was deeper power in the title than the English
scoffers knew.

The starting up of power-looms and the wonderful growth of woollen manufacture did not crowd
out homespun as speedily in America as in England.
When the poet Whittier set out from the Quaker
farmhouse to go to Boston to seek his fortune, he
wore a homespun suit every part of which, even
the horn buttons, was of domestic manufacture.
Many a man born since Whittier has grown to
manhood clothed for every-day wear wholly with
homespun ; and many a boy is living who was sent

to college dressed wholly in a "full-cloth" suit,
with horn buttons or buttons made of discs of
heavy leather.

During the Civil War spinning and weaving were
revived arts in the Confederate cities; and, as ever
in earlier days, proved a most valuable economic
resource under restricted conditions. In the home
of a friend in Charleston, South Carolina, an old,
worm-eaten loom was found in a garret where it had
lain since the embargo in 1812. It was set up in
1863, and plantation carpenters made many like it
for neighbors and fellow-citizens. All women in
the mountain districts knew how to use the loom,
and taught weaving to many others, both white and
black. A portion of the warp, which was cotton,
was spun at home; more was bought from a cotton-
factory. My friend sacrificed a great number of
excellent wool-mattresses ; this wool was spun into
yarn and used for weft, and formed a most grateful
and dignified addition to the varied, grotesque, and
interesting makeshifts of the wardrobe of the Southern Confederacy.

Though weaving on hand-looms in our Northern
and Middle states is practically extinct, save as to the
weaving of rag carpets (and that only in few communities), in the South all is different. In all the
mountain and remote regions of Kentucky, Tennes-

see, Georgia, the Carolinas, and I doubt not in
Alabama, both among the white and negro moun-
tain-dwellers, hand-weaving is still a household art.
The descendants of the Acadians in Louisiana still
weave and wear homespun.   The missions in the
mountains encourage spinning and weaving; and it
is pleasant to learn that many women not only pur-
sue these handicrafts for their home use, but some
secure a good living by hand-weaving, earning ten
cents a yard in weaving rag carpets.   The coverlet
patterns resemble the ones already described. Names
from Waynesville, North Carolina, are " Washington's Diamond Ring," " Nine Chariot Wheels";
from Pinehurst come " Flowery Vine," " Double
Table," "Cat Track," "Snow Ball and Dew Drop,"
" Snake Shed," " Flowers in the Mountains."   At
Pinehurst the old settlers, of sturdy Scotch stock, all
weave.   They make cloth, all cotton; cloth of cotton
warp and wool filling called drugget ; dimity, a
heavy cotton used for coverlets ; a yarn jean which
has wool warp and filling, and cotton jean which is
cotton warp and wool filling ; homespun is a heavy
cloth, of cotton and wool mixed.   All buy cotton
warp or " chain," as they call it, ready-spun from
the mills.   This is known by the name of bunch-
thread.   These Pinehurst weavers still use home-
made dyes.   Cotton is dyed black with dye made

by steeping the bark of the " Black Jack " or scrub-oak mixed with red maple bark.   Wool is dyed black with a mixture of gall-berry leaves and sumac berries ; for red they use a moss which they find growing on the rocks, and which may be the lichen *Roccella tinctoria* or dyer's-moss ; also madder root, and sassafras bark.   Yellow is dyed with laurel leaves, or " dyeflower," a yellow flower of the sunflower tribe ; laurel leaves and " dye-flower " together made orange-red. Blue is obtained from the plentiful wild indigo ; and for green, the cloth or yarn is first dyed blue with indigo, then boiled in a decoction of hickory bark and laurel leaves.   A bright yellow is obtained from a clay which abounds in that neighborhood, probably like a red ferruginous limestone found in Tennessee, which gives a splendid, fast color ; when the clay is baked and ground it gives a fine, artistic, dull red.   Purple dye comes from cedar tops and lilac leaves ; brown from an extract of walnut hulls.

The affectionate regard which all good workmen have for their tools and implements in handcrafts is found among these Southern weavers.   One assures me that her love for her loom is as for a human companion.   The machines are usually family heirlooms that have been owned for several generations, and are treasured like relics.

CHAPTER XI

HATCHELLING and carding, spinning and reeling, weaving and bleaching, cooking, candle and cheese making, were not the only household occupations of our busy grandmothers when they were young; a score of domestic duties kept ever busy their ready hands.

Some notion of the qualifications of a housekeeper over a century ago may be obtained from this advertisement in the *Pennsylvania Packet* of September 23, 1780:

" Wanted at a Seat about half a day's journey from Philadelphia, on which are good improvements and domestics, A single Woman of unsullied Reputation, an affable, cheerful, active and amiable Disposition; cleanly, industrious, perfectly qualified to direct and manage the female Concerns of country business, as raising small stock, dairying, marketing, combing, carding, spinning, knitting, sewing, pickling, preserving, etc., and occasionally to instruct two young Ladies in those Branches of Oeconomy, who, with their father, compose the Family. Such a person will be treated with respect and esteem, and meet with every encouragement due to such a character."

Respect and esteem, forsooth! and due encouragement to such a miracle of saintliness and capacity; light terms indeed to apply to such a character.

There is, in the library of the Connecticut Historical Society, a diary written by a young girl of Colchester, Connecticut, in the year 1775. Her name was Abigail Foote. She set down her daily work, and the entries run like this: —

" Fix'd gown for Prude, — Mend Mother's Riding-hood, — Spun short thread, — Fix'd two gowns for Welsh's girls, — Carded tow, — Spun linen, — Worked on Cheesebasket, — Hatchel'd flax with Hannah, we did 51 lbs. apiece, — Pleated and ironed, — Read a Sermon of Doddridge's, — Spooled a piece, — Milked the cows, — Spun linen, did 50 knots, — Made a Broom of Guinea wheat straw, — Spun thread to whiten, — Set a Red dye, — Had two Scholars from Mrs. Taylor's, — I carded two pounds of whole wool and felt Nationly, — Spun harness twine, — Scoured the pewter."

She tells also of washing, cooking, knitting, weeding the garden, picking geese, etc., and of many visits to her friends. She dipped candles in the spring, and made soap in the autumn. This latter was a trying and burdensome domestic duty, but the soft soap was important for home use.

All the refuse grease from cooking, butchering, etc., was stored through the winter, as well as wood-ashes from the great fireplaces. The first operation was to make the lye, to "set the leach." Many families owned a strongly made leach-barrel; others made a sort of barrel from a section of the bark of the white birch. This barrel was placed on bricks or set at a slight angle on a circular groove in a wood or stone base; then filled with ashes; water was poured in till the lye trickled or leached out through an outlet cut in the groove, into a small wooden tub or bucket. The water and ashes were frequently replenished as they wasted, and the lye accumulated in a large tub or kettle. If the lye was not strong enough, it was poured over fresh ashes. An old-time receipt says : —

" The great Difficulty in making Soap come is the want of Judgment of the Strength of the Lye. If your Lye will bear up an Egg or a Potato so you can see a piece of the Surface as big as a Ninepence it is just strong enough."

The grease and lye were then boiled together in a great pot over a fire out of doors. It took about six bushels of ashes and twenty-four pounds of grease to make a barrel of soap. The soft soap made by this process seemed like a clean jelly, and showed no trace of the repulsive grease that helped to form it.   A hard soap also was made with the tallow of the bayberry, and was deemed especially desirable for toilet use.   But little hard soap was purchased, even in city homes.

It was a common saying: "We had bad luck with our soap," or good luck.   The soap was always carefully stirred one way.   The " Pennsylvania Dutch " used a sassafras stick to stir it.   A good smart worker could make a barrel of soap in a day, and have time to sit and rest in the afternoon and talk her luck over, before getting supper.

This soft soap was used in the great monthly washings which, for a century after the settlement of the colonies, seem to have been the custom. The household wash was allowed to accumulate, and the washing done once a month, or in some households once in three months.

Thomas Tusser's rhymed instructions to good housekeepers as to the washing contain chiefly warnings to the housekeeper against thieves, thus : —

> " Dry sun, dry wind,
>   Safe bind, safe find.
> Go wash well, saith summer, with sun I shall dry;
> Go wring well, saith winter, with wind so shall I.
> To trust without heed is to venture a joint,
> Give tale and take count is a housewifely point."

Abigail Foote wrote of making a broom of Guinea wheat. This was not broom-corn, for that useful plant was not grown in Connecticut for the purpose of broom-making till twenty years or more after she wrote her diary. Brooms and brushes were made of it in Italy nearly two centuries ago. Benjamin Franklin, who was ever quick to use and develop anything that would benefit his native country, and was ever ready to take a hint, noted a few seeds of broom-corn hanging on an imported brush. He planted these seeds and raised some of the corn; and Thomas Jefferson placed broom-corn among the productions of Virginia in 1781. By this time many had planted it, but no systematic plan of raising broom-corn abundantly for the manufacture of brooms was planned till 1798, when Levi Dickenson, a Yankee farmer of Hadley, Massachusetts, planted half an acre. From this he made between one and two hundred brooms which he peddled in a horse-cart in neighboring towns. The following year he planted an acre; and the tall broom-corn with its spreading panicles attracted much attention. Though he was thought visionary when he predicted that broom manufacture would be the greatest industry in the county, and though he was sneeringly told that only Indians ought to make brooms, he persevered; and his neighbors finally planted and made brooms also. He carried brooms soon to Pittsfield, to New London, and in 1805 to Albany and Boston. So rapid was the increase of manufacture that in 1810 seventy thousand brooms were made in the county. Since then millions of dollars' worth have gone forth from the farms and villages in his neighborhood.

Mr. Dickenson at first scraped the seed from the brush with a knife; then he used a sort of hoe; then a coarse comb like a ripple-comb. He tied each broom by hand, with the help of a negro servant. Much of this work could be done by little girls, who soon gave great help in broom manufacture; though the final sewing (when the needle was pressed through with a leather "palm" such as sailors use) had to be done by the strong hands of grown women and men.

Doubtless Abigail Foote made many an "Indian broom," as well as her brooms of Guinea wheat, which may have been a special home manufacture of her neighborhood; for many fibres, leaves, and straws were used locally in broom-making.

Another duty of the women of the old-time household was the picking of domestic geese. Geese were raised for their feathers more than as food. In some towns every family had a flock, and their clanking was heard all day and sometimes all

s

night.   They roamed the streets all summer, eating grass by the highways and wallowing in the puddles. Sometimes they were yoked with a goose-yoke made of a shingle with a hole in it.   In midwinter they were kept in barnyards, but the rest of the year they spent the night in the street, each flock near the home of its owner.   It is said that one old goose of each flock always kept awake and stood watch; and it was told in Hadley, Massachusetts, that if a young man chanced to be out late, as for instance a-courting, his return home wakened the geese throughout the village, who sounded the unseasonable hour with a terrible clamor. They made so much noise on summer Sundays that they seriously disturbed church services; and became such nuisances that at last the boys killed whole flocks.

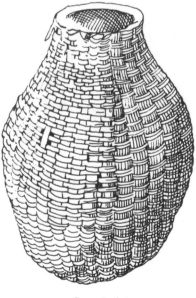

Goose Basket

Goose-picking was cruel work. Three or four times a year were the feathers stripped from the live birds. A stocking was pulled over the bird's head to keep it from biting. Sometimes the head was thrust into a goose basket. The pickers had to wear old clothes and tie covers over the hair, as the down flew everywhere. The quills, used for pens, were never pulled but once from a goose. Palladius, *On Husbondrie*, written in the fourth century, and Englished in the fifteenth century, tells of goose-picking : —

> " Twice a yere deplumed may they be,
> In spryngen tyme and harvest tyme."

The old Latin and English times for picking were followed in the New World. Among the Dutch, geese were everywhere raised; for feather-beds were, if possible, more desired by the Dutch than the English.

In a work entitled *Good Order established in Pennsylvania and New Jersey*, written by a Quaker in 1685, he urges that schools be provided where girls could be instructed in " the spinning of flax, sewing, and making all sorts of useful needle work, knitting of gloves and stockings, making of straw-works, as hats, baskets, etc., or any other useful art or mystery." It was a century before his " making of

straw-works " was carried out, not till larger im-
portations of straw hats and bonnets came to this
country.

When the beautiful and intricate straw bonnets
of Italian braid, Genoese, Leghorn, and others, were
brought here, they were too costly for many to purchase ; and many attempts, especially by country-
bred girls, were made to plait at home straw braids
to imitate these envied bonnets.   Many towns
claim the first American straw bonnet ; in fact, the
attempts were almost simultaneous.   To Betsey
Metcalf of Providence, Rhode Island, is usually
accorded the honor of starting the straw-hat business in America.   The earliest recorded effort to
manufacture straw head-wear is shown in a patent
given to Mrs. Sibylla Masters of Philadelphia, for
using palmetto and straw for hats.   This Mrs.
Masters was the first American, man or woman,
ever awarded a patent in England.   The first patent
issued by the United States to a woman was also
for an invention in straw-plaiting.   A Connecticut
girl, Miss Sophia Woodhouse, was given a prize for
" leghorn hats " which she had plaited ; and she
took out a patent in 1821 for a new material for
bonnets.   It was the stalks, above the upper joint,
of spear-grass and redtop grass growing so pro-
fusely in Weathersfield.   From this she had a

national reputation, and a prize of twenty guineas was given her the same year by the London Society of Arts. The wife of President John Quincy Adams wore one of these bonnets, to the great pride of her husband.

When the bonnet was braided and sewed into shape, it had to be bleached, for it was the dark natural straw. I don't know the domestic process in general use, but an ingenious family of sisters in Newburyport thus accomplished their bleaching. They bored holes in the head of a barrel; tied strings to each new bonnet; passed the strings through the holes and carefully plugged the openings with wood. This left the bonnets hanging inside the barrel, which was set over an old-fashioned foot-stove filled with hot coals on which sulphur had been placed. The fumes of the burning sulphur arose and filled the barrel, and were closely retained by quilts wrapped around it. When the bonnets were taken out, they were clear and white. The base of a lignum-vitæ mortar made into the proper shape with layers of pasteboard formed the mould on which the bonnet crown was pressed.

Even before they could spin girls were taught to knit, as soon as their little hands could hold the needles. Sometimes girls four years of age could knit stockings. Boys had to knit their own suspenders. All the stockings and mittens for the family, and coarse socks and mittens for sale, were made in large numbers. Much fine knitting was done, with many intricate and elaborate stitches ; those known as the " herring-bone " and " fox and geese " were great favorites. By the use of curious stitches initials could be knit into mittens ; and it is said that one young New Hampshire girl, using fine flaxen yarn, knit the whole alphabet and a verse of poetry into a pair of mittens ; which I think must have been long-armed mitts for ladies' wear, to have space enough for the poetry.

To knit a pair of double mittens was a sharp and long day's work. Nancy Peabody's brother of Shelburne, New Hampshire, came home one night and said he had lost his mittens while chopping in the woods. Nancy ran to a bundle of wool in the garret, carded and spun a big hank of yarn that night. It was soaked and scoured the next morning, and in twenty-four hours from the time the brother announced his loss he had a fine new pair of double mittens. A pair of double hooked and pegged mittens would last for years. Pegging, I am told, was heavy crocheting.

An elaborate and much-admired form of knitting was the bead bags and purses which were so fashionable in the early years of this century, though I have seen some knitted bags of colonial days.

Great variety and ingenuity were shown in these bags and purses. Some bore landscapes and figures; others were memorials done in black and white and purple beads, having so-called " mourning designs," such as weeping willows, gravestones, urns, etc., with the name of the deceased person and date of death. Beautiful bags were knitted to match wedding-gowns. Knitted purses were a favorite token and gift from fair hands to husband or lover. Watch chains were more unusual; they were knit in a geometrical design, were about a yard long and about three-eighths of an inch in diameter. One I saw had in tiny letters in gilt beads the date and the words " Remember the Giver." In all these knitted and crocheted bags the beads had to be strung by a rule in advance; in an elaborate pattern of many colors it may easily be seen that the mistake of a single bead in the stringing would spoil the entire design. They were therefore never a cheap form of decorative work. Five dollars was often paid for knitting a single bag. A varied group from the collection of Mr. J. Howard Swift of Chicago is here shown.

Netting was another decorative handiwork. Netted fringes for edging the coverlets, curtains, testers, and valances of high-post bedsteads were usually made of cotton thread or twine, and when tufted or tasselled were a pretty finish. A finer silk or cotton netting was used for trimming sacks and petticoats. A letter written by Mrs. Carrington from Mount Vernon in 1799 says of Mrs. President Washington: —

" Her netting' is a source of great amusement to her and is so neatly done that all the younger part of the family are proud of trimming their dresses with it, and have furnished me with a whole suit so that I shall appear ' a la domestique ' at the first party we have when I get home."

Netted purses and work-bags also were made similar to the knitted ones. A homelier and heavier netting of twine was often done at home for small fishing-nets.

Previous to the Revolution there was a boarding-school kept in Philadelphia in Second Street near Walnut, by a Mrs. Sarah Wilson. She thus advertised: —

" Young ladies may be educated in a genteel manner, and pains taken to teach them in regard to their behaviour, on reasonable terms. They may be taught all sorts fine needlework, viz., working on catgut or flowering muslin, sattin stitch, quince stitch, tent stitch, cross-stitch, open work, tambour, embroidering curtains or chairs, writing and cyphering. Likewise waxwork in all its several branches,

Knitted Bags

never as yet particularly taught here; also how to take profiles in wax, to make wax flowers and fruits and pin-baskets."

There was no limit to the beauty and delicacy of the embroidery of those days. I have seen the beautiful needlework cap and skirt worn by Governor Thomas Johnson of Maryland, when he was christened. The coat of arms of both the Lux and Johnson families, the name Agnes Lux and Anne Johnson, and the words "God bless the Babe" are embroidered upon them in most delicate fairy stitches. The babe grew up to be the governor of his state in Revolutionary times.

In an old book printed in 1821, a set of rules is given for teaching needlework, and it is doubtless exactly what had been the method for a century. The girls were first shown how to turn a hem on a piece of waste paper; then they proceeded to the various stitches in this order: to hem, to sew and fell a seam, to draw threads and hemstitch, to gather and sew on gathers, to make buttonholes, to sew on buttons, to do herring-bone stitch, to darn, to mark, to tuck, whip, and sew on a frill. There is also a long and tedious set of questions and answers like a catechism, explaining the various stitches.

There was one piece of needlework which was done by every little girl who was carefully brought up : she sewed a sampler.   These were worked in

various beautiful and difficult stitches in colored silks and wool on a strong, loosely woven canvas.

In English collections, the oblong samplers, long and narrow, are as a rule older than the square samplers ; and it is safe to believe the same of American samplers. Fortunately, many of them are dated, but this ancient one from the Quincy family has no date.   The oldest sampler I have ever seen is in the collection of antique articles now in Pilgrim Hall at Plymouth.   It was made by a daughter of the Pilgrims.   The verse embroidered on it reads : —

Fleetwood-Quincy
Sampler

" Lorea Standish is My Name.
 Lord Guide my Heart that I may do thy Will,
 And fill my Hands with such convenient skill
As will conduce to Virtue void of Shame,
And I will give the Glory to thy Name."

Similar verses, and portions of hymns, are often found on these samplers. A favorite rhyme was : —

" When I was young and in my Prime,
  You see how well I spent my Time.

And by my sampler you may see
What care my Parents took of me."

A very spirited verse is : —

" You'll mend your life to-morrow still you cry.
  In what far Country does To-morrow lie?
  It stays so long, is fetch'd so far, I fear
  'Twill prove both very old, and very dear."

Strange trees and fruits and birds and beasts,
wonderful vines and flowers, were embroidered on
these domestic tapestries.

In the hands of a skilful worker, the sampler
might become a thing of beauty and historical interest; and the stitches learned and practised on it
might be used on more ambitious pieces of work,
which often took the shape of the family coat of
arms. Such was the work of Mary Salter (Mrs.
Henry Quincy), who was born in 1726, and died in
1755. It is the arms of Salter and Bryan party per
pale upon a shield. Rich in embossed work in gold
and silver thread, it is a beautiful testimonial to the
deft and proficient hand of the young needlewoman
who embroidered it.

Sometimes pretentious pictures representing
events in public or family history, were embroidered in crewels on sampler linen. The largest and
funniest one I have ever seen was the boarding-

school climax of glory of Miss Hannah Otis, sister of the patriot James Otis. It is a view of the Hancock House, Boston Common, and vicinity, as they appeared from 1755 to 1760. Across its expanse Governor Hancock rides triumphantly; and the fair maid looking over the garden wall at the Charles River is Dorothy Quincy, afterwards Madam Hancock. This triumph of school-girl affection and needle-craft, wholly devoid of perspective or proportion, made a great sensation in Boston, in its day.

Another large piece of similar work is here represented. The original is in the library of the American Antiquarian Society at Worcester, Massachusetts. It is a view of the Old South Church, Boston; and with its hooped dames and coach and footman, has a certain value as indicating the costume of the times. It is dated 1756.

Familiar to the descendants of old New England families, are the embroidered mourning pieces. These are seldom more than a century old. On them weeping willows and urns, tombs and mourning figures, names of departed friends with dates of their deaths, and epitaphs were worked with vast skill, and were so much admired and were such a delightful home decoration, that it is no unusual thing to find these elaborate memento moris with

Colonial Embroidery, Old South Church, Boston

empty spaces for names and dates, waiting for some one to die, and still unfilled, unfinished, blankly commemorative of no one, while the industrious embroiderer has long since gone to the tomb she so deftly and eagerly pictured, and her name, too, is forgotten.

Tambour work was a favorite form of embroidery. In 1788 Madam Hesselius wrote thus in jest of her daughter, a Philadelphia miss: —

" To tambour on crape she has a great passion,
   Because here of late it has been much the fashion.
   The shades are dis-sorted, the spangles are scattered
   And for want of due care the crape has got tattered."

Tambouring with various stitches on different kinds of net made pretty laces; and these were apparently the laces usually worked and worn. In the form of rich veils and collars scores of intricate and beautiful stitches were used, and exquisite articles of wear were manufactured.

A strip of net footing pinned and sewn to paper, with reels of fine linen thread and threaded needle attached, is shown in the accompanying illustration just as it was left by the deft and industrious hands that have been folded for a century in the dust. The pattern and stitches in this design are simple; the design was first pricked in outline with a pin,

then worked in.   Other stitches and patterns, none
of them the most elaborate and difficult, are shown
in the infant's cap and collars, and the strips of
lace and "modesty-piece."

In the seventeenth century lace-making with

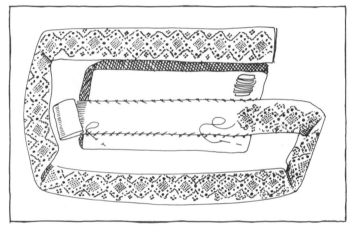

Net Footing and Lace

bobbins was taught; it is referred to in Judge
Sewall's diary; and a friend has shown me the
cushion and bobbins used by her far-away grandmother who learned the various stitches in London
at a guinea a stitch.

The feminine love of color, the longing for decoration, as well as pride in skill of needle-craft, found
riotous expansion in quilt-piecing.   A thrifty econ-

omy, too, a desire to use up all the fragments and
bits of stuffs which were necessarily cut out in the
shaping, chiefly of women's and children's garments, helped to make the patchwork a satisfaction.
The amount of labor, of careful fitting, neat piecing,
and elaborate quilting, the thousands of stitches that
went into one of these patchwork quilts, are to-day

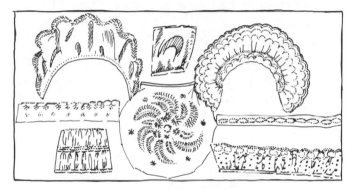

Collars, Caps, Laces, and "Modesty-piece"

almost painful to regard.   Women revelled in in
tricate and difficult patchwork; they eagerly exchanged patterns with one another; they talked over
the designs, and admired pretty bits of calico, and
pondered what combinations to make, with far more
zest than women ever discuss art or examine high
art specimens together to-day.   There was one
satisfactory condition in the work, and that was the

quality of the cottons and linens of which the patch-work was made. They were none of the slimsy, composition-filled, aniline-dyed calicoes of to-day. A piece of "chaney," "patch," or "copper-plate" a hundred years old will be as fresh to-day as when woven. Real India chintzes and palampours are found in these quilts, beautiful and artistic stuffs, and the firm, unyielding, high-priced, "real" French calicoes.

A sense of the idealization of quilt-piecing is given also by the quaint descriptive names applied to the various patterns. Of those the "Rising-sun," "Log Cabin," and "Job's Trouble" are perhaps the most familiar. "Job's Trouble" was simply honeycomb or hexagonal blocks. "To set a Job's Trouble," was to cut out an exact hexagon for a pattern (preferably from tin, otherwise from firm cardboard); to cut out from this many hexagons in stiff brown paper or letter paper. These were covered with the bits of calico with the edges turned under; the sides were sewed carefully together over and over, till a firm expanse permitted the removal of the papers.

The name of the pattern seldom gave an expression of its character. "Dove in the Window," "Rob Peter to Pay Paul," "Blue Brigade," "Fan-mill," "Crow's Foot," "Chinese Puzzle," "Flywheel," "Love-knot," "Sugar-bowl," are simply whims of fancy. Floral names, such as "Dutch Tulip," "Sunflower," "Rose of Sharon," "Blue-bells," "World's Rose," might suggest a love of flowers. Sometimes designs are appliqued on with some regard for coloring. I once saw a quilt that was a miracle of tedious work. The squares of white cotton each held a slender stem with two leaves of green or light brown calico, surmounted by a four-petalled flower of high-colored calico, — pink, red, blue, etc. This design was all carefully hemmed down. The effect was surprisingly Oriental.

When the patchwork was completed, it was laid flatly on the lining (often another expanse of patch-work), with layers of wool or cotton wadding between, and the edges were basted all around. Four bars of wood, about ten feet long, "the quiltin'-frame," were placed at the four edges, the quilt was sewed to them with stout thread, the bars crossed and tied firmly at corners, and the whole raised on chairs or tables to a convenient height. Thus around the outstretched quilt a dozen quilters could sit running the whole together with fanciful set designs of stitching. When about a foot on either side was wholly quilted, it was rolled upon its bar, and the work went on; thus the visible quilt diminished, like Balzac's Peau de Chagrin,

T

in a united and truly sociable work that required no special attention, in which all were facing together and all drawing closer together as the afternoon passed in intimate gossip. Sometimes several quilts were set up. I know of a ten days' quilting-bee in Narragansett in 1752.

In early days calicoes were not common, but every one had woollen garments and pieces, and the quilts made of these were of grateful warmth in bleak New England. All kinds of commonplace garments and remnants of decayed gentility were pressed into service in these quilts: portions of the moth-eaten and discarded uniforms of militia-men, worn-out flannel sheets dyed with some brilliant home-dye, old coat and cloak linings, well-worn petticoats. A magnificent scarlet cloak worn by a lord mayor of London and brought to America by a member of the Merritt family of Salisbury, Massachusetts, went through a series of adventures and migrations, and ended its days as small bits of vivid color casting a grateful glory and variety on a patchwork quilt in the Saco valley of Maine. To this day at vendues or sales of old country households in New England, there will be handed out great rolls of woollen pieces to be used for patchwork quilts or rag carpets, and they find purchasers.

These woollen quilts had a thin wadding, and were usually very closely quilted, so they were quite flat. They were called "pressed quilts." An old farm wife said to me in New Hampshire, "Girls won't take the trouble to make pressed quilts nowadays, it's as much as they'll do to tack a puff," that is, make a light quilt with thick wadding only tacked together from front to back, at regular intervals. A pressed quilt which I saw was quilted in inch squares. Another had a fan-pattern with sunflower leaf border; another was quilted in the elaborate pattern known as "feather-work."

As much ingenuity was exercised in the design of the quilting as in the pattern of the patchwork, and the marking for the quilt design was exceedingly tedious, since, of course, no drawings could be used. I remember seeing one quilt marked by chalking strings which were stretched tightly across at the desired intervals, and held up and snapped smartly down on the quilt, leaving a faint chalky line to guide the eye and needle. Another simple design was to quilt in rounds, using a saucer or plate to form a perfect circle.

The most elaborate quilt I know of is of silk containing portions of the wedding-dress of Esther Powel, granddaughter of Gabriel Bernon; she was married to James Helme in 1738. When her granddaughter was married in 1795, the quilt was still unfinished, and a woman was hired who worked on it for six months, putting a miracle of fine stitches in the quilting. I think she must have been very old and very slow, for the wages paid her were but twenty cents a week and "her keep," which was very small pay even in that day of small wages. When Washington came to Newport, this splendid quilt was sent to grace the bed upon which the hero slept.

I said a few summers ago to a farmer's wife who lived on the outskirts of a small New England hill-village: "Your home is very beautiful. From every window the view is perfect." She answered quickly: "Yes, but it's awful lonely for me, for I was born in Worcester; still I don't mind as long as we have plenty of quiltings." In answer to my questions she told me that the previous winter she had "kept count," and she had helped at twenty-eight "regular" quiltings, besides her own home patchwork and quilt-making, and much informal help of neighbors on plain quilts. Any one who has attended a county fair (one not too modernized and spoiled) and seen the display of intricate patchwork and quilting still made in country homes, can see that it is not an obsolete accomplishment.

A form of decorative work in which many women took great delight and became astonishingly skilful was what was known, or at any rate advertised, by the ambitious title of Papyrotamia. It was simply the cutting out of stiff paper of various decorative and ornamental designs with scissors. At the time of the Revolution it was evidently deemed a very high accomplishment, and the best pieces of work were carefully cherished, mounted on black paper, framed and glazed, and given to friends or bequeathed by will. One old lady is remembered as using her scissors with extraordinary deftness, and amusing herself and delighting her friends by occupying the hours of every afternoon visit with cutting out entirely by her trained eye various pretty and curious designs. Valentines in exceedingly delicate and appropriate patterns, wreaths and baskets of varied flowers, marine views, religious symbols, landscapes, all were accomplished. Coats of arms and escutch eons cut in black paper and mounted on white were highly prized. Portrait silhouettes were cut with the aid of a machine which marked and reduced mechanically a sharp shadow cast by the sitter's profile through candle-light on a sheet of white paper. Mrs. Lydia H. Sigourney wrote in rhyme of a revered friend of her youth, Mrs. Lathrop, of a period about a century ago : —

" Thy dextrous scissors ready to produce
  The flying squirrel or the long-neck'd goose,
  Or dancing girls with hands together join'd,
  Or tall spruce-trees with wreaths of roses twin'd,
  The well-dress'd dolls whose paper form display'd,
  Thy penknife's labor and thy pencil's shade."

I once found in an old lacquered box in a cupboard a paper packet containing all the cut-paper designs mentioned in this rhyme — and many more. The workmanship of the " spruce-trees with wreaths of roses twin'd " was specially marvellous. I plainly saw in that design a derivative of the English Maypole and encircling wreaths. This package was marked with the name of the paper-cutter, a Revolutionary dame who died at the beginning of this century. Her home was remote from the Norwich home of Mrs. Lathrop, and I know she never visited in Connecticut, yet she made precisely the same designs and indeed all the designs. This is but a petty proof among many other more decided ones of the fact that even in those days of scant communication and infrequent and contracted travel, there were as in our own times waves of feminine fancy work, of attempts at artistic expression, which flooded every home, and receding, left behind much decorative silt of varying but nearly universal uselessness and laborious commonplaceness.

One of the cut-paper landscapes of Madam Deming, a Boston lady who was a famous "papyrotamist," is here shown. It is now owned by James F.

Cut-paper Picture

Trott, Esq., of Niagara Falls. It is a view of Boston streets just previous to the Revolution. In that handsome volume, the *Ten Broeck Genealogical Record*, are reproductions of some of the landscape views by Albertina Ten Broeck at the same date.

They show the house and farm surroundings of the old Ten Broeck " Bouwerie," the ancestral home in New York, and give a wonderfully good idea of it. These are not in dead silhouette, for an appearance of shading is afforded by finely cut lines and intervening spaces. The highest form of cut-paper reproduction and decoration ever reached was by the English woman, Mrs. Delaney, who died in 1788, the friend of the Duchess of Portland, and intimate of George III. and his queen. She reproduced in colored paper, in what she called " paper mosaics," the entire flora of the United Kingdom, and it is said it was impossible at first sight to distinguish these flowers from the real ones.

CHAPTER XII

AT the time America was settled, rich dress was almost universal in Europe among persons of any wealth or station. The dress of plain people also, such as yeomen and small farmers and work-people, was plentiful and substantial, and even peasants had good and ample clothing. Materials were strongly and honestly made, clothing was sewed by hand, and lasted long. The fashions did not change from year to year, and the rich or stout clothes of one generation were bequeathed by will and worn by a second and even a third and fourth generation.

In England extravagance in dress in court circles, and grotesqueness in dress among all educated folk, had become abhorrent to that class of persons who were called Puritans; and as an expression of their dislike they wore plainer garments, and cut off their flowing locks, and soon were called Roundheads. The Massachusetts settlers who were Puritans determined to discourage extravagance in dress in the New World, and attempted to control the fashions.

The Massachusetts magistrates were reminded of
their duties in this direction by sanctimonious spur-
ring from gentlemen and ministers in England. One
such meddler wrote to Governor Winthrop in 1636:
" Many in your plantacions discover too much
pride." Another stern moralist reproved the colonists for writing to England " for cut work coifes,
for deep stammel dyes," to be sent to them in
America. Others, prohibited from wearing broad
laces, were criticised for ordering narrow ones, for
" going as farr as they may."

In 1634 the Massachusetts General Court passed
restricting sumptuary laws. These laws forbade the
purchase of woollen, silk, or linen garments, with
silver, gold, silk, or thread lace on them. Two
years later a narrow binding of lace was permitted
on linen garments. The colonists were ordered
not to make or buy any slashed clothes, except
those with one slash in each sleeve and another
slash in the back. " Cut works, imbroidd or needle
or capps bands & rayles," and gold or silver gir-
dles, hat-bands, belts, ruffs, and beaver hats were
forbidden. Liberty was thriftily given, however, to
the colonists to wear out any garments they chanced
to have unless in the form of inordinately slashed
apparel, immoderate great sleeves and rails, and long
wings, which could not possibly be endured.

In 1639 men's attire was approached and scanned, and "immoderate great breeches" were tabooed; also broad shoulder-bands, double ruffles and capes, and silk roses, which latter adornment were worn on the shoes.

In 1651 the Court again expressed its "utter detestation that men and women of meane condition, education, and calling, should take vppon them the garbe of gentlemen by wearinge of gold or silver lace, or buttons or poynts at their knees, or walke in great boots, or women of the same ranke to wear silke or tiffany hoods or scarfs."

Many persons were "presented" under this law, men boot-wearers as well as women hood-wearers. In Salem, in 1652, a man was presented for "excess in bootes, ribonds, gould and silver lace."

In Newbury, in 1653, two women were brought up for wearing silk hoods and scarfs, but they were discharged on proof that their husbands were worth £200 each. In Northampton, in the year 1676, a wholesale attempt was made by the magistrates to abolish "wicked apparell." Thirty-eight women of the Connecticut valley were presented at one time for various degrees of finery, and as of too small estate to wear silk. A young girl named Hannah Lyman was presented for "wearing silk in a fflaunting manner, in an offensive way and

garb not only before but when she stood presented."
Thirty young men were also presented for silk-
wearing, long hair, and other extravagances. The
calm flaunting of her silk in the very eyes of the
Court by sixteen-year-old Hannah was premonitory
of the waning power of the magistrates, for similar
prosecutions at a later date were quashed. By 1682
the tables were turned and we find the Court ar-
raigning the selectmen of five towns for not prose-
cuting offenders against these laws as in previous
years. In 1675 the town of Dedham had been
similarly warned and threatened, but apparently was
never prosecuted. Connecticut called to its aid in
repressing extravagant dress the economic power of
taxation by ordering that whoever wore gold or
silver lace, gold or silver buttons, silk ribbons, silk
scarfs, or bone lace worth over three shillings a yard
should be taxed as worth £150.

Virginia fussed a little over " excess in cloathes."
Sir Francis Wyatt was enjoined not to permit any
but the Council and the heads of Hundreds to wear
gold on their clothes, or to wear silk till they made
it — which was intended more to encourage silk-
making than to discourage silk-wearing. And it
provided that unmarried men should be assessed
according to their apparel, and married men according to that of their family. In 1660 Virginia

colonists were ordered to import no " silke stuffe in garments or in peeces except for whoods and scarfs, nor silver or gold lace, nor bone lace of silk or threads, nor ribbands wrought with gold or silver in them."

The ministers did not fail in their duty in attempting to march with the magistrates in the restriction and simplification of dress. They preached often against "intolerable pride in clothes and hair." Even when the Pilgrims were in Holland the preachers had been deeply disturbed over the dress of their minister's wife, Madam Johnson, who wore " lawn coives " and busks, and a velvet hood, and " whalebones in her petticoat bodice," and worst of all, "a topish hat." One of the earliest interferences of Roger Williams was when he instructed the women of Salem parish always to wear veils in public. But John Cotton preached to them the next Sunday, and he proved to the dames and goodwives that veils were a sign and symbol of undue subjection to their husbands, and Salem women soon proved their rights by coming barefaced to meeting.

Mr. Davenport preached about men's head-gear, that men must take off their hats, and stand up at the announcement of the text. And if New Haven men wore their hats in meeting, I can't see why they fussed so over the Quakers' broadbrims.

After a while the whole church interfered.   In
1769 the church at Andover put it to vote whether
" the parish Disapprove of the female sex sitting
with their Hats on in the Meeting-house in time of
Divine Service as being Indecent."   In the town
of Abington, in 1775, it was voted that it was " an
indecent way that the female sex do sit with their
hats and bonnets on to worship God."   Still another
town voted that it was the " Town's Mind " that
the women should take their bonnets off in meeting
and hang them " on the peggs."   We do not know
positively, but I suspect that the bonnets continued
to grace the heads instead of the pegs in Andover,
Abington, and other towns.

To know how the colonists were dressed, we have
to learn from the lists of their clothing which they
left by will, which lists are still preserved in court
records ; from the inventories of the garments furnished to each settler who came by contract ; from
the orders sent back to England for new clothing ;
from a few crude portraits, and from some articles
of ancient clothing which are still preserved.

When Salem was settled the Massachusetts Bay
Company furnished clothes to all the men who
emigrated and settled that town.   Every man had
four pairs of shoes, four pairs of stockings, a pair of
Norwich garters, four shirts, two suits of doublet

and hose of leather lined with oiled skin, a woollen suit lined with leather, four bands, two handkerchiefs, a green cotton waistcoat, a leather belt, a woollen cap, a black hat, two red knit caps, two pairs of gloves, a mandillion or cloak lined with cotton, and an extra pair of breeches. Little boys just as soon as they could walk wore clothes made precisely like their fathers': doublets which were warm double jackets, leather knee-breeches, leather belts, knit caps. The outfit for the Virginia planters was not so liberal, for the company was not so wealthy. It was called a "Particular of Apparell." It had only three bands, three pairs stockings, and three shirts instead of four. The suits were of canvas, frieze, and cloth. The clothing was doubtless lighter, because the climate of Virginia was warmer. There were no gloves, no handkerchiefs, no hat, no red knit caps, no mandillion, no extra pair of breeches. They had "a dozen points," which were simply tapes to hold up the clothing and fasten it together. The clothing of the Piscataquay planters varied but little from the others. They had scarlet waistcoats and cassocks of cloth, not of leather. We are apt to think of the Puritan settlers of New England as sombre in attire, wearing "sad-colored" garments, but green and scarlet waistcoats and scarlet caps certainly afforded a gay touch of color.

A young boy, about ten years old, named John Livingstone, was sent from New York to school in New England at the latter part of the seventeenth century. An "account of his new linen and clothes" has been preserved, and it gives an excellent idea of the clothing of a son of wealthy people at that time. It reads thus, in the old spelling: —

"Eleven new shirts,
4 pair laced sleves,
8 Plane Cravats,
4 Cravats with Lace,
4 Stripte Wastecoats with black buttons,
1 Flowered Wastecoat,
4 New osenbrig britches,
1 Gray hat with a black ribbon,
1 Gray hat with a blew ribbon,
1 Dousin black buttons,
1 Dousin coloured buttons,
3 Pair gold buttons,
3 Pair silver buttons,
2 Pair Fine blew Stockings,
1 Pair Fine red Stockings,
4 White Handkerchiefs,
2 Speckled Handkerchiefs,
5 Pair Gloves,
1 Stuff Coat with black buttons,
1 Cloth Coat,
1 Pair blew plush britches,
1 Pair Serge britches,
2 Combs,
1 Pair new Shooes,
Silk & Thred to mend his Cloathes."

Osenbrig was a heavy, strong linen. This would seem to be a summer outfit, and scarcely warm enough for New England winters. Other schoolboys at that date had deerskin breeches.

Leather was much used, especially in the form of tanned buckskin breeches and the deerskin hunters' jackets, which have always and deservedly been a favorite wear, since they are one of the most appropriate, useful, comfortable, and picturesque garments ever worn by men in any active outdoor life.

Soon in the larger cities and among wealthy folk a much more elaborate and varied style of dress became fashionable. The dress of little girls in families of wealth was certainly almost as formal and elegant as the dress

Calash, 1780

of their mammas, and it was a very hampering and stiff dress. They wore vast hoop-petticoats, heavy stays, and high-heeled shoes. Their complexions

U

were objects of special care; they wore masks of cloth or velvet to protect them from the tanning rays of the sun, and long-armed gloves. Little Dolly Payne, who afterwards became the wife of President Madison, went to school wearing "a white linen mask to keep every ray of sunshine from the complexion, a sunbonnet sewed on her head every morning by her careful mother, and long gloves covering the hands and arms." Our present love of outdoor life, of athletic sports, and our indifference to being sunburned, makes such painstaking vanity seem most unbearably tiresome.

In 1737 Colonel John Lewis sent from Virginia to England for a wardrobe for a young miss, a school-girl, who was his ward. The list reads thus: —

" A cap ruffle and tucker, the lace 5 shillings per Yard,
1 pair White Stays,
8 pair White Kid gloves,
2 pair coloured kid gloves,
2 pair worsted hose,
3 pair thread hose,
1 pair silk shoes laced,
1 pair morocco shoes,
1 Hoop Coat,
1 Hat,
4 pair plain Spanish shoes,
2 pair calf shoes,
1 mask,
1 fan,
1 necklace,
1 Girdle and buckle,
1 piece fashionable Calico,
4 yards ribbon for knots,
$1\frac{1}{2}$ yard Cambric,
A mantua and coat of lute-string."

In the middle of the century George Washington also sent to England for an outfit for his step-daughter, Miss Custis. She was four years old, and he ordered for her, pack-thread stays, stiff coats of silk, masks, caps, bonnets, bibs, ruffles, necklaces, fans, silk and cal-amanco shoes, and leather pumps. There were also eight pairs of kid mitts and four pairs of gloves; these with the masks show that this little girl's complexion was also to be well guarded.

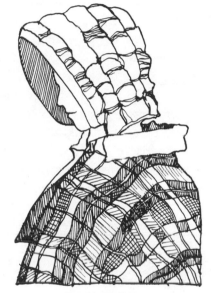

Pumpkin Hood, 1800

A little New England Miss Huntington, when twelve years old, was sent from Norwich, Connecticut, to be "fin-ished" in a Boston boarding-school. She had twelve silk gowns, but her teacher wrote home that she must have another gown of "a recently imported rich fabric," which was at once bought for her because it was "suitable for her rank and station."

Through the seventeenth and eighteenth centuries there was a constant succession of rich and gay fashions; for American dress was carefully modelled upon European, especially English modes. Men's wear was as rich as women's. An English traveller said that Boston women and men in 1740 dressed as gay every day as courtiers in England at a coronation. But with all the richness there was no wastefulness. The sister of the rich Boston merchant, Peter Faneuil, who built Faneuil Hall, sent her gowns to London to be turned and dyed, and her old ribbons and gowns to be sold. But her gowns, which are still preserved, are of magnificent stuffs.

New Yorkers were dressed in gauzes, silks, and laces; even women Quakers in Pennsylvania had to be warned against wearing hoop-petticoats, scarlet shoes, and puffed and rolled hair.

The family of so frugal a man as Benjamin Franklin did not escape a slight infection of the prevailing love for gay dress. In the *Pennsylvania Gazette* this advertisement appeared in 1750: —

"Whereas on Saturday night last the house of Benjamin Franklin of this city, Printer, was broken open, and the following things feloniously taken away, viz., a double necklace of gold beads, a womans long scarlet cloak almost new, with a double cape, a womans gown, of printed cotton of the sort called brocade print, very remarkable, the ground dark, with large red roses, and other large and yellow flowers, with blue in some of the flowers, with many green leaves; a pair of womens stays covered with white tabby before, and dove colour'd tabby behind, with two large steel hooks and sundry other goods, etc."

Southern dames, especially of Annapolis, Baltimore, and Charleston, were said to have the richest brocades and damasks that could be bought in London. Every sailing-vessel that came from Europe brought boxes of splendid clothing. The heroes of the Revolution had a high regard for dress. The patriot, John Hancock, was seen at noonday wearing a scarlet velvet cap, a blue damask gown lined with velvet, white satin embroidered waistcoat, black satin small-clothes, white silk stockings, and red morocco slippers. George Washington was most precise in his orders for his clothing, and wore the richest silk and velvet suits.

A true description of a Boston printer just after the Revolution shows his style of dress: —

"He wore a pea-green coat, white vest, nankeen small clothes, white silk stockings, and pumps fastened with silver buckles which covered at least half the foot from instep to toe. His small clothes were tied at the knees

with ribbon of the same colour in double bows, the ends
reaching down to the ancles.   His hair in front was well
loaded with pomatum, frizzled or craped and powdered.
Behind, his natural hair was augmented by the addition of
a large queue called vulgarly a false tail, which, enrolled
in some yards of black ribbon, hung half-way down his
back."

Many letters still exist written by prominent citizens of colonial times ordering clothing, chiefly
from Europe.   Rich laces, silk materials, velvet, and
fine cloth of light and gay colors abound.   Frequently they ordered nightgowns of silk and damask.   These nightgowns were not a garment worn
at night, but a sort of dressing-gown.   Harvard
students were in 1754 forbidden to wear them.
Under the name of banyan they became very fashionable, and men had their portraits painted in
them, for instance the portrait of Nicholas Boylston,
now in Harvard Memorial Hall.

With the increase of trade with China many
Chinese and East Indian goods became fashionable,
with hundreds of different names.   A few were of
silk or linen, but far more of cotton; among them
nankeens were the most imported and even for
winter wear.

Both men and women wore for many years great
cloaks or capes, known by various names, such as

roquelaures, capuchins, pelisses, etc. Women's shoes
were of very thin materials, and paper-soled.   They
wore to protect these frail shoes, when walking on
the ill-paved streets, various forms of overshoes,
known as goloe-shoes, clogs, pattens, etc.   When
riding, women in the colonies wore, as did Queen

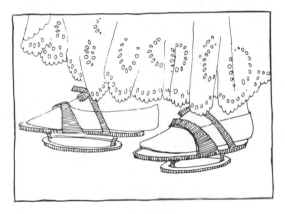

Colonial Pattens

Elizabeth, a safeguard, a long over-petticoat to protect the gown from mud and rain.   This was sometimes called a foot-mantle, also a weather-skirt.   A
traveller tells of seeing a row of horses tied to a
fence outside a Quaker meeting.   Some carried side
saddles, some men's saddles and pillions.   On the
fence hung the muddy safeguards the Quaker dames
had worn outside their drab petticoats.   Men wore

sherry-vallies or spatter-dashes to protect their gay breeches.

There was one fashion which lasted for a century and a half which was so untidy, so uncomfortable, so costly, and so ridiculous that we can only wonder that it was endured for a single season — I mean the fashion of wig-wearing by men. The first colonists wore their own natural hair. The Cavaliers had long and perfumed love-locks; and though the Puritans had been called Roundheads, their hair waved, also, over the band or collar, and often hung over the shoulder. The Quakers, also, wore long locks, as the lovely portrait of William Penn shows. But by 1675 wigs had become common enough to be denounced by the Massachusetts government, and to be preached against by many ministers; while other ministers proudly wore them. Wigs were called horrid bushes of vanity, and hundreds of other disparaging names, which seemed to make them more popular. They varied from year to year; sometimes they swelled out at the sides, or rose in great puffs, or turned under in heavy rolls, or hung in braids and curls and pig-tails; they were made of human hair, of horsehair, goat's-hair, calves' and cows' tails, of thread, silk, and mohair. They had scores of silly and meaningless names, such as "grave full-bottom," "giddy feather-top,"

"long-tail," "fox-tail," "drop-wig," etc. They
were bound and braided with pink, green, red, and
purple ribbons, sometimes all these colors on one
wig. They were very heavy, and very hot, and
very expensive, often costing what would be equal
to a hundred dollars to-day. The care of them was
a great item, often ten pounds a year for a single
wig, and some gentlemen owned eight or ten wigs.
Little children wore them. I have seen the bill for
a wig for William Freeman, dated 1754; he was a
child seven years old. His father paid nine pounds
for it, and the same for wigs for his other boys of
nine and ten. Even servants wore them; I read in
the *Massachusetts Gazette* of a runaway negro slave
who "wore off a curl of hair tied around his head
with a string to imitate a wig," which must have
been a comical sight. After wigs had become un-
fashionable, the natural hair was powdered, and was
tied in a queue in the back. This was an untidy,
troublesome fashion, which ruined the clothes; for
the hair was soaked with oil or pomatum to make
the powder stick.

Comparatively little jewellery was worn. A few
men had gold or silver sleeve-buttons; a few women
had bracelets or lockets; nearly all of any social
standing had rings, which were chiefly mourning-
rings. As these gloomy ornaments were given to

all the chief mourners at funerals, it can be seen that
a man of large family connections, or of prominent
social standing, might acquire a great many of them.
The minister and doctor usually had a ring at every
funeral they attended.   It is told of an old Salem
doctor, who died in 1758, that he had a tankard full

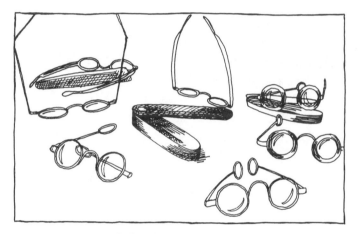

Eighteenth-century Spectacles

of mourning-rings which he had secured at funerals.
Men sometimes wore thumb-rings, which seems no
queerer than the fact that they carried muffs.   Old
Dr. Prince of Boston carried an enormous bearskin
muff.

Gloves also were gifts at funerals, sometimes in
large numbers.   At the funeral of the wife of Gov-

ernor Belcher, in 1738, over a thousand pairs were given away. Rev. Andrew Eliot, who was pastor of the North Church in Boston, had twenty-nine hundred pair of gloves given him in thirty-two years; many of these he sold. In all the colonies, whether settled by Dutch, English, French, German, or Swedes, gloves were universally given at funerals.

The early watches were clumsy affairs, often globose in shape, with a detached outer case.

To show how few of the first colonists owned either watches or clocks, we have the contemporary evidence of Roger Williams. When he rowed thirty miles down the bay, and disputed with the "Foxians" at Newport in 1672, it was agreed that each party should be heard in turn for a quarter of an hour. But no clock was available in Newport; and among the whole population that flocked to the debate, there was not a single watch. Williams says, "unless we had Clocks and Watches and Quarter Glasses (as in some Ships) it was impossible to be exactly punctual," so they guessed at the time.

Sun-dials were often set in the street in front of houses; and noon-marks on the threshold of the front door or window-sill helped to show the hour of the day.

CHAPTER XIII

JACK-KNIFE INDUSTRIES

CHEPA ROSE was one of those old-time chap-men known throughout New England as "trunk pedlers." Bearing on his back by means of a harness of stout hempen webbing two oblong trunks of thin metal, — probably tin, — for forty-eight years he had appeared at every considerable farmhouse throughout Narragansett and eastern Connecticut, at intervals as regular as the action and appearance of the sun, moon, and tides; and everywhere was he greeted with an eager welcome.

Chepa was, as he said, "half Injun, half French, and half Yankee." From his Indian half he had his love of tramping which made him choose the wandering trade of trunk pedler; his French half made him a good trader and talker; while his Yankee half endowed him with a universal Yankee trait, a "handiness," which showed in scores of gifts and accomplishments and knacks that made him as warmly greeted everywhere as were his attractive trunks.

He was a famous medicine-brewer; from the roots and herbs and barks that he gathered as he tramped along the country roads he manufactured a cough medicine that was twice as effective and twice as bitter as old Dr. Greene's; he made famous plasters, of two kinds, — plasters to stick and plasters to crawl, the latter to follow the course of the disease or pain; he concocted wonderful ink; he showed Jenny Greene how to bleach her new straw bonnet with sulphur fumes; he mended umbrellas, harnesses, and tinware; he made glorious teetotums which the children looked for as eagerly and unfailingly as they did for his tops and marbles, his ribbons and Gibraltars.

One day he came through the woods to John Helme's house carrying in his hand a stout birchen staff or small tree-trunk, which he laid down on the flat millstone imbedded in the grass at the back door, while he displayed and sold his wares and had his dinner. He then went out to the dooryard with little Johnny Helme, sat down on the millstone, lighted his pipe, opened his jack-knife, and discoursed thus : —

"Johnny, I'm going to tell you how to make an Injun broom. Fust, you must find a big birch-tree. There ain't so many big ones now of any kind as there useter be when we made canoes and plates and cradles, and water spouts, and troughs, and furnitoor out of the bark. But you must get a yellow birch-tree as straight as H and edzactly five inch acrost. Now, how kin ye tell how fur it is acrost a tree afore ye cut it off? I kin tell by the light of my eye, but that's Injun larnin'. Lemme tell you by book-larnin'. Measure it round, and make the string in three parts, and one part'll be what it is acrost. If it's nine inch round, it'll be three inch acrost, and so on. Now don't you forgit that. Wal! you must get a straight birch-tree five inch acrost where you cut it off, just like this one. Then make the stick six foot long. Then one foot and two inch from the big end cut a ring round the bark; wal! say two inch wide just like this. Then you take off all the bark below that ring. Then you begin a-slivering with a sharp jack-knife, leetle teeny flat slivers way up to the bark ring. When it's all slivered up thin and flat there'll be a leetle hard core left inside at the top, and you must cut it out careful. Then you take off the bark above the ring and begin slivering down. Leave a stick just big enough for a handle. Then tie this last lot of slivers down tight over the others with a hard-twisted tow string, and trim 'em off even. Then whittle off and scrape off a good smooth handle with a hole in the top to put a loop of cowhide in, to hang it up by orderly.

"Yes, Johnny, I've got just enough Injun in me to make a good broom; not enough to be ashamed of and not enough to be proud of. But you mustn't forgit this;

a moccasin's the best cover a man ever had on his feet in the woods; the easiest to get stuff for, the easiest to make, the easiest to wear. And a birch-bark canoe's the best boat a man can have on the river. It's the easiest to get stuff for, easiest to carry, the fastest to paddle. And a snowshoe's the best help a man can have in the winter. It's the easiest to get stuff for, the easiest to walk on, the easiest to carry. And just so a birch broom is the best broom a man or at any rate a woman can have; four best things and all of 'em is Injun. Now you just slip in and take that broom to Phillis. I see her the last time I was here a-using a mizrable store broom to clean her oven — and just ask her if I can't have a mug of apple-jack afore I go to bed."

If this scene had been laid in New Hampshire or Vermont instead of Narragansett, the Indian broom would have been no novelty to any boy or house-servant. For in the northern New England states, heavily wooded with yellow birch, every boy knew how to make the Indian brooms, and every household in country or town had them. There was a constant demand in Boston for them, and sometimes country stores had several hundred of the brooms at a time. Throughout Vermont seventy years ago the uniform price paid for making one of these brooms was six cents; and if the splints were very fine and the handle scraped with glass, it took nearly three evenings to finish it.   Indian squaws peddled them throughout the country for ninepence apiece.   Major Rob-

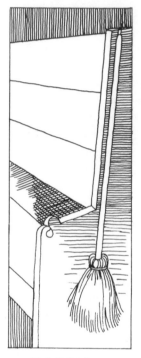

Birch Splint Broom

ert Randolph told in fashion-able London circles about the year 1750, that when he was a boy in New Hampshire he earned his only spending-money by making these brooms and carrying them on his back ten miles to town to sell them. Girls could whittle as well as boys, and often exchanged the birch brooms they made for a bit of ribbon or lace.

A simpler and less durable broom was made of hemlock branches.   A local rhyme says of them: —

" Driving at twilight the waiting cows,
With arms full-laden with hemlock boughs,
To be traced on a broom ere the coming day
From its eastern chambers should dance away."

The hemlock broom was simply a bunch of close-growing, full-foliaged hemlock branches tied tightly

together and wound around with hempen twine,
" traced," the rhyme says, with a sharply pointed
handle, which the boys had shaped and whittled,
driven well into the bound portion.   This making
of brooms for domestic use is but an example of
one of the many score of useful domestic and farm
articles which were furnished by the natural resources
of every wood-lot, adapted by the Yankee jack-knife
and a few equally simple tools, of which the gimlet
might take the second place.

It was so emphatically a wooden age in colonial
days that it seemed almost that there were no hard
metals used for any articles which to-day seem so
necessarily of metal.   Ploughs were of wood, and
harrows ; cart-wheels were often wholly of wood
without tires, though sometimes iron plates called
strakes held the felloes together, being fastened to
them by long clinch-pins.   The dish-turner and
cooper were artisans of importance in those days ;
piggins, noggins, runlets, keelers, firkins, buckets,
churns, dye-tubs, cowles, powdering-tubs, were made
with chary or no use of metal.

The forests were the wealth of the colonies in
more ways than one ; and it may be said that they
furnished both domestic winter employment and
toys for the boys.   The New England forests were
full of richly varied kinds of wood, suitable for

x

varied uses, with varied qualities — pliability, stiff-
ness, durability, weight, strength ; and it is surprising to see how quickly the woods were assigned to
fixed uses, even for toys ; in every state pop-guns
were made from elder; bows and arrows of hemlock;
whistles of chestnut or willow.

The Rev. John Pierpont wrote thus of the whittling of his childhood days : —

> " The Yankee boy before he's sent to school
> Well knows the mysteries of that magic tool —
> The pocket-knife. To that his wistful eye
> Turns, while he hears his mother's lullaby.
> And in the education of the lad,
> No little part that implement hath had.
> His pocket-knife to the young whittler brings
> A growing knowledge of material things,
> Projectiles, music, and the sculptor's art.
> His chestnut whistle, and his shingle dart,
> His elder pop-gun with its hickory rod,
> Its sharp explosion and rebounding wad,
> His corn-stalk fiddle, and the deeper tone
> That murmurs from his pumpkin-leaf trombone
> Conspire to teach the boy. To these succeed
> His bow, his arrow of a feathered reed,
> His windmill raised the passing breeze to win,
> His water-wheel that turns upon a pin.
> Thus by his genius and his jack-knife driven
> Ere long he'll solve you any problem given;

Make you a locomotive or a clock,
Cut a canal or build a floating dock :
Make anything in short for sea or shore,
From a child's rattle to a seventy-four.
Make it, said I — ay, when he undertakes it,
He'll make the thing and make the thing that
  makes it."

The boy's jack-knife was a possession so highly
desired, so closely treasured in those days when boys
had so few belongings, that it is pathetic to read

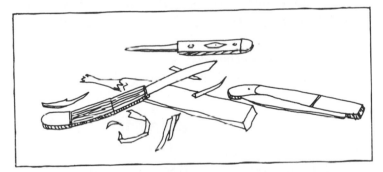

Barlow Jack-knives

of many a farm lad's struggles and long hours of
weary work to obtain a good knife.   Barlow knives
were the most highly prized for certainly sixty years,
and had, I am told, a vast popularity for over
a century.   May they forever rest in glorious
memory, as they lived the happiest of lots !   To be

the best beloved of a century of Yankee boys is indeed an enviable destiny.   A few battered old soldiers of this vast army of Barlow jack-knives still linger to show us the homely features borne by the century's well beloved : the Smithsonian Institution cherishes some of colonial days ; and from Deerfield Memorial Hall are shown three Barlow knives whose picture should appear to every American something more than the presentment of dull bits of wood and rusted metal.   These Yankee jack-knives were, said Daniel Webster, the direct forerunners of the cotton-gin and thousands of noble American inventions ; the New England boy's whittling was his alphabet of mechanics.

In this connection, let us note the skilful and utilitarian adaptation not only of natural materials for domestic and farm use, but also natural forms.   The farmer and his wife both turned to Nature for implements and utensils, or for parts adapted to shape readily into the implements and utensils of every-day life.   When we read of the first Boston settlers that "the dainty Indian maize was eat with clam-shells out of wooden trays," we learn of a primitive spoon, a clam-shell set in a split stick, which has been used till this century. Large flat clam-shells were used and highly esteemed by housewives, as skimming-shells in the

dairy, to skim cream from the milk. Gourd-
shells made capital bowls, skimmers, dippers, and
bottles ; pumpkin-shells, good seed and grain

holders. Turkey-
wings made an
ever-ready hearth-
brush. In the
forests were many
"crooked sticks"
that were more
useful than any
straight ones
could be. When
the mower wanted
a new snathe or
snead, as he called
it, for his scythe,
he found in the
woods a deformed
sapling that had
grown under a
log or twisted
around a rock in

Old Gourd Dishes

a double bend, which made it the exact shape desired.
He then whittled it, dressed it with a draw-shave,
fastened the nebs with a neb-wedge, hung it with
an iron ring, and was ready for the mowing-field.

Sled-runners were made from saplings bent at the root. The best thills for a cart were those naturally shaped by growth. The curved pieces of wood in the harness of a draught-horse, called the hames, to which the traces are fastened, could be found in twisted growths, as could also portions of ox-yokes. The gambrels used in slaughtering times, hay-hooks, long-handled pothooks for brick ovens, could all be cut ready-shaped.

The smaller underbrush and saplings had many uses. Sled and cart stakes were cut from some; long bean-poles from others; specially straight clean sticks were saved for whip-stocks. Sections of birch bark could be bottomed and served for baskets, or for potash cans, while capital feed-boxes could be made in the same way of sections cut from a hollow hemlock. Elm rind and portions of

Goose-yoke and Pig-yoke

brown ash butts were natural materials for chair-seats and baskets, as were flags for door-mats. Forked branches made geese and hog yokes. Hogs that ran at large had to wear yokes. It was ordered that these yokes should measure as long as twice and a half times the depth of the neck, while the bottom piece was three times the width of the neck.

In the shaping of heavy and large vessels such as salt-mortars, pig troughs, maple-sap troughs, the jack-knife was abandoned and the methods of the Indians adopted. These vessels were burnt and scraped out of a single log, and thus had a weighty stability and permanence. Wooden bread troughs were also made from a single piece of wood. These were oblong, trencher-shaped bowls about eighteen inches long; across the trough ran lengthwise a stick or rod on which rested the sieve, searse, or temse, when flour was sifted into the trough. The saying " set the Thames (or temse) on fire," meant that hard work and active friction would set the wooden temse on fire.

Sometimes the mould for an ox-bow was dug out of a log of wood. Oftener a plank of wood was cut into the desired shape as a frame or mould, and fastened to a heavy backboard. The ox-bow was steamed, placed in the bow-mould, pinned in, and then carefully seasoned.

The boys whittled cheese-ladders, cheese-hoops, and red-cherry butter-paddles for their mothers' dairy ; also many parts of cheese-presses and churns. To the toys enumerated by Rev. Mr. Pierpont, they added box-traps and " figure 4 " traps of various sizes for catching vari-sized animals.

Many farm implements other than those already named were made, and many portions of tools and implements ; among them were shovels, swingling-knives, sled-neaps, stanchions, handles for spades and bill-hooks, rake-stales, fork-stales, flails. A group of old farm implements from Memorial Hall, at Deerfield, is here given. The handleless scythe-snathe is said to have come over on the *Mayflower*.

The making of flails was an important and useful work. Many were broken and worn out during a great threshing. Both parts, the staff or handle, and the swingle or swiple, were carefully shaped from well-chosen wood, to be joined together later by an eelskin or leather strap.

The flail is little seen on farms to-day. Threshing and winnowing machines have taken its place. The father of Robert Burns declared threshing with a flail to be the only degrading and stultifying work on a farm; but I never knew another farmer who deemed it so, though it was certainly hard

work. Last autumn I visited the " Poor Farm "
on Quonsett Point in old Narragansett. In the
vast barn of that beautiful and sparsely occupied
country home, two powerful men, picturesque in
blue jeans tucked in
heavy boots, in scarlet
shirts and great straw
hats, were threshing out
grain with flails. Both
men were blind, one
wholly, the other par-
tially so — and were
" Town Poor." Their
strong, bare arms swung
the long flails in alter-
nate strokes with the
precision of clockwork,
bringing each blow
down on the piled-up
wheat-straw which cov-
ered the barn-floor, as
they advanced, one step-
ping backward while the
other stepped forward,

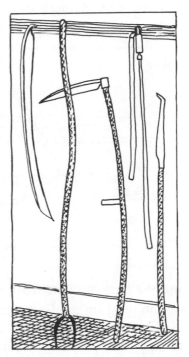

Mayflower Scythe-snathe, Pitchfork, Scythe,
Flail and Swingle, and Bill-hook

and then receded with
mechanical and rhythmic regularity, a step and a
blow, from one end of the long barn to the other.

The half-blind thresher could see the outline of the open door against the sunlight, and his steps and voice guided his sightless fellow-worker. Thus healthful and useful employment was given to two stricken waifs through the use of primitive methods, which no modern machine could ever have afforded;

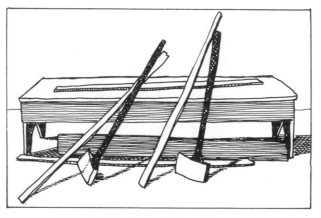

Old-time Axes and Riven Laths

and the blue sky and bay, with autumnal sunshine on the piled-up golden wheat on floor and in rack, idealized and even made of the threshers, paupers though they were, a beautiful picture of old-time farm-life.

Wood for axe-helves was carefully chosen, sawed, split, and whittled into shape. These were then scraped as smooth as ivory with broken glass.

Some men had a knack that was almost genius in shaping these axe-helves and selecting the wood for them. In a country where the broad-axe was so important an implement — used every day by every farmer; where lumbermen and loggers and ship-wrights swung the axe the entire day for many months, men were ready to pay double price for a well-made helve, so shaped as to let the heavy blow jar as little as possible the hand holding the helve. One Maine farmer boasted that he had made and sold five hundred axe-helves, and received a good price for them all; that some had gone five hundred miles out west, others a hundred miles " up country "; and of no one of them which he had set had it ever been said, as of the axe in Deuter-onomy, " When a man goeth into the wood to hew wood, and his hand fetcheth a stroke with the axe to cut down a tree, then the head slippeth from the helve."

A little money might be earned by cutting heel-pegs for shoemakers. These were made of a maple trunk sawed across the grain, making the circular board thin enough — a half inch or so — for the correct length of the pegs. The end was then marked in parallel lines, then grooved across at right angles, then split as marked into pegs with knife and mallet. A story is told of a farmer named

Meigs, who, on the winter ride to market in company with a score or more of his neighbors, stole
out at night from the tavern fireside where all were
gathered to the barn where the horses were put up.
There he took an oat-bag out of a neighbor's sleigh
and poured out a good feed for his own horse.   In
the morning it was found that his horse had not
relished the shoe-pegs that had been put in his
manger; and their telltale presence plainly pointed
out the thief.   These shoe-pegs were a venture of
two farmer boys which their father was taking to
town to sell for them, and in indignation the boys
thrust on the thief the name of Shoe-pegs Meigs,
which he carried to the end of his life.

When the boys had learned to use a few other
tools besides their jack-knives, as they quickly did,
they could get sawed staves from the sawmills and
make up shooks of staves bound with hoops of red
oak, for molasses hogsheads.   These would be
shipped to the West Indies, and form an important link in the profitable rum and slave round of
traffic that bound Africa, New England, and the
West Indies so closely together in those days.   A
constant occupation for men and boys was making
rived or shaved shingles.   They were split with a
beetle and wedge.   A smart workman could by
sharp work make a thousand a day.   There may

still be occasionally found in what were well-wooded pine regions, in shed or barn-lofts, or in old wood-houses, a stout oaken frame or rack such as was at one time found in nearly every house. It was known as a bundling-mould or shingling-mould. At the bottom of this strong frame were laid straight sticks and twisted withes which extended up the sides. Upon these were evenly packed the shingles, two hundred and fifty in number, known as a "quarter." The withes or "binders" were twisted strongly around when the number was full. The mould held them firmly in place while being tied. These were sealed by law and shipped. Cullers of staves were regularly appointed town officers. The dimensions of the shingles were given by law and rule; fifteen inches was the length for one period of time, and the bundling-mould conformed to it.

Daniel Leake of Salisbury, New Hampshire, made during his lifetime and was paid for a million shingles. During the years he was accomplishing this colossal work he cleared three hundred acres of land, tapped for twenty years at least six hundred maple-trees, making sometimes four thousand pounds of sugar a year. He could mow six acres a day, giving nine tons of hay; his strong, long arms cut a swath twelve feet wide. *In his spare time* he worked as a cooper, and he was a famous drum-maker. Truly there were giants in those days. I love to read of such vigorous, powerful lives; they seem to be of a race entirely different from our own. Still, among our New England forbears I doubt not many of us had some such giants, who conquered for us the earth and forests.

One mark the shingling industry left on the household. In the sawing of blocks there would always be some too knotty or gnarled to split into shingles. These were what were known in the vernacular as "on-marchantable shingle-bolts." They formed in many a pioneer's home and in many a pioneer school-house good solid seats for children and even grown people to sit on. And even in pioneer meeting-houses these blocks could sometimes be seen.

Other fittings for the house were whittled out. Long, heavy, wooden hinges were cut from horn-beam for cupboard and closet doors; even shed doors were hung on wooden hinges as were house doors in the earliest colonial days. Door-latches were made of wood, also oblong buttons to fasten chamber and cupboard doors.

New England housekeepers prized the smooth, close-grained bowls which the Indians made from the veined and mottled knots of maple-wood. They

were valued at what seems high prices for wooden
utensils and were often named and bequeathed in
wills.   Maple-wood has been used and esteemed by
many nations for cups and bowls.   The old English and German vessel known as a mazer was made
of maple-wood, often bound and tipped with silver.

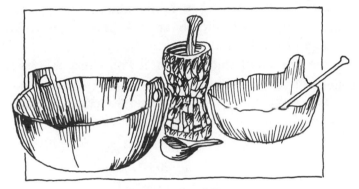

Indian Knot-bowls and Mortar

Spenser speaks in his *Shepheard's Calendar* of
"a mazer yrought of the maple wood."   A well-
known specimen in England bears the legend in
Gothic text : —

> "In the Name of the Trinitie
> Fille the kup and drinke to me."

Sometimes a specially skilful Yankee would rival
the Indians in shaping and whittling out these
bowls.   I have seen two really beautiful ones carved

with double initials, and one with a Scriptural reference, said to be the work of a lover for his bride. Another token of affection and skill from the whittler were carved busks, which were the broad and strong strips of wood placed in corsets or stays to help to form and preserve the long-waisted, stiff figure then fashionable. One carved busk bears initials and an appropriately sentimental design of arrows and hearts.

On the rim of spinning-wheels, on shuttles, swifts, and on niddy-noddys or hand-reels I have seen lettering by the hands of rustic lovers. A finely carved legend on a hand-reel reads : —

> " POLLY GREENE, HER REEL.
>> Count your threads right
>> If you reel in the night
>> When I am far away.
>>> June, 1777."

Perhaps some Revolutionary soldier gave this as a parting gift to his sweetheart on the eve of battle.

On his powder-horn the rustic carver bestowed his best and daintiest work. Emblem both of war and of sport, it seemed worthy of being shaped into the highest expression of his artistic longing. A chapter, even a book, might be filled with the romantic history and representations of American

powder-horns; patriotism, sentiment, and adventure shed equal halos over them. Months of the
patient work of every spare moment was spent in
beautifying them, and their quaintness, variety, and
individuality are a never-ceasing delight to the antiquary. Maps, plans, legends, verses, portraits,
landscapes, family history, crests, dates of births,
marriages, and deaths, lists of battles, patriotic
and religious sentiments, all may be found on
powder-horns. They have in many cases proved
valuable historical records, and have sometimes
been the only records of events. Mr. Rufus A.
Grider, of Canajoharie, has made colored drawings
of about five hundred of these powder-horns, and
of canteens or drinking-horns. It is unfortunate
that the ordinary processes of book-illustration give
too scant suggestion of the variety, beauty, and
delicacy of their decoration, to permit the reproduction of some of these powder-horns in these
pages.

These habits of employing the spare moments of
farm-life in the manufacture from wood of farm implements and various aids to domestic comfort,
were not peculiar to New England farmers, nor
invented by them. The old English farmer-author,
Thomas Tusser, in his rhymed book, *Five Hundred
Points of Good Husbandry*, written in the sixteenth

Y

century (which Southey declared to be one of the most curious and formerly one of the most popular books in our language), was careful to give instructions in his "remembrances" and "doings" as to similar industries on the English farm and manor house. He says: —

> "Yokes, forks, and such other let bailie spy out
> And gather the same as he walketh about;
> And after, at leisure, let this be his hire,
> To beath them and trim them at home by the fire."

To beath is to heat unseasoned wood to harden and straighten it.

> "If hop-yard or orchard ye mean for to have,
> For hop-poles and crotches in lopping go save.

> "Save elm, ash, and crab tree for cart and for plow,
> Save step for a stile of the crotch of a bough;
> Save hazel for forks, save sallow for rake:
> Save hulver and thorn, thereof flail for to make."

The Massachusetts Bay settlers came chiefly from the vicinity, many from the same county, where Tusser lived and farmed, and where his points of good husbandry were household words; so they had in their English homes as had their grandfathers before them, the knowledge and habit of saving and utilizing the various woods on the farm, and of occupying every spare minute with the useful jack-knife. The varied and bountiful trees of the New World stimulated and emphasized the whittling habit until it became universally accepted as a distinguishing New England characteristic, a Yankee trait.

This constant employment of every moment of the waking hours contributed to impart to New Englanders a regard and method of life which is spoken of by many outsiders with contempt, namely, a closely girded and invariable habit of economy. Children brought up in this way knew the value of everything in the household, knew the time it took to produce it, for they had labored themselves, and they grew to take care of small things, not to squander and waste what they had been so long at work on. This, instead of being a thing to sneer at, is one of the very best elements in a community, one of the best securities of character. For sudden leaps to fortune are given to but few, and are seldom lasting, and the results of sudden inflations are more disastrous even to a community than to isolated individuals, as may be abundantly proved by the early history of Virginia. It was not meanness that made the wiry New England farmer so cautious and exacting in trade, when the pennies he saved sent his son through college. It was not meanness which made him refuse to spend money;

he had no money to spend, and it was a high sense
of honor that kept him from running in debt.   It
was not meanness which so justly ordered conditions
and cared for the unfortunate that even in those
days of horrible drunkenness often there would not
be a pauper in the entire village.   It has been a reproach that in some towns the few town poor were
vendued out to be cared for; the mode was harsh in
its wording, and unfeeling in method, but in reality
the pauper found a home.   I have known cases
where the pauper was not only supported but
cherished in the families to whose lot she fell.

CHAPTER XIV

TRAVEL, TRANSPORTATION, AND TAVERNS

W HEREVER the earliest colonists settled in America, they had to adopt the
modes of travel and the ways of getting from place to place of their prede-
cessors and new neighbors, the Indians. These
were first — and generally — to walk on their
own stout legs ; second, to go wherever they could
by water, in boats. In Maryland and Virginia,
where for a long time nearly all settlers tried to
build their homes on the banks of the rivers and
bays, the travel was almost entirely by boats ; as it
was between settlements on all the great rivers, the
Hudson, Connecticut, and Merrimac.

Between the large settlements in Massachusetts —
Boston, Salem, and Plymouth — travel was preferably, when the weather permitted, in boats. The colonists went in canoes, or pinnaces, shaped and made
exactly like the birch-bark canoes of the Canadian
Indians to-day ; and in dugouts, which were formed
from hollowed pine-logs, usually about twenty feet

325

long and two or three feet wide ; both of these were made for them by the Indians.   It was said that one Indian, working alone, felling the pine-tree by the primitive way of burning and scraping off the charred parts with a stone tool called a celt (for the Indians had no iron or steel axes), then cutting off the top in the same manner, then burning out part of the interior, then burning and scraping and shaping it without and within, could make one of these dugouts in three weeks. The Indians at Onondaga still make the wooden mortars they use in the same tedious way.

When the white men came to America in great ships, the Indians marvelled much at the size, thinking they were hollowed out of tree-trunks as were the dugouts, and wondered where such vast trees grew.

The Swedish scientific traveller, Kalm, who was in America in 1748, was delighted with the Indian canoes and dugouts.   He found the Swede settlers using them constantly to go long distances to market.   He said : —

" They usually carry six persons who however by no means must be unruly, but sit at the bottom of the canoe in the quietest manner possible lest the boat upset.   They are narrow, round below, have no keel and may be easily overset.   So when the wind is brisk the people make for the land.   Larger dugouts were made for war-canoes which would carry thirty or forty savages."

These boats usually kept close to the shore, both in calm and windy weather, though the natives were not afraid to go many miles out to sea in the dugouts.

The lightness of the birch-bark canoe made it specially desirable where there were such frequent overland transfers.   It was and is a beautiful and perfect expression of natural and wild life; as Long-fellow wrote : —

> " . . . the forest's life was in it,
> All its mystery and magic,
> All the lightness of the birch tree,
> All the toughness of the cedar,
> All the larch's supple sinews,
> And it floated on the river
> Like a yellow leaf in autumn."

The French governor and missionaries all saw and admired these birch-bark canoes.   Father Char-levoix wrote a beautiful and vivid description of them.   All the early travellers noted their ticklish balance.   Wood, writing in 1634, said, " In these cockling fly-boats an Englishman can scarce sit without a fearful tottering," and Madam Knights a century later said in her vivid English of a trip in one : —

" The Cannoo was very small and shallow, which greatly
terrify'd me and caused me to be very circumspect, sitting
with my hands fast on each side, my eyes steady, not daring so much as to lodge my tongue a hair's bredth more on
one side of my mouth than tother, nor so much as think
on Lott's wife, for a very thought would have oversett our
wherry."

When boats and vessels were built by the colonists, they were in forms or had names but little
used to-day. Shallop, ketch, pink, and snow are

A Gundalow at the Landing

rarely heard.   Sloops were early built, but schooner is a modern term.   Batteau and periagua still are used; and the gundalow, picturesque with its lateen sail, still is found on our northern New England shores.

The Indians had narrow foot-paths in many places through the woods.   On them foot-travel was possible, though many estuaries and rivers intersected the coast; for the narrow streams could be crossed on natural ford-ways, or on rude bridges of fallen trees, which the English government ordered to be put in place.

As late as 1631 Governor Endicott would not go from Salem to Boston to visit Governor Winthrop because he was not strong enough to wade across the fords.   He might have done as Governor Winthrop did the next year when he went to Plymouth to visit Governor Bradford (and it took him two days to get there); he might have been carried across the fords pickaback by an Indian guide.

The Indian paths were good, though only two or three feet wide, and in many places the savages kept the woods clear from underbrush by burning over large tracts.   When King Philip's War took place, all the land around the Indian settlements in Narragansett and eastern Massachusetts was so free of brush that horsemen could ride everywhere

freely through the woods.   Some of the old paths
are famous in our history.   The most so was the
Bay Path, which ran from Cambridge through
Marlborough, Worcester, Oxford, Brookfield, and
on to Springfield and the Connecticut River.   Holland's beautiful story called by the name of the
path gives its history, its sentiment, and much that
happened on it in olden times.

When new paths were cut through the forests,
the settlers "blazed" the trees, that is, they chopped
a piece of the bark off tree after tree standing on
the side of the way.   Thus the "blazes" stood out
clear and white in the dark shadows of the forests,
like welcome guide-posts, showing the traveller his
way.   In Maryland roads turning off to a church
were marked by slips or blazes cut near the ground.

In Maryland and Virginia what were known as,
and indeed are still called, rolling-roads were cut
through the forest.   They were narrow roads adown
which hogsheads of tobacco, fitted with axles, could
be drawn or rolled from inland plantations to the
river or bay side; sometimes the hogsheads were
simply rolled by human propulsion, not dragged
on these roads.

The broader rivers soon had canoe-ferries.   The
first regular Massachusetts ferry from Charlestown
to Boston was in 1639.   It carried passengers for

threepence apiece.   From Chelsea to Boston was
fourpence.   In 1636 the Cambridge ferryman
charged but half a penny, as so many wished to
attend the Thursday lecture in the Boston churches.
We learn from the Massachusetts Laws that often
a rider had to let his horse cross by swimming over,
being guided from the ferry-boat; he then paid no
ferriage for the horse.   After wheeled vehicles were
used, these ferries were not large enough to carry
them properly.   Often the carriage had to be taken
apart, or towed over, while the horse had his fore
feet in one canoe-ferry and his hind feet in another,
the two canoes being lashed together.   The rope-
ferry lingered till our own day, and was ever a picturesque sight on the river.   As soon as roads were
built there were, of course, bridges and cart-ways,
but these were only between the closely neighboring towns.   Usually the bridges were merely
" horse-bridges " with a railing on but one side.

After the period of walking and canoe-riding had
had its day, nearly all land travel for a century was
on horseback, just as it was in England at that
date.   In 1672 there were only six stage-coaches
in the whole of Great Britain ; and a man wrote
a pamphlet protesting that they encouraged too
much travel.   Boston then had one private coach.
Women and children usually rode seated on a pil-

lion behind a man. A pillion was a padded cushion with straps which sometimes had on one side a sort of platform-stirrup. One way of progress which would help four persons ride part of their journey was what was called the ride-and-tie system. Two of the four persons who were travelling started on their road on foot; two mounted on the saddle and pillion, rode about a mile, dismounted, tied the horse, and walked on. When the two who had started on foot reached the waiting horse, they mounted, rode on past the other couple for a mile or so, dismounted, tied, and walked on; and so on. It was also a universal and courteous as it was a pleasant custom for friends to ride out on the road a few miles with any departing guest or friend, and then bid them God speed agatewards.

In 1704 a Boston schoolmistress named Madam Knights rode from Boston to New York on horseback. She was probably the first woman to make the journey, and it was a great and daring undertaking. She had as a companion the "post." This was the mail-carrier, who also rode on horseback. One of his duties was to assist and be kind to all persons who cared to journey in his company. The first regular mail started from New York to Boston on January 1, 1673. The postman carried two "portmantles," which were crammed with letters and parcels.   He did not change horses till he reached Hartford.   He was ordered to look out and report the condition of all ferries, fords, and roads.   He had to be "active, stout, indefatigable, and honest."   When he delivered his mail it was laid on a table at an inn, and any one who wished looked over all the letters, then took and paid the postage (which was very high) on any addressed to himself.   It was usually about a month from this setting out of "the post" in winter, till his return. As late certainly as 1730 the mail was carried from New York to Albany in the winter by a "foot-post."   He went up the Hudson River, and lonely enough it must have been; probably he skated up when the ice was good.   This mail was only sent at irregular intervals.

In 1760 there were but eight mails a year from Philadelphia to the Potomac River, and even then the post-rider need not start till he had received enough letters to pay the expenses of the trip.   It was not till postal affairs were placed in the capable and responsible hands of Benjamin Franklin that there were any regular or trustworthy mails.

The journal and report of Hugh Finlay, a post-office surveyor in 1773 of the mail service from Quebec to St. Augustine, Florida, tells of the vicissitudes of mail-matter even at that later day.   In

some places the deputy, as the postmaster was
called, had no office, so his family rooms were
constantly invaded.   Occasionally a tavern served as
post-office; letters were thrown down on a table
and if the weather was bad, or smallpox raged, or
the deputy were careless, they were not forwarded
for many days.   Letters that arrived might lie on
the table or bar-counter for days for any one to pull
over, until the owner chanced to arrive and claim
them.   Good service could scarcely be expected
from any deputy, for his salary was paid according
to the number of letters coming to his office; and
as private mail-carriage constantly went on, though
forbidden by British law, the deputy suffered.
" If an information were lodg'd but an informer
wou'd get tar'd and feather'd, no jury wou'd find
the fact."   The government-riders were in truth
the chief offenders.   Any ship's captain, or wagon-
driver, or post-rider could carry merchandise;
therefore small sham bundles of paper, straw, or
chips would be tied to a large sealed packet or
letter, and both be exempt from postage paid to the
Crown.

The post-rider between Boston and Newport
loaded his carriage with bundles real and sham,
which delayed him long in delivery.   He bought
and sold on commission along this road; and in

violation of law he carried many letters to his own profit. He took twenty-six hours to go eighty miles. Had the Newport deputy dared to complain, he would have incurred much odium and been declared a " friend of slavery and oppression."

"Old Herd," the rider from Saybrook to New York, had been in the service forty-six years and had made a good estate. He coolly took postage of all way-letters as his perquisite; was a money carrier and transferrer, all advantage to his own pocket; carried merchandise; returned horses for travellers; and when Finlay saw him he was waiting for a yoke of oxen he was paid for fetching along some miles. A Pennsylvania post-rider, an aged man, occupied himself as he slowly jogged along by knitting mittens and stockings. Not always were mail portmanteaux properly locked; hence many letters were lost and the pulling in and out of bundles defaced the letters.

Of course so much horseback riding made it necessary to have horse-blocks in front of nearly all houses. In course of time stones were set every mile on the principal roads to tell the distance from town to town. Benjamin Franklin set milestones the entire way on the post-road from Boston to Philadelphia. He rode in a chaise over the road; and a machine which he had invented was

attached to the chaise; and it was certainly the first
cyclometer that went on that road, over which so
many cyclometers have passed during the last five
years. It measured the miles as he travelled.
When he had ridden a mile he stopped; from a
heavy cart loaded with milestones, which kept
alongside the chaise, a stone was dropped which
was afterwards set by a gang of men.

A number of old colonial milestones are still standing. There is one in Worcester, on what was the
" New Connecticut Path"; one in Springfield on
the " Bay Path," and there are several of Benjamin
Franklin's setting, one being at Stratford, Connecticut.

The inland transportation of freight was carried
on in the colonies just as it was in Europe, on the
backs of pack-horses. Very interesting historical
evidence in relation to the methods of transportation
in the middle of the eighteenth century may be found
in the ingenious advertisement and address with which
Benjamin Franklin raised transportation facilities for
Braddock's army in 1755. This is one of his most
characteristic literary productions. Braddock's ap-
peals to the Philadelphia Assembly for a rough
wagon-road and wagons for the army succeeded in
raising only twenty-five wagons. Franklin visited
him in his desolate plight and agreed to assist him,
and appealed to the public to send to him for the

use of the army a hundred and fifty wagons and fifteen hundred pack-horses; for the latter Franklin offered to pay two shillings a day each, as long as used, if provided with a pack-saddle. Twenty horses were sent with their loads to the camp as gifts to the British officers. As a good and definite list of the load one of these pack-horses was expected to carry (as well as a record of the kind of provisions grateful to an officer of that day) let me give an inventory: —

Six pounds loaf-sugar,
Six pounds muscovado sugar,
One pound green tea,
One pound bohea tea,
Six pounds ground coffee,
Six pounds chocolate,
One-half chest best white biscuit,
One-half pound pepper,
One quart white vinegar,
Two dozen bottles old Madeira wine,

Two gallons Jamaica spirits,
One bottle flour of mustard,
Two well-cured hams,
One-half dozen cured tongues,
Six pounds rice,
Six pounds raisins,
One Gloucester cheese,
One keg containing 20 lbs. best butter.

The wagons and horses were all lost after Braddock's defeat, or were seized by the French and Indians, and Franklin had many anxious months of responsibility for damages from the owners; but I am confident the officers got all the provisions.

Franklin gathered the wagons in York and Lancaster; no two English shires could have done better at that time than did these Pennsylvania counties.

In Pennsylvania, western Virginia, and Ohio, pack-horses long were used, and a pretty picture is drawn by Doddridge and many other local historians of the trains of these horses with their gay collars and stuffed bells, as, laden with furs, ginseng, and snakeroot, they filed down the mountain roads to the towns, and came home laden with salt, nails, tea, pewter plates, etc. At night the horses were hobbled, and the clappers of their bells were loosened; the ringing prevented the horses being lost. The animals started on their journey with two hundred pounds' burden, of which part was provender for horse and man, which was left at convenient relays to be taken up on the way home. Two men could manage fifteen pack-horses, which were tethered successively each to the pack-saddle of the one in front of him. One man led the foremost horse, and the driver followed the file to watch the packs and urge on the laggards. Their numbers were vast; five hundred were counted at one time in Carlisle, Pennsylvania, going westward. It was a costly method of transportation. Mr. Howland says that in 1784 the expense of carrying a ton's weight from Philadelphia to Erie by pack-horses was $249.   It is interesting to note that the routes taken by those men, skilled only in humble wood-craft, were the same ones followed in later years by the engineers of the turnpikes and railroads.

As the roads were somewhat better in Pennsylvania than in some other provinces, and more needed, so wagons soon were far greater in number; indeed, during the Revolution nearly all the wagons and horses used by the army came from that state.   There was developed in Pennsylvania by the soft soil of these many roads, as well as by various topographical conditions, a splendid example of a true American vehicle, one which was for a long time the highest type of a commodious freight-carrier in this or any other country — the Conestoga wagon, "the finest wagon the world has ever known."   They were first used in any considerable number about 1760.   They had broad wheel-tires, and one of the peculiarities was a decided curve in the bottom, analogous to that of a galley or canoe, which made it specially fitted for traversing mountain roads; for this curved bottom prevented freight from slipping too far at either end when going up or down hill.   This body was universally painted a bright blue, and furnished with sideboards of an equally vivid red.   The wagon-bodies were arched over with six or eight stately

Conestoga Wagon

bows, of which the middle ones were the lowest,
and the others rose gradually to front and rear till
the end bows were nearly of equal height.   Over
them all was stretched a strong, white, hempen
cover, well corded down at the sides and ends.
These wagons could be loaded up to the bows, and
could carry four to six tons in weight.   The rates
between Philadelphia and Pittsburgh were about
two dollars a hundred pounds.   The horses, four
to seven in number, were magnificent, often matched
throughout; some were all dapple-gray, or all bay.
The harnesses, of best materials and appearance,
were costly; each horse had a large housing of

deerskin or heavy bearskin trimmed with deep scarlet fringe ; while the head-stall was tied with bunches
of gay ribbons.   Bell-teams were common; each
horse except the saddle-horse then had a full set of
bells tied with high-colored ribbons.

The horses were highly fed ; and when the driver,
seated on the saddle-horse, drew rein on the prancing
leader and flourished his fine bull-hide London
whip, making the silk snap and tingle round the
leader's ears, every horse started off with the ponderous load with a grace and ease that was beautiful
to see.

The wagons were first used in the Conestoga valley, and most extensively used there ; and the sleek
powerful draught-horses known as the Conestoga
breed were attached to them, hence their name.
These teams were objects of pride to their owners,
objects of admiration and attention wherever they
appeared, and are objects of historical interest and
satisfaction to-day.

Often a prosperous teamster would own several
Conestoga wagons, and driving the leading and
handsomest team himself would start off his proud
procession.   From twenty to a hundred would follow in close row.   Large numbers were constantly
passing.   At one time ten thousand ran from Philadelphia to other towns.   Josiah Quincy told of the

road at Lancaster being lined with them. The scene on the road between the Cumberland valley and Greensburg, where there are five distinct and noble mountain ranges, — Tuscarora, Rays Hill, Alleghany, Laurel Hills, and Chestnut Ridge, — when a long train of white-topped Conestoga wagons appeared and wound along the mountain sides, was picturesque and beautiful with a charm unparalleled to-day.

> "—— Many a fleet of them
> In one long upward winding row.
> It ever was a noble sight
> As from the distant mountain height
>   Or quiet valley far below,
> Their snow-white covers looked like sail."

There were two classes of Conestoga wagons and wagoners. The "Regulars," or men who made it their constant and only business; and "Militia." A local poet thus describes these outfits : —

> "Militia-men drove narrow treads,
>   Four horses and plain red Dutch beds,
>   And always carried grub and feed."

They were farmers or common teamsters who made occasional trips, usually in winter time, and did some carriage for others, and drove but four horses with their wagons. The "Regulars" had broad tires, carried no feed for horses nor food for themselves, but both classes of teamsters carried coarse mattresses and blankets, which they spread side by side, and row after row, on the bar-room

"American Stage-wagon"

floor of the tavern at which they " put up." Their horses when unharnessed fed from long troughs hitched to the wagon-pole. The wagons that plied between the Delaware and the small city of Pittsburgh were called Pitt-teams.

The life of the Conestoga wagon did not end

even with the establishment of railroads in the Eastern states ; farther and farther west it penetrated, ever chosen by emigrants and travellers to the frontiers ; and at last in its old age it had an equal career of usefulness as the " prairie-schooner," in which vast numbers of families safely crossed the prairies of our far West. The white tilts of the wagons thus passed and repassed till our own day.

Four-wheeled wagons were but little used in New England till after the War of 1812. Two-wheeled carts and sleds carried inland freight, which was chiefly transported over the snow in the winter.

The Conestoga wagon of the past century was far ahead of anything in England at that date ; indeed Mr. C. W. Ernst, the best authority I know on the subject, says we had in every way far better traffic facilities at that time than England. In other ways we excelled. Though Finlay found many defects in the postal service in 1773, he also found the Stavers mail-coach plying between Boston and Portsmouth long before England had such a thing. Mr. Ernst says : " The Stavers mail-coach was stunning ; used six horses when roads were bad, and never was late. They had no mail-coaches in England till after the Revolution, and I believe Massachusetts men introduced the idea in England."

We are apt to grow retrospectively sentimental

over the delights, æsthetic and physical, of ancient stage-coach days.   Those days are not so ancient as many fancy.   The first stage-coach which ran directly from Philadelphia to New York in 1766 — and primitive enough it was — was called " the flying-machine, a good stage-wagon set on springs."

Wayside Inn

Its swift trip occupied two days in good weather. It was but a year later than the original stage-coach between Edinburgh and Glasgow.   At that time, in favorable weather, the coach between London and Edinburgh made the trip in thirteen days. The London mail-coach in its palmiest days could make this trip in forty-three hours and a half. As early as 1718 Jonathan Wardwell advertised that he would run a stage to Rhode Island. In 1767 a stage-coach was run during the summer months between Boston and Providence; in 1770 a stage-chaise started between Salem and Boston and a post-chaise between Boston and Portsmouth the following year. As early as 1732 some common-carrier lines had wagons which would carry a few passengers. Let us hear the testimony of some travellers as to the glorious pleasure of stage-coach travelling. Describing a trip between Boston and New York towards the end of the last century President Quincy of Harvard College said:—

"The carriages were old and the shackling and much of the harness made of ropes. One pair of horses carried us eighteen miles. We generally reached our resting-place for the night if no accident intervened, at ten o'clock, and after a frugal supper went to bed, with a notice that we should be called at three next morning, which generally proved to be half-past two, and then, whether it snowed or rained, the traveller must rise and make ready, by the help of a horn-lantern and a farthing candle, and proceed on his way over bad roads, sometimes getting out to help the coachman lift the coach out of a quagmire or rut, and arrived in New York after a week's hard travelling, wondering at the ease as well as the expedition with which our journey was effected."

The *Columbia Centinel* of April 24, 1793, advertised a new line of " small genteel and easy stage-

Old Pigskin and Deerskin Travelling-trunks

carriages " from Boston to New York with four
inside passengers, and smart horses. Many of the
announcements of the day have pictures of the

coaches. They usually resemble market wagons with round, canvas-covered tops, and the driver is seated outside the body of the wagon with his feet on the foot-board. Trunks were small, covered with deerskin or pigskin, studded with brass nails; and each traveller took his trunk under his seat and feet.

The poet, Moore, gives in rhyme his testimony of Virginia roads in 1800 : —

> " Dear George, though every bone is aching
>   After the shaking
>   I've had this week over ruts and ridges,
>   And bridges
>   Made of a few uneasy planks,
>   In open ranks,
>   Over rivers of mud whose names alone
>   Would make knock the knees of stoutest man."

The traveller Weld, in 1795, gave testimony that the bridges were so poor that the driver had always to stop and arrange the loose planks ere he dared cross, and he adds : —

" The driver frequently had to call to the passengers in the stage to lean out of the carriage first on one side then on the other, to prevent it from oversetting in the deep roads with which the road abounds. ' Now, gentlemen, to the right,' upon which the passengers all stretched their bodies half-way out of the carriage to balance on that side. ' Now, gentlemen, to the left,' and so on."

The coach in which this pleasure trip was taken is shown in the illustration entitled "American Stage-wagon." It is copied from a first edition of *Weld's Travels*.

Ann Warder, in her journey from Philadelphia to New York in 1759, notes two overturned and abandoned stage-wagons at Perth Amboy; and many other travellers give similar testimony. In 1796 the trip from Philadelphia to Baltimore took five days.

The growth in stage-coaches and travel came with the turnpike at the beginning of this century. In transportation and travel, improvement of road-ways is ever associated with improvement of vehicles. The first extensive turnpike was the one between Philadelphia and Lancaster, built in 1792. The growth and the cost of these roads may be briefly mentioned by quoting a statement from the annual message of the governor of Pennsylvania in 1838, that that commonwealth then had two thousand five hundred miles of turnpikes which had cost $37,000,000.

Many of these turnpikes were beautiful and splendid roads; for instance, the " Mohawk and

Hudson Turnpike," which ran in a straight line from Albany to Schenectady, was ornamented and shaded with two rows of the quickly growing and fashionable poplar-trees and thickly punctuated with taverns. On one turnpike there were sixty-five taverns in sixty miles. The dashing stage-coach accorded well with this fine thoroughfare.

With the splendid turnpikes came the glorious coaching days. In 1827 the Traveller's Register reported eight hundred stage-coaches arriving, and as many leaving Boston each week. The forty-mile road from Boston to Providence sometimes saw twenty coaches going each way. The editor of the *Providence Gazette* wrote: "We were rattled from Boston to Providence in four hours and fifty minutes — if any one wants to go faster he may go to Kentucky and charter a streak of lightning." There were four rival lines on the Cumberland road, — the National, Good Intent, Pioneer, and June Bug. Some spirited races the old stage-road witnessed between the rival lines. The distance from Wheeling to Cumberland, one hundred and thirty-two miles, was regularly accomplished in twenty-four hours. No heavy luggage was carried and but nine passengers; fourteen coaches rolled off together — one was a mail-coach with a horn. Relays were every ten miles; teams were changed before the coach ceased rocking; one driver boasted of changing and harnessing his four horses in four minutes.   Lady travellers were quickly thrust in the open door and their bandboxes after them.   Scant time was there for refreshment, save by uncorking of bottles.   The keen test and acute rivalry between drivers came in the delivery of the President's Message.   Dan Gordon carried the message thirty-two miles in two hours and thirty minutes, changing horses three times.   Bill Noble carried the message from Wheeling to Hagerstown, a hundred and eighty-five miles, in fifteen and a half hours.

In 1818 the Eastern Stage Company was chartered in the state of New Hampshire.   The route was this: a stage started from Portsmouth at 9 A.M.; passengers dined at Topsfield; thence through Danvers and Salem; back the following day, dining at Newburyport.   The capital stock was four hundred and twenty-five shares at a hundred dollars par.   In 1834 the stock was worth two hundred dollars a share.   The company owned several hundred horses.   It was on a coach of this line that Henry Clay rode from Pleasant Street, Salem, to Tremont House, Boston, in exactly an hour; and on the route extended to Portland, Daniel Webster was carried at the rate of sixteen English miles an hour from Boston to Portland to sign the Ashburton Treaty.

The middle of the century saw the beginning of the end of coaching in all the states that had been colonies.   Further west the old stage-coach had to trundle in order to exist at all: Ohio, Indiana, Missouri, across the plains, and then over the Rocky Mountains to Salt Lake.   The road from

Old-time Rocky Mountain Mail-coach

Carson to Plainville gave the crack ride, and the driver wore yellow kid gloves.   The coach known as the Concord wagon, drawn by six horses, still makes cheerful the out-of-the-way roads of our Western states, and recalls the life of olden times. The story of spirited and gay life still exists in the Wells Fargo Express.   The usefulness of the Con-

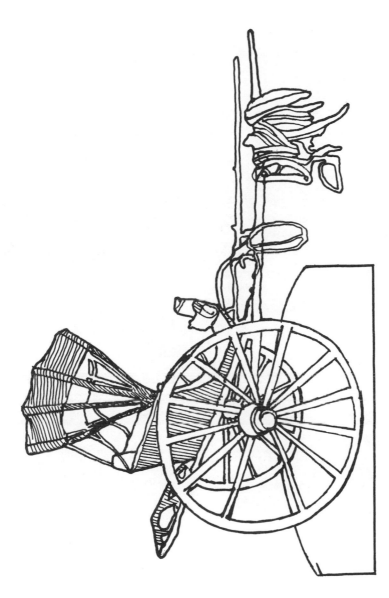

Brother Jonathan's Chaise

cord coach is not limited to the western nor the northern portion of our continent; in South America it flourishes, banishing all rivals.

Canal travel and transportation were proposed at the close of provincial days, and a few short canals were built. Benjamin Franklin was early awake to their practicability and value. Among the stock-owners of the Dismal Swamp Canal was George Washington, and he was equally interested in the Potomac Canal.

The Erie Canal, first proposed to the New York legislature in 1768, was completed in 1825. There was considerable passenger travel on this canal at "a cent and a half a mile, a mile and a half an hour." Horace Greeley has given an excellent picture of this leisurely travel; it was asserted by some that stage-coaches were doomed by the canal-boat, but they continued to exist till they encountered a more formidable rival.

Until turnpike days all small carriages were two-wheeled; chaises, chairs, and sulkies were those generally used. The chaise and harness used by Jonathan Trumbull — "Brother Jonathan" — are here shown. With regard to private conveyances, whether coaches, chaises, or chairs, the colonies kept close step from earliest days with the mother-countries. Randolph noted with envy the Boston

2 A

coaches of the seventeenth century. Parson Thatcher was accused and reprehended in 1675 for making visits with a coach and four. Coaches were taxed both in England and America; so we know exactly how plentiful they were. There were as many in Massachusetts in 1750 in proportion to the number of inhabitants as there were in England in 1830. Judge Sewall's diary often refers to private coaches; and one of the most amusing scenes it depicts is his continued and ingenious argument when wooing Madam Winthrop for his third wife, when she stipulated that he should keep a coach, and his frugal mind disposed him not to do it.

Coach-building prospered in the colonies; Lucas and Paddock in Boston, Ross in New York, made beautiful and rich coaches. Materials were ample

Campbell Coach

and varied in the New World for carriage-building;
horseflesh — not over-choice, to be sure — became
over-plentiful; it was said that no man ever walked
in America save a vagabond or a fool.   A coach
made for Madam Angelica Campbell of Schenectady, New York, by coach-builder Ross, in 1790,

Dutch Sleigh in New York.   From an old print

is here shown.   It is now owned by Mr. John D.
Campbell of Rotterdam, New York.

Sleighs were common in New York a half-cen-
tury before they were in Boston.   Madam Knights
noted the fast racing in sleighs in New York when
she was there in 1704.

One other curious conveyance of colonial days should be spoken of, — a sedan-chair. This was a strong covered chair fastened on two bars with handles like a litter, and might be carried by two or four persons. When sedan-chairs were so much used in England, they were sure to be somewhat used in cities in America. One was presented to Governor Winthrop as early as 1646, portion of a capture from a Spanish galleon. Judge Sewall wrote in 1706, " Five Indians carried Mr. Bromfield in a chair." This was in the country, down on Cape Cod, and doubtless four Indians carried him while one rested. As late as 1789 Eliza Quincy saw Dr. Franklin riding in a sedan-chair in Philadelphia.

The establishment and building of roads, bridges, and opening of inns show that mutual interest which marks civilization, and separates us from the lonely, selfish life of a savage. Soon inns were found everywhere in the Northern colonies. In New England, New York, and Pennsylvania an inn was called an ordinary, a victualling, a cook-shop, or a tavern before we had our modern word hotel.

Board was not very high at early inns ; the prices were regulated by the different towns. In 1633 the Salem innkeeper could only have sixpence for a meal. This was at the famous Anchor Tavern, which was kept as a hostelry for nearly two centuries. At the Ship Tavern, board, lodging, wine at dinner, and beer between meals cost three shillings a day. Great care was taken by the magistrates to choose responsible men and women to keep taverns, and they would not permit too many taverns in one town.   At first the tavern-keeper could not sell sack (which was sherry), nor stronger intoxicating liquor to travellers, but he could sell beer, provided it was good, for a penny a quart.   Nor could he sell cakes or buns except at a wedding or funeral. He could not allow games to be played, nor singing or dancing to take place.

We know from Shakespeare's plays that the different rooms in English inns had names.   This was also the custom in New England.   The Star Chamber, Rose and Sun Chamber, Blue Chamber, Jerusalem Chamber, were some of them.   Many of the taverns of Revolutionary days and some of colonial times are still standing.   A few have even been taverns since first built; others have served many other uses.   A well-preserved old house, built in 1690 in Sudbury, Massachusetts, was originally known as the Red Horse Tavern, but has acquired greater fame as the Wayside Inn of Longfellow's Tales.   Its tap-room with raftered ceiling and cage-like bar with swinging gate is a picturesque room, and is one of the few old tap-rooms left unaltered in New England.

Every inn had a name, usually painted on its

Swing-sign from Grosvenor Inn, Pomfret, Connecticut

swinging sign-board, with some significant emblem. These names were simply repetitions of old English tavern-signs until Revolutionary days, when patriotic landlords eagerly invented and adopted names significant of the new nation.   The scarlet coat of

King George became the blue and buff of George Washington; and the eagle of the United States took the place of the British lion.

The sign-board was an interesting survival of feudal times, and with its old-time carved and forged companions, such as vanes and weathercocks, door-knockers and figureheads, formed a picturesque element of decoration and symbolism. Many chapters might be written on historic, commemorative, emblematic, heraldic, biblical, humorous, or significant signs, nearly all of which have vanished from public gaze, as has disappeared also the general incapacity to read, which made pictorial devices a necessity. Gilders, painter-stainers, smiths, and joiners all helped to make the tavern-sign a thing of varied workmanship if not of art. It is said that Philadelphia excelled in the quantity and quality of her sign-boards. With fair roads for colonial days, the best and amplest system of transportation, and the splendid Conestoga wagons, great inns multiplied throughout Pennsylvania. In Baltimore both taverns and signs were many and varied, from the Three Loggerheads to the Indian Queen with its "two hundred guest-rooms with a bell in every room," and the Fountain Inn built around a shady court, with galleries on every story, like the Tabard Inn at Southwark.

The swinging sign-board of John Nash's Tavern at Amherst, Massachu-

Sign-board, John Nash's Tavern, Amherst, Massachusetts

setts, is here reproduced from the *History of Amherst*. It is a good type of the ordinary sign-board which was found hanging in front of every tavern a century ago.

In Virginia and the Carolinas taverns were not so plentiful nor so necessary; for a traveller might ride from Maryland to Georgia, and be sure of a welcome at every private house on the way. Some planters, eager for company and news, stationed negroes at the gate to invite passers-by on the post-road to come into the house and be entertained. Berkeley, in his *History of Virginia*, wrote : —

"The inhabitants are very courteous to travellers, who need no other recommendation than being human creatures. A stranger has no more to do but to inquire upon the road where any gentleman or good housekeeper lives, and then he may depend upon being received with hospitality. This good-nature is so general among their people, that the gentry, when they go abroad, order their principal servants to entertain all visitors with everything the plantation affords; and the poor planters who have but one bed, will often sit up, or lie upon a form or couch all night, to make room for a weary traveller to repose himself after his journey."

So universal was this custom of free entertainment that it was a law in Virginia that unless there had been a distinct agreement to pay for board and shelter, no pay could be claimed from any guest, no matter how long he remained. In the few taverns that existed prices were low, about a shilling a dinner; and it was ordered that the meal must be wholesome and good.

The governor of New Netherlands at first entertained all visitors to New Amsterdam at his house in the fort. But as commerce increased he found this hospitality burdensome, and a Harberg or tavern was built; it was later used as a city hall.

In England throughout the seventeenth century, and indeed much later, traversing the great cities by night was a matter of some danger. The streets were ill-lighted, were full of holes and mud and filth, and were infested with thieves. Worse still, groups of drunken and dissipated young men of wealth, calling themselves Mohocks, Scourers, and other names, roamed the dark streets armed with swords and bludgeons, assaulting, tormenting, and injuring every one whom they met, who had the ill fortune to be abroad at night.

There was nothing of that sort known in American cities; there was little noise or roistering, no highway robbery, comparatively little petty stealing. The streets were ill-paved and dirty, but not foul with the accumulated dirt of centuries as in London. The streets in nearly all cities were unlighted. In 1697 New Yorkers were ordered to have a lantern and candle hung out on a pole from every seventh house. And as the watchman walked around he called out, " Lanthorn, and a whole candell-light. Hang out your lights." The watchman was called a rattle-watch, and carried a long staff and a lantern and a large rattle or klopper, which he struck to frighten away thieves. And all night long he called out each hour, and told the weather. For instance, he called out, " Past midnight, and all's well "; "One o'clock and fair winds," or " Five o'clock and cloudy skies." Thus one could lie safe in bed and if he chanced to waken could know that the friendly rattle-watch was near at hand, and what was the weather and the time of night.   In 1658 New York had in all ten watchmen, who were like our modern police; to-day it has many thousands.

In New England the constables and watch were all carefully appointed by law.   They carried black staves six feet long, tipped with brass, and hence were called tipstaves.   The night watch was called a bell-man.   He looked out for fire and thieves and other disorders, and called the time of the night, and the weather.   The pay was small, often but a shilling a night, and occasionally a " coat of kersey."   In large towns, as Boston and Salem, thirteen " sober, honest men and householders " were the night watch.   The highest in the community, even the magistrates, took their turn at the watch, and were ordered to walk two together, a young man with " one of the soberer sort."

CHAPTER XV

THE first building used as a church at the Plymouth colony was the fort, and to it the Pilgrim fathers and mothers and children walked on Sunday reverently and gravely, three in a row, the men fully armed with swords and guns, till they built a meeting-house in 1648. In other New England settlements, the first services were held in tents, under trees, or under any shelter. The settler who had a roomy house often had also the meeting. The first Boston meeting-house had mud walls, a thatched roof, and earthen floor. It was used till 1640, and some very thrilling and inspiring scenes were enacted within its humble walls. Usually the earliest meeting-houses were log houses, with clay-filled chinks, and roofs thatched with reeds and long grass, like the dwelling-houses. At Salem is still preserved one of the early churches. The second and more dignified form of New England meeting-house was usually a square wooden building with a truncated pyramidal roof, surmounted often with a belfry, which served as a lookout station and held a bell, from which the bell-rope hung down to the floor in the centre of the church aisle. The old church at Hingham, Massachusetts, still

The "Old Ship," Hingham, Massachusetts, 1680

standing and still used, is a good specimen of this shape. It was built in 1681, and is known as the "Old Ship," and is a comely and dignified building. As more elegant and costly dwelling-houses were built, so were better meeting-houses; and the third form with lofty wooden steeple at one end, in the style of architecture invented by Sir Christopher Wren, after the great fire of London, multiplied and increased until every town was graced with an example. In all these the main body of the edifice remained as bare, prosaic, and undecorated as were the preceding churches, while all the ambition of both builders and congregation spent itself in the steeple. These were so varied and at times so beautiful that a chapter might be written on New England steeples. The Old South Church of Boston is a good example of this school of ecclesiastical architecture, and is a well-known historic building as well.

The earliest meeting-houses had oiled paper in the windows, and when glass came it was not set with putty, but was nailed in. The windows had what were termed "heavy current side-shutters." The outside of the meeting-house was not "colored," or "stained" as it was then termed, but was left to turn gray and weather-stained, and sometimes moss-covered with the dampness of the great shadowing hemlock and fir trees which were usually planted around New England churches. The first meeting-houses were often decorated in a very singular and grotesque manner. Rewards were paid by all the early towns for killing wolves; and any person who killed a wolf brought the head to the meeting-house and nailed it to the outer wall; the fierce grinning heads and splashes of blood made a grim and horrible decoration.   All kinds of notices were also nailed to the meeting-house door where all of the congregation might readily see them, — notices of town-meetings, of sales of cattle or farms, lists of town-officers, prohibitions from selling guns to the Indians, notices of intended marriages, vendues, etc.   It was the only meeting-place, the only method of advertisement.   In front of the church was usually a row of stepping-stones or horse-blocks, for nearly all came on horseback; and often on the meeting-house green stood the stocks, pillory, and whipping-post.

A verse from an old-fashioned hymn reads thus:

"New England's Sabbath day
    Is heaven-like, still, and pure,
When Israel walks the way
    Up to the temple's door.
The time we tell
    When there to come,
    By beat of drum,
Or sounding shell."

The first church at Jamestown, Virginia, gathered the congregation by beat of drum; but while attendants of the Episcopal, Roman Catholic, and

Dutch Reformed churches in the New World were in general being summoned to divine service by the ringing of a bell hung either over the church or in the branches of a tree by its side, New England Puritans were summoned, as the hymn relates, by drum, or horn, or shell. The shell was a great conch-shell, and a man was hired to blow it — a mournful sound — at the proper time, which was usually nine o'clock in the morning. In Stockbridge, Massachusetts, the church-shell was afterwards used for many years as a signal to begin and stop work in the haying field. In Windsor, Connecticut, a man walked up and down on a platform on the top of the meeting-house and blew a trumpet to summon worshippers. Many churches had a church drummer, who stood on the roof or in the belfry and drummed ; a few raised a flag as a summons, or fired a gun.

Within the meeting-house all was simple enough : raftered walls, puncheon and sanded or earthen floors, rows of benches, a few pews, all of unpainted wood, and a pulpit which was usually a high desk overhung by a heavy sounding-board, which was fastened to the roof by a slender metal rod. The pulpit was sometimes called a scaffold. When pews were built they were square, with high partition walls, and had narrow, uncomfortable seats round three sides. The word was always spelled " pue " ; and they were sometimes called " pits." A little girl in the middle of this century attended a service in an old church which still retained the old-fashioned square pews ; she exclaimed, in a loud voice, " What ! must I be shut in a closet and sit on a shelf ? " These narrow, shelf-like seats were usually hung on hinges and could be turned up against the pew-walls during the long psalm-tunes and prayers ; so the members of the congregation could lean against the pew-walls for support as they stood. When the seats were let down, they fell with a heavy slam that could be heard half a mile away in the summer time, when the windows of the meeting-house were open. Lines from an old poem read : —

> " And when at last the loud Amen
> Fell from aloft, how quickly then
> The seats came down with heavy rattle,
> Like musketry in fiercest battle."

A few of the old-time meeting-houses, with high pulpit, square pews, and deacons' seats, still remain in New England. The interior of the Rocky Hill meeting-house at Salisbury, Massachusetts, is here shown. It fully illustrates the words of the poet : —

2 B

" Old house of Puritanic wood
    Through whose unpainted windows streamed
On seats as primitive and rude
    As Jacob's pillow when he dreamed,
The white and undiluted day — "

The seats were carefully and thoughtfully assigned by a church committee called the Seating Com-

Rocky Hill Meeting-house, Salisbury, Massachusetts, 1785

mittee, the best seats being given to older persons of wealth and dignity who attended the church. Whittier wrote of this custom : —

" In the goodly house of worship, where in order due and fit,
    As by public vote directed, classed and ranked the people
        sit.

Mistress first and good wife after, clerkly squire before
the clown,
From the brave coat lace-embroidered to the gray coat
shading down."

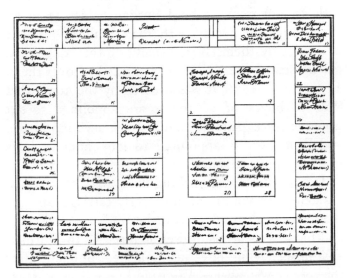

Plan for Seating the Meeting-house

Many of the plans for "seating the meeting-
house" have been preserved; the pews and their
assigned occupants are clearly designated. A copy
is shown of one now in Deerfield Memorial Hall.

In the early meeting-houses men and women sat
on separate sides of the meeting-house, as in Quaker
meetings till our own time. Sometimes a group of

young women or of young men were permitted to
sit in the gallery together.   Little girls sat beside
their mothers or on footstools at their feet, or sometimes on the gallery stairs; and I have heard of a
little cage or frame to hold Puritan babies in meeting.   Boys did not sit with their families, but were
in groups by themselves, usually on the pulpit and
gallery stairs, where tithing-men watched over them.
In Salem, in 1676, it was ordered by the town that
"all ye boyes of ye towne are appointed to sitt
upon ye three paire of stairs in ye meeting-house,
and Wm. Lord is appointed to look after ye boys
upon ye pulpitt stairs."

In Stratford the tithing-man was ordered to
"watch over youths of disorderly carriage, and see
they behave themselves comelie, and use such raps
and blows as is in his discretion meet."   In Durham
any misbehaving boy was punished publicly after
the service was over.   We would nowadays scarcely
seat twenty or thirty active boys together in church
if we wished them to be models of attention and
dignified behavior; but after the boys' seats were
removed from the pulpit stairs they were all turned
in together in a "boys' pew" in the gallery.   There
was a boys' pew in Windsor, Connecticut, as late as
1845, and pretty noisy it usually was.   A certain
small boy in Connecticut misbehaved himself on

Sunday, and his wickedness was specified by the justice of peace as follows : —

"A Rude and Idel Behaver in the meeting hous. Such as Smiling and Larfing and Intiseing others to the Same Evil. Such as Larfing or Smiling or puling the hair of his nayber Benoni Simkins in the time of Publick Worship. Such as throwing Sister Penticost Perkins on the Ice, it being Saboth day, between the meeting hous and his plaes of abode."

I can picture well the wicked scene; poor, meek little Benoni Simpkins trying to behave well in meeting, and not cry out when the young "wanton gospeller" pulled her hair, and unfortunate Sister Perkins tripped up on the ice by the young rascal. Another vain youth in Andover, Massachusetts, was brought up before the magistrate, and it was charged that he "sported and played, and by Indecent gestures and wry faces caused laughter and misbehavior in the beholders." The girls were just as wicked; they slammed down the pew-seats. Tabatha Morgus of Norwich "prophaned the Lord's daye" by her "rude and indecent behavior in Laughing and playing in ye tyme of service." On Long Island godless boys "ran raesses" on the Sabbath and "talked of vane things," and as for Albany children, they played hookey and coasted down hill on Sunday to the scandal of every one evidently, except their parents. When the boys were separated and families sat in pews together, all became orderly in meeting.

The deacons sat in a "Deacons' Pue" just in front of the pulpit; sometimes also there was a " Deaf Pue " in front for those who were hard of hearing. After choirs were established the singers' seats were usually in the gallery; and high up under the beams in a loft sat the negroes and Indians.

If any person seated himself in any place which was not assigned to him, he had to pay a fine, usually of several shillings, for each offence. But in old Newbury men were fined as high as twenty-seven pounds each for persistent and unruly sitting in seats belonging to other members.

The churches were all unheated. Few had stoves until the middle of this century. The chill of the damp buildings, never heated from autumn to spring, and closed and dark throughout the week, was hard for every one to bear. In some of the early log-built meeting-houses, fur bags made of wolfskins were nailed to the seats; and in winter church attendants thrust their feet into them. Dogs, too, were permitted to enter the meeting-house and lie on their masters' feet. Dog-whippers or dog-pelters were appointed to control and expel them when they became unruly or unbearable. Women

and children usually carried foot-stoves, which were
little pierced metal boxes that stood on wooden
legs, and held hot coals.   During the noon inter-
mission the half-frozen church attendants went to
a neighboring house or tavern, or to a noon-house

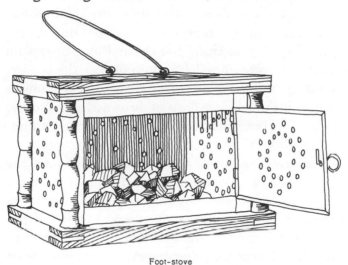

Foot-stove

to get warm.   A noon-house or "Sabba-day house,"
as it was often called, was a long low building built
near the meeting-house, with horse-stalls at one end
and a chimney at the other.   In it the farmers kept,
says one church record, " their duds and horses."
A great fire of logs was built there each Sunday,
and before its cheerful blaze noonday luncheons of

brown bread, doughnuts, or gingerbread were eaten, and foot-stoves were filled. Boys and girls were not permitted to indulge in idle talk in those noon-houses, much less to play. Often two or three families built a noon-house together, or the church built a " Society-house," and there the children had a sermon read to them by a deacon during the " nooning "; sometimes the children had to explain aloud the notes they had taken during the sermon in the morning. Thus they throve, as a minister wrote, on the " Good Fare of brown Bread and the Gospel." There was no nearer approach to a Sunday-school until this century.

The services were not shortened because the churches were uncomfortable. By the side of the pulpit stood a brass-bound hour-glass which was turned by the tithing-man or clerk, but it did not hasten the closing of the sermon. Sermons two or three hours long were customary, and prayers from one to two hours in length. When the first church in Woburn was dedicated, the minister preached a sermon nearly five hours long. A Dutch traveller recorded a prayer four hours long on a Fast Day. Many prayers were two hours long. The doors were closed and watched by the tithing-man, and none could leave even if tired or restless unless with good excuse. The singing of the psalms was tedious

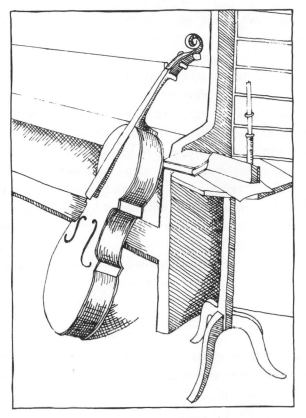

Bass-viol, Psalm-book and Pitch-pipe

and unmusical, just as it was in churches of all denominations both in America and England at that date. Singing was by ear and very uncertain, and the congregation had no notes, and many had no psalm-books, and hence no words. So the psalms were " lined " or " deaconed " ; that is, a line was read by the deacon, and then sung by the congregation. Some psalms when lined and sung occupied half an hour, during which the congregation stood. There were but eight or nine tunes in general use, and even these were often sung incorrectly. There were no church organs to help keep the singers together, but sometimes pitch-pipes were used to set the key. Bass-viols, clarionets, and flutes were played upon at a later date in meeting to help the singing. Violins were too associated with dance music to be thought decorous for church music. Still the New England churches clung to and loved their poor confused psalm-singing as one of their few delights, and whenever a Puritan, even in road or field, heard the distant sound of a psalm-tune he removed his hat and bowed his head in prayer.

Contributions at first were not collected by the deacons, but the entire congregation, one after another, walked up to the deacons' seat and placed gifts of money, goods, wampum, or promissory notes in a box. When the services were ended, all remained in the pews until the minister and his wife had walked up the aisle and out of the church.

The strict observance of Sunday as a holy day was one of the characteristics of the Puritans. Any profanation of the day was severely punished by fine or whipping. Citizens were forbidden to fish, shoot, sail, row, dance, jump, or ride, save to and from church, or to perform any work on the farm. An infinite number of examples might be given to show how rigidly the laws were enforced. The use of tobacco was forbidden near the meeting-house. These laws were held to extend from sunset on Saturday to sunset on Sunday; for in the first instructions given to Governor Endicott by the company in England, it was ordered that all in the colony cease work at three o'clock in the afternoon on Saturday. The Puritans found support of this belief in the Scriptural words, " The evening and the morning were the first day."

A Sabbath day in the family of Rev. John Cotton was thus described by one of his fellow-ministers : —

" He began the Sabbath at evening, therefore then performed family duty after supper, being longer than ordinary in exposition. After which he catechized his children and servants, and then returned to his study. The morning following, family worship being ended, he retired into his study until the bell called him away. Upon his return from meeting (where he had preached and prayed some hours), he returned again into his study (the place of his labor and prayer), unto his favorite devotion ; where having a small repast carried him up for his dinner, he continued until the tolling of the bell. The public service of the afternoon being over, he withdrew for a space to his pre-mentioned oratory for his sacred addresses to God, as in the forenoon, then came down, repeated the sermon in the family, prayed, after supper sang a Psalm, and toward bedtime betaking himself again to his study he closed the day with prayer. Thus he spent the Sabbath continually."

The Virginia Cavaliers were strict Church of England men and the first who came to the colony were strict Sunday-keepers. Rules were laid down to enforce Sunday observance. Journeys were forbidden, boat-lading was prohibited, also all profanation of the day by sports, such as shooting, fishing, game-playing, etc. The offender who broke the Sabbath laws had to pay a fine and be set in the stocks. When that sturdy watch-dog of religion and government — Sir Thomas Dale — came over, he declared absence from church should be punishable by death; but this severity never was executed. The captain of the watch was made to play the same part as the New England tithing-man. Every Sunday, half an hour before service-time, at the last tolling of the bell, the captain stationed sentinels, then searched all the houses and commanded and forced all (except the sick) to go to church. Then, when all were driven churchwards before him, he went with his guards to church himself.

Captain John Smith, in his *Pathway to erect a Plantation,* thus vividly described the first places of divine worship in Virginia : —

"Wee did hang an awning, which is an old saile, to three or foure trees to shadow us from the Sunne; our walls were railes of wood; our seats unhewed trees till we cut plankes; our Pulpit a bar of wood nailed to two neighbouring trees. In foul weather we shifted into an old rotten tent; this came by way of adventure for new. This was our Church till we built a homely thing like a barne set upon Cratchets, covered with rafts, sedge, and earth; so also was the walls; the best of our houses were of like curiosity, that could neither well defend from wind nor rain.

"Yet we had daily Common Prayer morning and evening;

Bruton Parish Church, Williamsburgh, Virginia

every Sunday two sermons; and every three months a holy Communion till our Minister died: but our Prayers daily with an Homily on Sundays we continued two or three years after, till more Preachers came."

A timber church sixty feet long took the place of this mud and clay chapel, and this was in turn replaced by the brick one whose ruined arches are still standing. The wooden church saw the most pompous ceremony of the day when the governor, De La Warre, or Delaware as we now call it, in full dress, attended by all his councillors and officers and fifty halbert-bearers in scarlet cloaks, filed within its flower-decked walls.

This decoration of flowers was significant of the difference between the church edifices of the Puritans and of the Cavaliers. The churches of the Southern colonies were, as a rule, much more richly furnished. Many were modelled in shape after the old English churches and were built of stone, though Jonathan Boucher, the colonial clergyman, could write that the greater number of the Southern churches were, at the time of the Revolution, "composed of wood, without spires, or towers or steeples or bells, placed in retired and solitary spots and contiguous to springs or wells." Many of the churches and the chapels-of-ease stood by the waterside, and to the services came the church attendants

Pohick Church, Mount Vernon, Virginia

in canoes, periaugers, dugouts, etc. It made an animated scene upon the water, as the boats came rowing in and as they departed after the service.

Sometimes the seats were comfortably cushioned, and they were carefully assigned as in the Puritan meetings. In some Virginia churches seats in the galleries were deemed the most dignified. There was a pew for the magistrates, another for the magistrates' ladies; pews for the representatives and church-wardens, vestrymen, etc. Persons crowded into pews above their stations, just as in New Eng-

land, and were promptly displaced. Groups of
men built pews together, and there were schoolboys' galleries and pews.

The first clergyman in Virginia, Robert Hunt,
a true man of God, came as a missionary, and he
and others were men of marked intellect and religion, but in the eighteenth century the pay was too
small and uncertain to attract any great men from
the Church of England, and church attendance
dwindled and became irregular. For in Virginia
the parish was expected to receive any clergyman
sent them from England, a rule which often proved
unsatisfactory; and deservedly so, since some very
disreputable offshoots of English families were
thrust upon the Virginia churches. In the Carolinas, where the church chose its own clergyman,
harmony and affection prevailed in the parishes as
it did among the New England Puritans. Though
the Virginians did not always love their clergymen, still they were ever steadfast in their affection to their church, and regarded it as the only
church.

Sunday was not observed with as much rigidity
in New Netherland as in New England, but strict
rules and laws were made for enforcing quiet during service-time. Fishing, gathering berries or nuts,
playing in the streets, working, going on pleasure

trips, all were forbidden. On Long Island shooting of wild fowl, carting of grain, travelling for pleasure, all were punished. In Revolutionary times a cage was set up in City Hall Park, near the present New York Post-office, in which boys were confined who did not properly regard the Sabbath.

Before the Dutch settlers had any churches or domines, as they called their ministers, they had *krankbesoeckers*, or visitors of the sick, who read sermons to an assembled congregation every Sunday. The first church at Albany was much like the Plymouth fort, simply a blockhouse with loopholes through which guns could be fired. The roof was mounted with three cannon. It had a seat for the magistrates and one for the deacons, and a handsome octagonal pulpit which had been sent from Holland, and which still exists. The edifice had a chandelier and candle sconces and two low galleries. The first church in New Amsterdam was of stone, and was seventy-two feet long.

A favorite form of the Dutch churches was six or eight sided, with a high pyramidal roof, topped with a belfry and a weather-vane. Usually the windows were so small and of glass so opaque that the church was very dark. A few of the churches were poorly heated with high stoves perched up on pillars, the Albany and Schenectady churches among them, but

2 c

all the women carried foot-stoves, and some of the men carried muffs.

Almost as important as the domine was the *voorleezer* or chorister, who was also generally the bell-ringer, sexton, grave-digger, funeral in-

viter, schoolmaster, and sometimes town clerk. He " tuned the psalm"; turned the hour-glass; gave out the psalms on a hanging board to the congregation; read the Bible; gave up notices to the domine by sticking the papers in the end of a cleft stick and holding it up to the high pulpit.

Dutch Reformed Church, Bushwick, Long Island, 1711. From an old print

The deacons had control of all the church money. In the middle of the sermon they collected contributions by passing *sacjes*. These were small cloth or vel-

vet bags hung on the end of a pole six or eight
feet long. A French traveller told that the Dutch
deacons passed round "the old square hat of the
preacher" on the end of a stick for the contributions. Usually there was a little bell on the *sacje*
which rung when a coin was dropped in.

In many Dutch churches the men sat in a row of
pews around the wall while the women were seated
on chairs in the centre of the church. There were
also a few benches or pews for persons of special
dignity, or for the minister's wife.

There were many other colonists of other religious faiths: the Roman Catholics in Maryland and
the extreme Southern colonies; the Quakers in
Pennsylvania; the Baptists in Rhode Island; the
Huguenots, Lutherans, Moravians; but all enjoined
an orderly observance of the Sabbath day. And it
may be counted as one of the great blessings of the
settlement of America, one of the most ennobling
conditions of its colonization, that it was made at a
time when the deepest religious feeling prevailed
throughout Europe, when devotion to some religion was found in every one, when the Bible was a
newly found and deeply loved treasure; when the
very differences of religious belief and the formation
of new sects made each cling more lovingly and
more earnestly to his own faith.

CHAPTER XVI

COLONIAL NEIGHBORLINESS

IF the first foundation of New England's strength and growth was godliness, its next was neighborliness, and a firm rock it proved to build upon. It may seem anomalous to assert that while there was in olden times infinitely greater independence in each household than at present, yet there was also greater interdependence with surrounding households.

It is curious to see how completely social ethics and relations have changed since olden days. Aid in our families in times of stress and need is not given to us now by kindly neighbors as of yore; we have well-arranged systems by which we can buy all that assistance, and pay for it, not with affectionate regard, but with current coin. The colonist turned to any and all who lived around him, and never turned in vain for help in sickness, or at the time of death of members of his household; for friendly advice; for culinary aids to a halting appetite; for the preparation for feasting an exceptional number of persons ; in short, in any unusual emergency, as well as in frequent every-day coöperation in log-rolling, stone-piling, stump-pulling, wall-building, house-raising, etc., — all the hard and exhausting labor on the farm.

The word "coöperation" is modern, but the thing itself is as old as civilization. In a new country where there was much work to be done which one man or one family could not do, under the mechanical conditions which then existed, a working together, or union of labor was necessary for progress, indeed, almost for obtaining a foothold.

The term "log-rolling" is frequently employed in its metaphorical sense in politics, both by English and American writers who have vague knowledge of the original meaning of the word. A log-rolling in early pioneer days, in the Northern colonies and in western Virginia and the central states, was a noble example of generous coöperation, where each gave of his best — his time, strength, and good will ; and where all worked to clear the ground in the forest for a home-farm for a neighbor who might be newly come and an entire stranger, but who in turn would just as cheerfully and energetically give his work for others when it was needed.

With the vanishing of the log-rolling, and a score of similar kindly usages and customs, has gone from our communities all traces of the old-time exalted type of neighborliness. We nowadays have generalized our sentiments; we have more philanthropy and less neighborliness; we have more love for mankind and less for men. We are independent of our neighbors, but infinitely more dependent on the world at large. The personal element has been removed to a large extent from our social ethics. We buy nursing and catering just as we hire our houses built and buy our corn ready ground. Doubtless everything we buy is infinitely better; nevertheless, our loss in affectionate zeal is great.

The plantation was the unit in Virginia; in New England it was the town. The neighborly helpfulness of the New England settlers extended from small to great matters; it formed communal privileges and entered into every department of town life. For instance, the town of Gloucester in 1663 granted a right to a citizen for running a small saw-mill for twenty-one years. In return for this right the grantee was to sell boards to Gloucester men at "one shilling per hundred better cheape than to strangers" — and was to receive pay "raised in the towne." Saco and Biddeford, in Maine, ordered that fellow-townsmen should have preference in every employment. Other towns ordered certain persons to buy provisions "of the towns-men in preference."

Reading would not sell any of its felled timber out of the town. Thus the social compact called a town extended itself also into all the small doings of daily life, and the mutual helpfulness made mutual interests that proved no small element of the force which bound all together in 1776 in a successful struggle for independence.

In outlying settlements and districts this feeling of mutual dependence and assistance was strong enough to give a name which sometimes lingered long. "The Loomis Neighborhood," "The Mason Neighborhood," "The Robinson Neighborhood" were names distinctive for half a century, and far more distinguishing and individual than the Greenville, Masontown, and Longwood that succeeded them.

There was one curious and contradictory aspect of this neighborliness, this kindliness, this thought for mutual welfare, and that was its narrowness, especially in New England, as regards the limitations of space and locality. It is impossible to judge what caused this restraint of vision, but it is certain that in generality and almost in universality, just as soon as any group of settlers could call themselves a town, these colonists' notions of kindliness and thoughtfulness for others became distinctly and rigidly limited to their own townspeople. The town was their whole world. Without doubt this was partly the result of the lack of travelling facilities and ample communication, which made townships far more separated and remote from each other than states are to-day, and made difficult the possibility of speedy or full knowledge of strangers.

This caused a constant suspicion of all newcomers, especially those who chanced to enter with scant introduction, and made universal a custom of " warning out " all strangers who arrived in any town. This formality was gone through with by the sheriff or tithing-man. Thereafter should the warned ones prove incapable or unsuccessful or vicious, they could not become a charge upon the town, but could be returned whence they came with despatch and violence if necessary. By this means, and by various attempts to restrict the powers of citizens to sell property to newcomers, the town kept a jealous watch over the right of entry into the corporation.

Dorchester in 1634 enacted that " no man within the Plantation shall sell his house or lott to any man without the Plantation whome they shall dislike off." Providence would not permit a proprietor to sell to any " but to an Inhabitant " without consent of the town. New Haven would neither sell nor let ground to a stranger. Hadley would sell no land to any until after three years' occupation, and then only with approval of the "Town's Mind." In 1637 the General Court very reasonably questioned whether towns could legally restrain individuals from disposal of their own property, but the custom was so established, so in touch with the narrow exclusiveness of the colonists, that it still prevailed. The expression of the town of Watertown when it would sell lots only to freemen of the congregation, because it wished no strange neighbors, but only " to sitt down there close togither," was the sentiment of all the towns. One John Stebbins, who had twice served as a soldier of Watertown and lived there seven years, could not get a town lot.

The legal process of warning out of town had an element of the absurd in it, and in one case that of mystery, namely : a sheriff appeared before the woebegone intruder, and said, half laughing, " I warn you off the face of the earth." " Let me get my hat before I go," stammered the terrified wanderer, who ran into the house for his hat and was never seen by any mortal eye in that town afterwards. It has become a tradition of local folk-lore that he literally vanished from the earth at the command of the officer of the law.

The harboring of strangers, even of relatives who

were not local residents, was a frequent source of bickering between citizens and magistrates, as well as a constant cause of arbitration between towns. A widow in Dorchester was not permitted to entertain her own son-in-law from another town, and her neighbor was fined in 1671 "under distress" for housing his own daughter. She was a married woman, and alleged she could not return to her husband on account of the inclement weather.

As time passed on and immigration continued, freemen clung closely to their right to keep out strangers and outsiders. From the Boston Town Records of 1714 we find citizens still prohibited from entertaining a stranger without giving notice to the town authorities, and a description of the stranger and his circumstances. Boston required that all coming from Ireland should be registered "lest they become chargeable." Warnings and whippings out of town still continued. All this was so contrary to the methods of colonies in other countries, such as the Barbadoes, Honduras, etc., where extraordinary privileges were offered settlers, free and large grants of land, absolvment from past debts, etc., that it makes an early example of the curious absorbing and assimilating power of American nationality, which ever grew and grew even against such clogs and hampering restrictions.

In the Southern colonies the same kindliness existed as in the North, but the conditions differed. John Hammond, of Virginia, wrote in 1656, in his *Leah and Rachel*: —

" The Country is not only plentifull, but pleasant and profitable, pleasant in regard of the extraordinary good neighbourhood and loving conversation they have one with another.

" The inhabitants are generally affable, courteous, and very assistant to Strangers (for what but plenty makes hospitality and good neighbourhood) and no sooner are they settled, but they will be visiting, presenting and advising the strangers how to improve what they have, how to better their way of livelihood."

In summer when fresh meat was killed, the neighbors shared the luxury, and in turn gave of their slaughter. Hammond adds: —

" If any fall sick and cannot compass to follow his crops which would soon be lost, the adjoining neighbour, or upon request more joyn together and work it by spells, until he recovers; and that gratis, so that no man may by sickness loose any part of his year's work.

" Let any travell, it is without charge and at every house is entertainment as in a hostelry."

It was the same in the Carolinas. Ramsay, the early historian of South Carolina, said that hospitality was such a virtue that innkeepers complained

that their business was not worth carrying on.   The
doors of citizens were open to all decent travellers,
and shut to none.

The plantations were in many counties too far
apart for any coöperative labor, and the planters
were not men of such vast strength or so great personal industry, even in their own affairs, as were the
Yankees.   There were slaves on each plantation to
do all the hard work of lifting, etc.   But in out-of-
the-way settlements the Virginia planters' kindliness
was shown in a vast and unbounded hospitality, a
hospitality so insatiable that it watched for and way-
laid travellers to expend a welcome and lavish atten-
tions upon.   Negroes were stationed at the planter's
gate where it opened on the post-road or turnpike,
to hail travellers and assure them of a hearty welcome at the " big house up yonder."   One writer
says of the planters : —

" Their manner of living is most generous and open :
strangers are sought after with Greediness to be invited."

The *London Magazine* of the year 1743 published
a series of papers entitled *Itinerant Observations in
America*.   It was written with a spirited pen which
thus pleasantly describes simple Maryland hospitality, not of men of vast wealth but of very poor
folk : —

"With the meaner Sort you find little else to drink but Water amongst them when their Cyder is spent, but the Water is presented you by one of the barefooted Family in a copious Calabash, with an innocent Strain of good Breeding and Heartiness, the Cake baking on the Hearth, and the prodigious Cleanliness of everything around you must needs put you in Mind of the Golden Age, the Times of ancient Frugality and Purity. All over the Colony a universal Hospitality reigns, full Tables and open Doors; the kind Salute, the generous Detention speak somewhat like the roast-Beef Ages of our Forefathers."

There came a time when this Southern hospitality became burdensome. With the exhaustion of the soil and competition in tobacco-raising, the great wealth of the Virginians was gone. But visitors did not cease; in fact, they increased. The generous welcome offered to kinsmen, friends, and occasional travellers was sought by curiosity-hunters and tourists who wanted to save a tavern-bill. Nothing could be more pathetic than the impoverishment of Thomas Jefferson through these impositions. Times and conditions had changed, but Jefferson felt bound in honor to himself and his state to keep the same open hand and ready welcome as of yore. His overseer describes his own hopeless efforts to keep these travelling friends and admirers from eating his master out of house and home: —

" They were there all times of the year; but about the middle of June the travel would commence from the lower part of the State to the Springs, and then there was a perfect throng of visitors. They travelled in their own carriages and came in gangs, the whole family with carriage and riding horses and servants, sometimes three or four such gangs at a time. We had thirty-six stalls for horses and only used ten of them for the stock we kept there. Very often all the rest were full, and I had to send horses off to another place. I have often sent a wagon-load of hay up to the stable, and the next morning there would not be enough left to make a bird's nest. I have killed a fine beef, and it would all be eaten up in a day or two."

The final extinction of old-time hospitality in Virginia came not from a death of hospitable intent, but from an entire vanishing of the means to furnish entertainment. And the Civil War drove away even the lingering ghost.

Many general customs existed in the early colonies which were simply exemplifications of neighborliness put in legal form. Such were the systems of common lands and herding. This was an old Aryan custom which existed many centuries ago, and has ever been one of the best ways of uniting any settlement of people, especially a new settlement; for it makes the interest of one the interest of all, and promotes union rather than selfishness.

Common lands were set off and common herds existed in many of the Northern colonies; cowherds or "cow-keeps" were appointed and paid by the town to care throughout the summer for all the cattle owned by the inhabitants. This was an intelligent provision; for it saved much work of individuals during the months when farmers had so much hard work to do, and so short a time to do it in. In Albany and New York the cowherd and "a chosen proper youngster" — in other words, a good, steady boy — went through the town at sunrise sounding a horn, which the cattle heard and knew; and they quickly followed him to green pastures outside the town. There they lingered till nearly sunset, when they were brought home to the church, and the owners were again warned by the horn of the safe return of their cattle, and that it was milking time. Sometimes the cowherd received part of his pay in butter or cheese. In Cambridge, Massachusetts, Cowherd Rice, in 1635, agreed to take charge of one hundred cows for three months for ten pounds. The town also paid two men or boys to help him the first two weeks, and one man a week longer; he kept the cows alone after that, for the intelligent cattle had fallen into habits of order and obedience to his horn. He had to pay threepence fine each time he failed to bring in all the cattle at night.

On Long Island and in Connecticut there were cowherds, calf-keepers, and pound-keepers. The calf-keepers' duties were to keep the calves away from the cows, water them, protect them, etc. In Virginia and Maryland there were cow-pens in early days, and cowherds; but in the South the cattle generally roamed wild through the forests, and were known to their owners by earmarks. In all communities earmarks and other brands of ownership on cattle, horses, sheep, and swine were very important, and rigidly regarded where so much value was kept in domestic cattle. These earmarks were registered by the town clerk in the town records, and were usually described both in words and rude drawings. One of my great-great-grandfather's earmarks for his cows was a "swallow-fork slit in both ears"; another was a slit under the ear and a "half-penny mark on the foreside of the near ear." This custom of herding cattle in common lasted in some out-of-the-way places to this century, and even lingered long in large cities such as Boston, where cows were allowed to feed on Boston Common till about 1840. In Philadelphia until the year 1795 a cowherd stood every morning at the corner of Dock and Second streets, blew his horn, tramped off to a distant pasture followed by all the cows of his neighborhood, who had run out to him as soon as

they heard the familiar sound. He led them back
to the same place at night, when each returned alone
to her own home.

Sheep-herds or shepherds in colonial days also
took charge of the sheep of many owners in herd-
walks, or ranges, by day, and by night in sheep-
folds built with fences and gates.

Fence-viewers were men who were appointed by
the town for common benefit to take charge of
building and keeping in repair the fences that surrounded the "great lotts" or commons; that is,
the enclosed fields which were the common property
of each town, in which all farmers living near could
place their cattle. The fence-viewers saw that each
man worked a certain amount each year on these
"pales" as the fences were called, or paid his share
for the work of others. Each farmer or cow-owner
usually built about twenty feet of fence for each cow
which he pastured in the "great lotts." The fence-
viewers also examined the condition of fences around
private lands; noted breaks and ordered repairs.
For if cattle broke through a poorly made fence,
and did damage to crops, the fence-owner had to
stand the loss, while if the fences were good and
strong, proving the cattle unruly and destructive,
the owner of the cattle had to pay. All the colonies
were watchful over the safe-keeping of fences. In

2 D

1659 the Dutch rulers of New Amsterdam (now New York) ordered that for "stripping fences of rails and posts" the offender should be whipped and branded, and for a second offence he could be punished by death.   This seems cruelly severe, but that year there was a great scarcity of grain and other food, and if the fences were pulled down, cattle could get into fields and eat up the growing crops, and famine and death might result.

Sometimes a common field was fenced in and planted with Indian corn.   In this case the fence served to keep the cattle out, not in.   This was always the case in Virginia.

Hay-wards were, as the name indicates, men to keep watchful care over the growing hay.   For instance, in Hadley, Massachusetts, in 1661, Goodman Montague was chosen hay-ward by the town.   He was to have twelvepence for each cow or hog, two shillings for each horse, and twenty pence for each twenty sheep that he found loose in any field or meadow, and successfully turned out.   The owner of the animal was to pay the fine.   At a later date these hay-wards were called field-drivers.   They are still appointed in many towns and cities, among them Boston.

Hog-reeves were men appointed by the citizens to look after their hogs that roamed the roads and streets, to see that all those swine had rings in their noses, were properly marked, and did not do damage to crops. Many towns had hog-reeves till this century; for until seventy years ago hogs ran freely everywhere, even in the streets of our great cities. It was a favorite jest to appoint a newly married man hog-reeve. When Ralph Waldo Emerson was married and became a householder in Concord, the young philosopher was appointed to that office. Sometimes a single swineherd was hired to take care of the roving swine. The two Salem swineherds or swine-keepers in 1640 were to have sixpence for each hog they drove daily to pasture from April to November. These and many other public offices were simply a form of legalized coöperation; a joining together of neighbors for public good.

The neighborly assistance given to new settlers began with the clearing of the ground for occupancy. The girdling of trees was easy and speedy, but it was discountenanced as dangerous and hideous, and was not frequently practised. A chopping-bee was a universal method among pioneers of clearing ground in newly settled districts, or even in older townships in Vermont, New Hampshire, and Maine, where great tracts of land were left for many years in the original growth. Sometimes this bee was held to clear land for a newly married man, or a new neighbor, or one who had had bad luck; but it was just as freely given to a prosperous farmer, though plentiful thanks and plentiful rum were the only rewards of the willing workers.

All the strong men of the township repaired at an early hour to the tract to be cleared, and with powerful blows attacked the great trees. A favorite way of bringing the day's work and the day's excitement to a climax was by a "drive." This was made by chopping half-way into the trunks of a great group or circle of trees — under-cutting it was called — so that by a few powerful and well-driven blows at the monarch of the group, and perhaps a few well-concerted pulls on a rope, the entire group could be felled together, the leader bringing down with his spreading branches in his mighty fall his fellows in front of him, and they in turn their neighbors, with a crash that shook the earth and made the mountains ring. It was dangerous work; accidents were frequent; the records of death at log-rollings are pathetic to read and to think of, in a country where the loss of a sturdy man meant so much to some struggling household. A heavy and sudden gust of wind might blow down a small tree, which had been carelessly "under-cut," and thus give an unexpected and premature collapse of the simple machinery of the grand finale.

A century ago a New Hampshire woman and her
husband went out into the forest primeval; he cut
down a few trees, made a little clearing termed a
cut-down wherein a tiny patch of sky and cloud
and scant sunlight could be seen overhead, but no
sunrise or sunset, and built a log house of a single
room — a home. With the opening spring came
one day a group of kindly settlers from distant
clearings and settlements, some riding from ten
miles away the previous day. In front of the log
house they chopped all the morning long with
sturdy arms and swinging blows, yet felled nothing,
till in the afternoon when all was ready for the final
blow at the towering leader, which by its fall should
lay low a great sloping tract for a dooryard and
home field. As the noble trees fell at last to the
earth with a resounding crash, lo! in the opening
there appeared to the startled eyes of the settler's
wife, as if rising out of heaven, a neighbor in her
loneliness — Mount Kearsage, grand, serene, and
beautiful, crowned with the glories of the setting
sun, standing guard over a smiling lake at its foot.
And every day through her long and happy life till
ninety-six years old, as she looked at the splendid
mountain, standing as it will till time shall be no
more, did she thank God for His gift, for that
noble companionship which came so suddenly, so

inspiringly, upon the cramped horizon of her lonely forest home.

After the trees were all felled, it was no longer a "cut-down" but an "opening." This was made preferably in the spring. The fallen trees were left some months on the ground to dry in the summer sun, while the farmer turned to other work on his farm, or, if he were starting in life, hired out for the summer. In the autumn the tops were set on fire, and the lighter limbs usually burned out, leaving the great charred tree-trunks. Then came what was known as a piling-bee, a perfect riot of hard work, cinders, and dirt. Usually the half-burned tree-trunks were "niggered off" in Indian fashion, by burning across with a smaller stick of wood till the long log was in lengths which could be dragged by the farmers with their oxen and horses into vast piles and again set on fire. Another treat of rum accompanied this day's work. The word "log-rolling" was often applied to the latter bee, and occasionally the felling of trees and dragging into piles for firing was done in a single log-rolling.

Sometimes before the opening was cleared it was planted. The spring rains and melting snows carried the fertilizing ashes deep into the soil. Corn was planted and "dug in"; rye was sowed and "hacked in." The crops were astonishing; the

grain grew among the fallen logs and stumps in riot-
ing luxuriance. A stump-pulling was another occasion for a friendly bee, to clear off and put into
comely shape the new field.

Another exhibition of coöperation was in a
stone-hauling or a stone-bee. Some of the rocky
fields of hard New England would defy a lifetime of
work of one man and a single yoke of oxen. With
judicious blasting, many oxen, strong arms, and
willing hearts the boulders and ledges were tamed.
Stone walls eight feet wide, such as may be seen in
Hopkinton, New Hampshire, stand as monuments
of the patience, strength, skill, and coöperation of
our forbears.

To show the struggle and hard work willingly
done for a home, let me give the statement in 1870
of a respected citizen, the historian of Norridgewock, Maine, when he was over ninety years old.
He served an apprenticeship of eight years till he
was twenty-one, then bought on credit a tract of
fifty acres in the primeval woods. On eight acres
he felled the trees and left them through the winter.
In April, 1801, he spent three weeks in burning off
the logs and clearing as well as possible by hand-
work three acres. These he sowed with wheat and
rye, buying the seed on credit. He hired a yoke
of oxen for one day and did what harrowing he

could in that short time, grubbing around the stumps with a hoe for two more days. The crop grew, as did all others on similar soil, amazingly. The two bushels of seed-wheat yielded fifty-two bushels, the bushel of rye thirty bushels. On his other five acres among the fallen trees he planted corn, and raised a hundred and twenty-eight bushels. He adds : —

"When I could leave my work on my new land I worked out haying and other work. I made shoes in the Fall, taught school in the Winter, paid for my board and some clothing, but husbanded my resources to pay for my land. At the end of the year found myself worth two hundred dollars. I continued to clear up four acres each year till I had cleared the fifty acres, planted an orchard and erected suitable farm buildings and fences."

Six years later he married and prospered. In eleven years he was worth two thousand dollars; he filled, during his long life, many positions of trust and of profit, and did many and varied good deeds; he continued in active life till he was ninety years old. At his death he left a considerable fortune. It is an interesting picture of the value of honorable economy and thrift; a typical New England picture, with a certain vigor and stimulus about it that makes it pleasing.

A "raising" might be of a church or a school-house, or of a house or barn for a neighbor. All the strong men far and near turned out to help, tools were lent, and many strong hands and arms made quick work. Often the frame of a whole side of a house — the broadside — was fastened together on the ground. After it was laid out and pinned together, shores of long poles were attached to the plates with ox-chains, and it was literally lifted into place by the united strength of the entire band of men and boys. Sometimes women pulled on the rope to express their good will and helpfulness. Then the other sides were put up, and the cross-beams, braces, and studding all pinned and nailed into place. Afterwards the huge rafters were raised for the roof. Each man was assigned in the beginning to his place and work, and worked faithfully when his turn came. When the ridge-pole was put in place, the building was christened, as it was called, by breaking over it a bottle of rum. Often the house was literally given a name. Sitting astride the ridge-pole, one poet sang: —

> " Here's a mighty fine frame
>   Which desarves a good name,
>   Say what shall we call it ?
>   The timbers all straight,
>   And was hewed fust rate,
>   The frame is well put together.

> It is a good frame
> That desarvcs a good name,
> Say! what shall we name it?"

Another, a Rochester, New Hampshire, frame was celebrated in verse which closed thus: —

> "The Flower of the Plain is the name of this Frame,
> We've had exceeding good Luck in raising the Same."

It was not luck that made these raisings a success, it was skill and strength; skill and powers of endurance which could overcome and surmount even the quantity of vile New England rum with which the workmen were plied throughout the day. Accidents were frequent, and often fatal. A great frame of a meeting-house, or a vast barn with forty or fifty men at work on it, could not collapse without loss of life and much injury of limb.

In the work of these raisings the highest as well as the humblest citizens took part. Truly a man could glow with the warmth of home even in a bare and scantily furnished house, at the thought that the walls and rafters were held in place by the kind wishes and deeds of all his friends and neighbors.

There is nothing in nature so unnatural, so singular in quality, as the glittering artificiality of the early morning in the country the day after a heavy, drifting, New England snowstorm. For a day and a night the wildly whirling snow that " driving o'er the fields seems nowhere to alight" has restrained the outlook, and every one has turned depressed from that outside life of loneliness and gloom. The following morning always opens with an excessively bright and dazzling sunshine which is not like any other sunshine in any place or season, but is wholly artificial, like the lime-light of a theatre. We always run eagerly to the window to greet once more the signs of life and cheerfulness; but the landscape is more devoid of life and reality than during any storm of wind and snow and sleet, no matter how dark and lowering. There is a changed aspect in everything; it is metallic, and everything is made of the same horrible white metal. Nothing seems familiar; not only are the wonted forms and outlines vanished, and all their varied textures and materials and beautiful diversity of color gone also, but there is a steely immobility restraining every thing which is so complete that it seems as if it were a shell that could never be broken.

> " We look upon a world unknown,
>   On nothing we can call our own."

It is no longer a real landscape but an artificial encircling diorama of meaningless objects made of vast unshaded sheets of white glazed Bristol-board,

painted with white enamel, warranted not to crack;
with the garish high-lights put in crystallized alum
or possibly powdered glass.   It is without life, or
atmosphere, or reality; it has nothing but the million reflections of that artificial and repellent sunshine.   In a quarter of an hour, even in a few
minutes, it is agonizingly monotonous to the spirit
as it is painful to the eye; then, like a veritable oasis
of color and motion in an unmovable glittering
white desert, a sound and sight of beautiful and
active life appears.   Around the bend of the road
comes slow and straining down the hill, as has come
through the glaring artificial sunlight after every
heavy snowstorm for over a century past, a long
train of oxen with a snow-plough "breaking out"
the old post-road.   Beautiful emblems of patient
and docile strength, these splendid creatures are
never so grateful to the sight as now.   Their slow
progress down the hill has many elements to make
it interesting; it is historic.   Ever since the township
was thickly settled enough for families to have any
winter communication with each other, whether for
school, church, mail, or doctor, this road has been
broken out in precisely this same way.

In nearly all scattered townships in New England
the custom prevails to-day just as it did a century
and more ago even in large towns, and a description

of the present "breaking out" is that of the past also. The work is now usually done in charge of road-surveyors or the road-masters, who are often appointed from the remote points of the township. There is, therefore, much friendly rivalry to see which surveyor will first reach the centre of the town — and the tavern. Beginning at sunrise with his own yoke of oxen hitched to a snow-plough, each road-master breaks through the drift to the nearest neighbor, who adds his yoke to the other, and so from neighbor to neighbor till sometimes fifteen or twenty yoke of oxen are hitched in a long line to the plough. Sometimes a pair of wild young steers are hitched, plunging and kicking, with the sober elders. By this time the first yoke often begins to show signs of distress by lolling out the tongue, a sure symptom of overwork in oxen, and they are left at some farmer's barn to cool down.

Whittier thus describes the scene of breaking out the winter roads in his *Snow-Bound :* —

> " Next morn we wakened with the shout
> Of merry voices high and clear ;
> And saw the teamsters drawing near
> To break the drifted highways out.
> Down the long hillside treading slow
> We saw the half-buried oxen go,

Shaking the snow from heads uptost,
Their straining nostrils white with frost.
Before our door the straggling train
Drew up, an added team to gain.
The elders threshed their hands a-cold,
Passed, with the cider mug, their jokes
From lip to lip."

Thus are the white snow-waste and the drifted
roads turned by cheerful coöperation into a midwinter visiting where every neighbor can exchange
greetings with the other, young and old. For of
course school does not keep, and the boys crowd on
the snow-plough or try their new snowshoes, and the
men of the various families who do not go with
the oxen hitch up the sleighs, pods, and pungs and
follow the snow-plough, and the young men send a
volley of snowballs against every house where any
fair maid lives. And at the tavern in the afternoon
is a great sight, greater in ante-temperance days than
now: scores of yoke of oxen at the door, the horse-
sheds full of horses and sleighs, all the lads and
men of the township within. There is rivalry in
the method of breaking. One road-master always
used a snow-plough; another lashed an ordinary
plough on either side of a narrow ox-sled; a third
used a coarse harrow weighted down with a group
of standing boys. This broke up the drifts in a

wonderful manner. The deeper drifts often have to be shovelled out partly by hand. After the road to the tavern is broken, the road to the school-house, the doctor's house, and the meeting-house come next.

The roads thus made were not permitted in former days to be cut up idly by careless use; many town-ships forbade by law the use of narrow sleds and sleighs. The roads were narrow at best; often when two sleighs met the horses had to be unharnessed, and the sleighs lifted past over each other. On lonely hill-roads or straight turnpikes, where team-sters could see some distance ahead, turnouts were made where one sleigh could wait for another to pass.

After there had been a heavy fall of snow and the roads were well broken, the time was always chosen where any logging was done to haul logs to the sawmill on ox-sleds. An interesting sled was used which had an interesting name, — chebobbin. One writer called it a cross between a tree and a bob-sled. It was made by a close and ingenious adapta-tion of natural forms of wood, which made excellent runners, cross-bars, etc.; they were fastened together so loosely that they readily adjusted themselves to the inequalities of the wood-roads. The word and article are now almost obsolete. In some localities chebobbin became tebobbin and tarboggin, all three being adaptations in nomenclature, as they were in form, of the Indian toboggan or moose-sled, — a sledge with runners or flat bottom of wood or bark, upon which the red men drew heavy loads over the snow. This sledge has become familiar to us in the light and strong Canadian form now used for the delightful winter sport of tobogganing.

On these chebobbins great logs were hitched together by chains, and dragged down from the upland wood-lots. Under these mighty loads the snow-tracks got an almost icy polish, prime sledding for country sleighing parties. Sometimes a logging-bee was made to clear a special lot for a neighbor, and a band of wood-choppers worked all day together. It was cheerful work, though the men had to stand all day in the snow, and the thermometer was below zero. But there was no cutting wind in the forest, and the exercise kept the blood warm. Many a time a hearty man would drop his axe to wipe the sweat from his brow. Loose woollen frocks, or long-shorts, two or three over each other, were warm as are the overlapping feathers of a bird; a few had buckskin or sheepskin waistcoats; their hands were warmly covered with home-knit mittens. In later days all had heavy well-greased boots, but in the early years of such pioneer settlements, as the towns of New Hampshire and Vermont, all could not afford to wear boots. Their place was well supplied by heavy woollen stockings, shoes, and an over-covering of old stockings, or cloth soaked in neat's-foot oil; this was deemed a positive preventive of frozen feet.

It was the custom both among men and women to join forces on a smaller scale and have a little neighborly visiting by what was called "change-work." For instance, if two neighbors both were to make soap, or both to make apple-butter, or both to make up a rag carpet, instead of each woman sitting at home alone sewing and fitting the carpet, one would take her thimble and go to spend the day, and the two would sew all day long, finish and lay the carpet at one house. In a few days the visit would be returned, and the second carpet be finished. Sometimes the work was easier when two worked together. One man could load logs and sled them down to the sawmill alone, but two by "change-work" could accomplish the task much more rapidly and with less strain.

Even those evil days of New England households, the annual house-cleaning, were robbed of some of their dismal terrors by what was known as a "whang," a gathering of a few friendly women neighbors to assist one another in that dire time, and thus speed and shorten the hours of misery.

2 E

For any details of domestic life of colonial days
the reader has ever to turn to the diary of Judge
Samuel Sewall of Boston, just as the student of
English life of the same date turns to the diary of
Samuel Pepys.   Sewall was a Puritan of the narrow
type of the later days of Puritanism; and there is
little of warmth or beauty in his pages, save that
throughout them there shines with gentle radiance
the unconscious record of a pure and never-dying
neighborliness, the neighborliness of an upright and
reserved but deeply tender Christian.   No thoughtful person can read the simple and meagre, but
wholly self-forgetful entries which reveal this trait
of character without a feeling of profound respect
and even affection for Sewall.   He was the richest
man in town, and one of the most dignified of citizens, a busy man full of many cares and plans.   But
he watched by the bedside of his sick and dying
neighbors, those of humble station as well as his
friends and kinsfolk, nursing them with tender care,
praying with them, bringing appetizing gifts, and
also giving pecuniary aid to the household.   He
afforded even more homely examples of neighborly
feeling; he sent " tastes of his dinner " many times
to friends and neighbors.   This pleasant custom
lingered till the present day in New England; I
saw last summer, several times, covered treasures

of housewifery being carried in petty amounts, literally "a taste," to tempt tired appetites or lonely
diners.   The gift of a portion of the over-bountiful
supply for the supper of a wedding, a reception,
etc., went by the expressive name of "cold party."

In rural Pennsylvania a charming and friendly custom prevailed among country folk of all nationalities
— the "metzel-soup," the "taste" of sausage-mak-
ing.   This is the anglicized form of *Metzelsuppe*;
metzeln means to kill and cut to pieces — especially for sausage meat.   When each farmer butch-
ered and made sausage, a great dish heaped with
eight or ten pounds of the new sausages was sent
to each intimate friend.   The recipient would in
turn send metzel-soup when his family killed and
made sausage.   If the metzel-soup were not returned, the minister promptly learned of it and
set at work to effect a reconciliation between the
offended parties.   The custom is dying out, and in
many towns is wholly vanished.

Sewall seemed to regard it as a duty, and doubtless it was also a pleasure, to pray for and with
dying friends.   His is not the only old-time diary
that I have read in which those long prayers are
recorded, nor are his surprised occasional records of
the impatience of dying friends the only ones I
have seen.   A very sick man, even though he were

a Puritan, might occasionally tire of the prayers of laymen.

Sewall was ever ready to signify his good will and interest in his neighbors' advancing fortunes, by driving a nail at a ship-building or a pin at a house-raising, by laying a stone in a wall or a foundation of a house, the latter, apparently, in the case of some very humble homes. He, the Judge of the Supreme Court, served on the watch, walking and guarding the streets and his neighbors' safety just as faithfully as did the humblest citizen.

CHAPTER XVII

OLD-TIME FLOWER GARDENS

ADJOINING the street through which I always, in my childhood, walked slowly each Sunday, on my way to and from church, was a spot to detain lingering footsteps — a beautiful garden laid out and tenanted like the gardens of colonial days, and serene with the atmosphere of a worthy old age; a garden which had been tended for over half a century by a withered old man and his wife, whose golden wedding was spent in the house they had built, and in the garden they had planted when they were bride and groom. His back was permanently bowed with constant weeding and pruning and planting and hoeing, and his hands and face were brown as the soil he cultivated. The "hot-glowing" crimson peonies, seedlings which the wife had sown in her youth, had become great shrubs, fifteen or twenty feet in circumference. The flowering shrubs were trees. Vigorous borders of box crowded across the paths and towered on either side, till one could scarcely walk through

them. There were beautiful fairy groves of fox
gloves "gloriously freckled, purple, and white,"
and tall Canterbury bells; and at stiffly regular
intervals were set flowering almonds, St. Peter's
wreath, Persian lilacs, "Moses in the burning
bush," which shrub was rare in our town, and
"laburnums rich in streaming gold, syringas ivory
pure." At the lower ends of the flower borders
were rows of "honey-blob" gooseberries, and aged
currant bushes, gray with years, overhung by a few
patriarchal quince and crab-apple trees, in whose
low-spreading gnarled branches I spent many a
summer afternoon, a happy visitor, though my own
home garden was just as beautiful, old-fashioned,
and flower-filled.

The varying grades of city streets had gradually
risen around the garden until it lay depressed several feet below the level of the adjoining streets, a
pleasant valley, — like Avalon, —

> " Deep-meadowed, happy, fair, with orchard lawns,
> And bowery hollows crown'd with summer seas."

A flight of stone steps led down to it, — steps
very steep, narrow, and slippery with green moss,
and ladies'-delights that crowded and blossomed in
every crack and crevice of the stones. On each
side arose terraces to the street, and in the spring

these terraces flushed a mass of vivid, glowing rose-
color from blooming moss-pink, forming such a
glory that pious church-going folk from the other
end of the town did not think it wicked to walk
thither, on a Sunday morn in May, to look at the
rosy banks that sloped to the valleyed garden, as
they had walked there in February or March to see

> "Winter, slumbering in the open air,
> Wear on his smiling face a dream of spring,"

in the shape of the first crocuses and snowdrops
that opened beside a snow-drift still lingering on a
shaded bank; and to watch the first benumbed
honey-bees who greeted every flower that bloomed
in that cherished spot, and who buzzed in bleak
March winds over the purple crocus and "blue
flushing" grape-hyacinth as cheerfully as though
they were sipping the scarlet poppies in sunny
August.

The garden edges and the street were overhung
by graceful larches and by thorny honey-locust trees
that bore on their trunks great clusters of powerful
spines and sheltered in their branches an exceedingly unpleasant species of fat, fuzzy caterpillars,
which always chose Sunday to drop on my garments
as I walked to church, and to go with me to meeting, and in the middle of the long prayer to parade

on my neck, to my startled disgust and agitated whisking away, and consequent reproof for being noisy in meeting.

What fragrances arose from that old garden, and were wafted out to passers-by! The ever-present, pungent, dry aroma of box was overcome or tempered, through the summer months, by a succession of delicate flower-scents that hung over the garden-vale like an imperceptible mist; perhaps the most perfect and clear among memory's retrospective treasures was that of the pale fringed "snow-pink," and later, "sweet william with its homely cottage smell." Phlox and ten-weeks stock were there, as everywhere, the last sweet-scented flowers of autumn.

At no time was this old garden sweeter than in the twilight, the eventide, when all the great clumps of snowy phlox, night-rockets, and luminous evening primrose, and all the tangles of pale yellow and white honeysuckle shone irradiated; when,

> "In puffs of balm the night air blows
> The burden which the day foregoes,"

and scents far richer than any of the day — the "spiced air of night" — floated out in the dusky gloaming.

Though the old garden had many fragrant leaves

and flowers, their delicate perfume was sometimes fairly deadened by an almost mephitic aroma that came from an ancient blossom, a favorite in Shakespeare's day — the jewelled bell of the noxious crown-imperial. This stately flower, with its rich color and pearly drops, has through its evil scent been firmly banished from our garden borders.

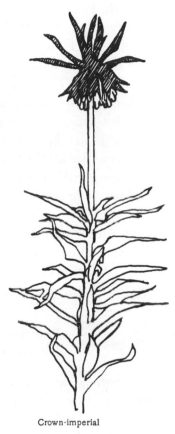

Crown-imperial

One of the most cheerful flowers of this and of my mother's garden was the happy-faced little pansy that under various fanciful folk-names has ever been loved. Like Montgomery's daisy, it "blossomed everywhere." Its Italian name means "idle thoughts"; the German, "little stepmother." Spenser called it "pawnce." Shakespeare said maidens called it "love-in-idleness," and Drayton named it

"heartsease."   Dr. Prior gives these names —
"Herb Trinity, Three Faces under a Hood, Fancy
Flamy, Kiss Me, Pull Me, Cuddle Me unto You,
Tickle my Fancy, Kiss Me ere I Rise, Jump Up
and Kiss Me, Kiss Me at the Garden Gate, Pink of
my Joan."   To these let me add the New England
folk-names — bird's-eye, garden-gate, johnny-jump-
up, kit-run-about, none-so-pretty, and ladies'-de-
light.   All these testify to the affectionate and
intimate friendship felt for this laughing and fairly
speaking little garden face, not the least of whose
endearing qualities was that, after a half-warm, snow-
melting week in January or February, this bright-
some little "delight" often opened a tiny blossom
to greet and cheer us — a true "jump-up-and-kiss-
me," and proved by its blooming the truth of the
graceful Chinese verse, —

> "Ere man is aware
> That the spring is here
> The plants have found it out."

Another dearly loved spring flower was the daffodil, the favorite also of old English dramatists
and poets, and of modern authors as well, when we
find that Keats names a daffodil as the thing of
beauty that is a joy forever.   Perhaps the happiest
and most poetic picture of daffodils is that of Dora

Wordsworth, when she speaks of them as "gay and glancing, and laughing with the wind." Perdita, in *The Winter's Tale*, thus describes them in her ever-quoted list: "Daffodils that come before the swallow dares and take the winds of March with beauty." Most cheerful and sunny of all our spring flowers, they have never lost their old-time popularity, and they still laugh at our bleak March winds.

Bouncing-bet and her comely hearty cousins of the pink family made delightsome many a corner of our home garden. The pinks were Jove's own flowers, and the carthusian pink, china pink, clove pink, snow pink, plumed pink, mullein pink, sweet william, maltese cross, ragged robin, catch-fly, and campion, all made gay and sweet the summer. The clove pink was the ancestor of all the carnations.

The richest autumnal glory came from the cheerful marigold, the "golde" of Chaucer, and "marybud" of Shakespeare. This flower, beloved of all the old writers, as deeply suggestive and emblematic, has been coldly neglected by modern poets, as for a while it was banished from modern town gardens; but it may regain its popularity in verse as it has in cultivation. In farm gardens it has always flourished, and every autumn has "gone to bed with the sun and with him risen weeping," and has given

forth in the autumn air its acrid odor, which to me
is not disagreeable, though my old herbal calls its
"a very naughty smell."

A favorite shrub in our garden, as in every country dooryard, was southernwood, or lad's-love. A
sprig of it was carried to meeting each summer Sunday by many old ladies, and with its finely dissected,
bluish-green foliage, and clean pungent scent, it was
pleasant to see in the meeting-house, and pleasant
to sniff at. The "virtues of flowers" took a prominent place in the descriptions in old-time botanies.
The southernwood had strong medicinal qualities,
and was used to cure "vanityes of the head."

"Take a quantitye of Suthernwood and put it upon
kindled coales to burn and being made into powder mix it
with the oyle of radishes and anoynt a balde place and you
shall see great experiences."

It was of power as a love charm. If you placed
a sprig in each shoe and wore it through the day
when you were in love, you would then also in some
way "see great experiences."

In the tender glamour of happy association, all
flowers in the old garden seem to have been loved
save the garish petunias, whose sickish odor grew
more offensive and more powerful at nightfall and
made me long to tear them away from their dainty

garden-fellows, and the portulaca with its fleshy, worm-like stems and leaves, and its aggressively pushing habits, "never would be missed." Perhaps its close relation to the "pusley," most hated of weeds, makes us eye it askance.

There was one attribute of the old-time garden, one part of nature's economy, which added much to its charm — it was the crowding abundance, the over-fulness of leaf, bud, and blossom. Nature there displayed no bare expanses of naked soil, as in some too-carefully-kept modern parterres; the dull earth was covered with a tangle of ready-growing, self-sowing, lowly flowers, that filled every space left unoccupied by statelier garden favorites, and crowded every corner with cheerful, though unostentatious, bloom. And the close juxtaposition, and even intermingling, of flowers with herbs, vegetables, and fruits gave a sense of homely simplicity and usefulness, as well as of beauty. The soft, purple eyes of the mourning-bride were no less lovely to us in "our garden" because they opened under the shade of currant and gooseberry bushes; and the sweet alyssum and candytuft were no less honey-sweet. The delicate, pinky-purple hues of the sweet peas were not dimmed by their vivid neighbors at the end of the row of poles — the scarlet runners. The adlumia, or mountain fringe, was a special vine of our own and known by a special name — virgin's bower. With its delicate leaves, almost as beautiful as a maidenhair fern, and its dainty pink flower, it festooned the ripening corn as wantonly and luxuriantly as it encircled the snowball and lilac bushes.

Though "colored herbs" were cultivated in England in the seventeenth and eighteenth centuries as carefully as were flowers, — striped hollies, variegated myrtles, and bays being the gardener's pride, — yet in our old American gardens few plants were grown for their variegated or odd-colored foliage. The familiar and ever-present ribbon-grass, also called striped grass, canary grass, and gardener's garters, — whose pretty expanded panicles formed an almost tropical effect at the base of the garden hedge; the variegated wandering jew, the striped leaves of some varieties of day-lilies; the dusty-miller, with its "frosty pow" (which was properly a house plant), fill the short list. The box was the sole evergreen.

And may I not enter here a plea for the preservation of the box-edgings of our old garden borders? I know they are almost obsolete — have been winter-killed and sunburned — and are even in sorry disrepute as having a graveyard association, and as being harborers of unpleasant and unwelcome garden visitors. One lover of old ways thus indignantly mourns their passing : —

"I spoke of box-edgings. We used to see them in little country gardens, with paths of crude earth. Nowadays, it has been discovered that box harbours slugs, and we are beginning to have beds with tiled borders, while the walks are of asphalt. For a pleasure-ground in Dante's *Inferno* such materials might be suitable."

For its beauty in winter alone, the box should still find a place in our gardens. It grows to great size. Bushes of box in the deserted garden at Vaucluse in Newport, Rhode Island, are fifteen feet in height, and over them spread the branches of forest trees that have sprung up in the garden beds since that neglected pleasaunce was planted, over a century ago. The beautiful border and hedges of box at Mount Vernon, the home of Washington, plead for fresh popularity for this old-time favorite.

Our mothers and grandmothers came honestly by their love of gardens. They inherited this affection from their Puritan, Quaker, or Dutch forbears, perhaps from the days when the famous hanging gardens of Babylon were made for a woman. Bacon says : " A garden is the purest of human pleasures, it is the greatest refreshment to the spirits of man." A garden was certainly the greatest refreshment to

Flower Garden, Mount Vernon

the spirits of a woman in the early colonial days, and the purest of her pleasures — too often her only pleasure.

Quickly, in tender memory of her fair English home, the homesick goodwife, trying to create a semblance of the birthplace she still loved, planted the seeds and roots of homely English flowers and herbs that grew and blossomed under bleak New England skies, and on rocky New England shores, as sturdily and cheerfully as they had sprung up and bloomed by the green hedgerows and door-sides in the home beyond the sea.

In the year 1638, and again in 1663, an English gentleman named John Josselyn came to New England. He published, in 1672, an account of

these two visits. He was a man of polite reading
and of culture, and as was the high fashion for
gentlemen of his day, had a taste for gardening and
botany. He made interesting lists of plants which
he noted in America under these heads : —

    " 1. Such plants as are common with us in England.
    " 2. Such plants as are proper to the country.
    " 3. Such plants as are proper to the country and have
no names.
    " 4. Such plants as have sprung up since the English
planted and kept cattle in New England.
    " 5. Such Garden-Herbs among us as do thrive there
and of such as do not."

This last division is the one that specially interests us, since it is the earliest and the fullest account
of the gardens of our forefathers, after they had
tamed the rugged shores of the New World, and
made them obey the rule of English husbandry.
They had " good store of garden vegetables and
herbs ; lettuce, sorrel, parsley, mallows, chevril,
burnet, summer savory, winter savory, thyme, sage,
carrots, parsnips, beets, radishes, purslain, beans " ;
" cabbidge growing exceeding well ; pease of all sorts
and the best in the world ; sparagus thrives exceedingly, musk mellons, cucumbers, and pompions."
For grains there were wheat, rye, barley, and oats.
    2 F

There were other garden herbs and garden flowers :
spearmint, pennyroyal, ground-ivy, coriander, dill,
tansy ; " feverfew prospereth exceedingly ; white
sattin groweth pretty well, and so doth lavender-
cotton; gilly flowers will continue two years ; horse-
leek prospereth notably ; hollyhocks ; comferie with
white flowers ; clary lasts but one summer ; sweet-
bryer or eglantine ; celandine but slowly ; blood-
wort but sorrily, but patience and English roses
very pleasantly."

Patience and English roses very pleasantly in
truth must have shown their fair English faces to
English women in the strange land.   Dearly loved
had these brier-roses or dog-roses been in England,
where, says the old herbalist, Gerard, " children with
delight make chains and pretty gewgawes of the
fruit; and cookes and gentlewomen make tarts and
suchlike dishes for pleasure thereof."   Hollyhocks,
feverfew, and gillyflowers must have made a sunshine in the shady places in the new home.   Many
of these garden herbs are now common weeds or
roadside blossoms.   Celandine, even a century ago,
was " common by fences and among rubbish."
Tansy and elecampane grow everywhere.   Sweetbrier is at home in New England pastures and roadsides.   Spearmint edges our brooks.   Ground-ivy
is a naturalized citizen.   It is easy to note that the

flowers and herbs beloved in gardens and medicinal
waters and kitchens "at home" were the ones trans-
planted here.   "Clary-water" was a favorite tonic
of Englishmen of that day.

The list of "such plants as have sprung up since
the English planted" should be of interest to every

Abigail Adams Garden, Quincy, Massachusetts

one who has any sense of the sentiment of association, or interest in laws of succession.   The Spanish
proverb says : —

> " More in the garden grows
> Than the gardener sows."

The plantain has a history full of romance; its
old Northern names — *Wegetritt* in German, *Weeg-*

bree in Dutch, *Viebred* in Danish, and *Weybred* in Old English, all indicating its presence in the much-trodden paths of man — were not lost in its new home, nor were its characteristics overlooked by the nature-noting and plant-knowing red man. It was called by the Indian "the Englishman's foot," says Josselyn, and by Kalm also, a later traveller in 1740; "for they say where an Englishman trod, there grew a plantain in each footstep." Not less closely did such old garden weeds as motherwort, groundsel, chickweed, and wild mustard cling to the white man. They are old colonists, brought over by the first settlers, and still thrive and triumph in every kitchen garden and back yard in the land. Mullein and nettle, henbane and wormwood, all are English emigrants.

The Puritans were not the only flower-lovers in the new land. The Pennsylvania Quakers and Mennonites were quick to plant gardens. Pastorius encouraged all the Germantown settlers to raise flowers as well as fruit. Whittier says of him in his *Pennsylvania Pilgrim:* —

> "The flowers his boyhood knew
> Smiled at his door, the same in form and hue,
> And on his vines the Rhenish clusters grew."

It gives one a pleasant notion of the old Quaker,

George Fox, to read his bequest by will of a tract of land near Philadelphia " for a playground for the children of the town to play on and for a garden to plant with physical plants, for lads and lassies to know simples, and learn to make oils and ointments."

Among Pennsylvanians the art of gardening reached the highest point. The landscape gardening was a reproduction of the best in England. Our modern country places cannot equal in this respect the colonial country seats near Philadelphia. Woodlands and Bush Hill, the homes of the Hamiltons, Cliveden, of Chief Justice Chew, Fair Hill, Belmont, the estate of Judge Peters, were splendid examples. An ecstatic account of the glories and wonders of some of them was written just after the Revolution by a visitor who fully understood their treasures, the Rev. Manasseh Cutler, the clergyman, statesman, and botanist.

In Newport, Rhode Island, where flowers ever seem to thrive with extraordinary luxuriance, there were handsome gardens in the eighteenth century. A description of Mr. Bowler's garden during the Revolution reads thus: —

" It contains four acres and has a grand aisle in the middle. Near the middle is an oval surrounded with espaliers of fruit-trees, in the centre of which is a pedestal,

on which is an armillary sphere with an equatorial dial.
On one side of the front is a hot-house containing orange-
trees, some ripe, some green, some blooms, and various
other fruit-trees of the exotic kind and curious flowers.
At the lower end of the aisle is a large summer-house, a
long square containing three rooms, the middle paved with
marble and hung with landscapes.   On the right is a large
private library adorned with curious carvings.   There are
espaliers of fruit-trees at each end of the garden and curious
flowering shrubs.   The room on the left is beautifully
designed for music and contains a spinnet.   But the whole
garden discovered the desolations of war."

In the Southern colonies men of wealth soon had
beautiful gardens.   In an early account of South
Carolina, written in 1682, we find : —

"Their Gardens are supplied with such European Plants
and Herbs as are necessary for the Kitchen, and they
begin to be beautiful and adorned with such Flowers as to
the Smell or Eye are pleasing or agreeable,: viz.: the Rose,
Tulip, Carnation, Lilly, etc."

By the middle of the century many exquisite
gardens could be seen in Charleston, and they
were the pride of Southern colonial dames.   Those
of Mrs. Lamboll, Mrs. Hopton, and Mrs. Logan
were the largest.   The latter flower-lover in 1779,
when seventy years old, wrote a treatise on flower-
raising called *The Gardener's Kalendar*, which was

read and used for many years. Mrs. Laurens had another splendid garden. Those Southern ladies and their gardeners constantly sent specimens to England, and received others in return. The letters of the day, especially those of Eliza Lucas Pinckney, ever interested in floriculture and arboriculture, show a constant exchange with English flower-lovers.

Beverley wrote of Virginia, in 1720: "A garden is nowhere sooner made than there." William Byrd and other travellers, a few years later, saw many beautiful terraced gardens in Virginian homes. Mrs. Anne Grant writes at length of the love and care the Dutch women of the past century had for flowers: —

"The care of plants such as needed peculiar care or skill to rear them, was the female province. Every one in town or country had a garden. Into the garden no foot of man intruded after it was dug in the spring. I think I see yet what I have so often beheld — a respectable mistress of a family going out to her garden, in an April morning, with her great calash, her little painted basket of seeds, and her rake over her shoulders, to her garden of labours. A woman in very easy circumstances and abundantly gentle in form and manners would sow and plant and rake incessantly."

In New York, before the Revolution, were many

Old Garden, Ellenville, New York

beautiful gardens, such as that of Madam Alexander
on Broad Street, where in their proper season grew
"paus bloemen of all hues, laylocks and tall May
roses and snowballs intermixed with choice vegetables and herbs all bounded and hemmed in by
huge rows of neatly clipped box edgings." We
have a pretty picture also, in the letters of Catha-
rine Rutherfurd, of an entire company gathering
rose-leaves in June in Madam Clark's garden, and
setting the rose-still at work to turn their sweet-
scented spoils into rose-water.

A trade in flower and vegetable seeds formed a
lucrative and popular means by which women could
earn a livelihood in colonial days. I have seen in

one of the dingy little newspaper sheets of those days, in the large total of nine advertisements, contained therein, the announcements, by five Boston seedswomen, of lists of their wares.

The earliest list of names of flower-seeds which I have chanced to note was in the *Boston Evening Post* of March, 1760, and is of much interest as showing to us with exactness the flowers beloved and sought for at that time. They were "hollyhook, purple Stock, white Lewpins, Africans, blew Lewpins, candy-tuff, cyanus, pink, wall-flower, double larkin-spur, venus navelwort, brompton flock, princess feather, balsam, sweet-scented pease, carnation, sweet williams, annual stock, sweet feabus, yellow lewpins, sunflower, convolus minor, catch-fly, ten week stock, globe thistle, globe amaranthus, nigella, love-lies-bleeding, casent hamen, polianthus, canterbury bells, carnation poppy, india pink, convolus major, Queen Margrets." This is certainly a very pretty list of flowers, nearly all of which are still loved, though sometimes under other names — thus the Queen Margrets are our asters. And the homely old English names seem to bring the flowers to our very sight, for we do not seem to be on very friendly intimacy, on very sociable terms with flowers, unless they have what Miss Mitford calls "decent, well-wearing English names"; we can have no flower memories, no affections that cling to botanical nomenclature. Yet nothing is more fatal to an exact flower knowledge, to an acquaintance that shall ever be more than local, than a too confident dependence on the folk-names of flowers. Our bachelor's-buttons are ragged sailors in a neighboring state; they are corn-pinks in Plymouth, ragged ladies in another town, blue bottles in England, but cyanus everywhere. Ragged robin is, in the garden of one friend, a pink, in another it flaunts as London-pride, while the true glowing London-pride has half a dozen pseudonyms in as many different localities, and only really recognizes itself in the botany. An American cowslip is not an English cowslip, an American primrose is no English primrose, and the English daisy is no country friend of ours in America.

What cheerful and appropriate furnishings the old-time gardens had; benches full of straw bee-skepes and wooden beehives, those homelike and busy dwelling-places; frequently, also, a well-filled dovecote. Sometimes was seen a sun-dial — once the every-day friend and suggestive monitor of all who wandered among the flowers of an hour; now known, alas! only to the antiquary. Sentiment and even spirituality seem suggested by the sun-dial, yet few remain to cast their instructive shadow before our sight.

One stood for years in the old box-bordered
garden at Homogansett Farm, at Wickford, in old
Narragansett.   Governor Endicott's dial is in the
Essex Institute, at Salem; and my forbear, Jacob
Fairbanks, had one dated 1650, which is now in
the rooms of the Dedham Historical Society.   Dr.
Bowditch, of Boston, had a sun-dial which was thus
inscribed: —

> " With warning hand I mark Times rapid flight
> From life's glad morning to its solemn night.
> And like God's love I also show
> Theres light above me, by the shade below."

Another garden dial thus gives, "in long, lean
letters," its warning word : —

> " You'll mend your Ways To-morrow
>   When blooms that budded Flour ?
> Mortall!   Lern to your Sorrow
> Death may creep with his Arrow
> And pierce yo'r vitall Marrow
> Long ere my warning Shadow
>   Can mark that Hour."

These dials are all of heavy metal, usually lead;
sometimes with gnomon of brass.   But I have heard
of one which was unique ; it was cut in box.

At the edge of the farm garden often stood the
well-sweep, one of the most picturesque adjuncts of

the country dooryard. Its successor, the roofed
well with bucket, stone, and chain, and even the
homely long-handled pump, had a certain appro-
priateness as part of the garden furnishings.

Old Well-sweep

So many thoughts crowd upon us in regard to
the old garden; one is the age of its flowers. We
have no older inhabitants than these garden plants;
they are old settlers. Clumps of flower-de-luce,

double buttercups, peonies, yellow day-lilies, are certainly seventy-five years old.   Many lilac bushes a century old still bloom in New England, and syringas and flowering currants are as old as the elms and locusts that shade them.

This established constancy and yearly recurrence of bloom is one of the garden's many charms.   To those who have known and loved an old garden in which,

> " There grow no strange flowers every year,
>   But when spring winds blow o'er the pleasant places,
>   The same dear things lift up the same fair faces,"

and faithfully tell and retell the story of the changing seasons by their growth, blossom, and decay, nothing can seem more artificial than the modern show-beds of full-grown plants which are removed by assiduous gardeners as soon as they have flowered, to be replaced by others, only in turn to bloom and disappear.   These seem to form a real garden no more than does a child's posy-bed stuck with short-stemmed flowers to wither in a morning.

And the tiresome, tasteless ribbon-beds of our day were preceded in earlier centuries by figured beds of diverse-colored earths — and of both we can say with Bacon, " they be but toys, you may see as good sights many times in tarts."

The promise to Noah, " while the earth remaineth seed-time and harvest shall not cease," when heeded in the garden, brings various interests. The seed-time, the springing-up of familiar favorites, and the cherishing of these favorites through their in-gathering of seeds or bulbs or roots for another year, bring pleasure as much as does their inflorescence.

Another pathetic trait of many of the old-time flowers should not be overlooked—their persistent clinging to life after they had been exiled from the trim garden borders where they first saw the chill sun of a New England spring. You see them growing and blooming outside the garden fence, against old stone walls, where their up-torn roots have been thrown to make places for new and more popular favorites. You find them cheerfully spreading, pushing along the foot-paths, turning into vagrants, becoming flaunting weeds. You see them climbing here and there, trying to hide the deserted chimneys of their early homes, or wandering over and hiding the untrodden foot-paths of other days. A vivid imagination can shape many a story of their life in the interval between their first careful planting in colonial gardens and their neglected exile to highways and byways, where the poor bits of depauperated earth can grow no more lucrative harvest.

The sites of colonial houses which are now destroyed, the trend, almost the exact line of old roads, can be traced by the cheerful faces of these garden-strays. The situation of old Fort Nassau, in Pennsylvania, so long a matter of uncertainty, is said to have been definitely determined by the familiar garden flowers found growing on one of these disputed sites. It is a tender thought that this indelible mark is left upon the face of our native land through the affection of our forbears for their gardens.

The botany tells us that bouncing-bet has "escaped from cultivation " — she has been thrust out, but unresentfully lives and smiles; opening her tender pinky-opalescent flowers adown the dusty roadsides, and even on barren gravel-beds in railroad cuts. Butter-and-eggs, tansy, chamomile, spiked loose-strife, velvet-leaf, bladder-campion, cypress spurge, live-for-ever, star of Bethlehem, money-vine, — all have seen better days, but now are flower-tramps. Even the larkspur, beloved of children, the moss-pink, and the grape-hyacinth may sometimes be seen growing in country fields and byways. The homely and cheerful blossoms of the orange-tawny ephemeral lily, and the spotted tiger-lily, whose gaudy colors glow with the warmth of far Cathay — their early home — now make gay many of our roadsides and crowd upon the sweet cinnamon roses of our grandmothers, which also are undaunted garden exiles.

Driving once along a country road, I saw on the edge of a field an expanse of yellow bloom which seemed to be an unfamiliar field-tint. It proved to be a vast bed of coreopsis, self-sown from year to year; and the blackened outlines of an old cellar wall in its midst showed that in that field once stood a home, once there a garden smiled.

I am always sure when I see bouncing-bet, butter-and-eggs, and tawny lilies growing in a tangle together that in their midst may be found an un-trodden door-stone, a fallen chimney, or a filled-in well.

Still broader field expanses are filled with old-country plants. In June a golden glory of bud and blossom covers the hills and fields of Essex County in Massachusetts from Lynn to Danvers, and Ryal Side to Beverly; it is the English gorse or woad-wax, and by tradition it was first brought to this country in spray and seed as a packing for some of the household belongings of Governor Endicott. Thrown out in friendly soil, the seeds took root and there remain in the vicinity of their first American homes. It is a stubborn squatter, yielding only to scythe, plough, and hoe combined.

Chicory or blue weed was, it is said, brought from England by Governor Bow-doin as food for his sheep. It has spread till its extended presence has been a startling surprise to all English visiting botanists. It hurts no one's fields, for it invades chiefly waste and neglected land — the "dear common flower" — and it has redeemed many a city suburb of vacant lots, many a railroad ash heap from the abomination of desolation.

Whiteweed or ox-eye daisy, a far greater pest than gorse or chicory, has been carried intentionally to many a township by homesick settlers whose descendants to-day rue the sentiment of their ancestors.

Fraxinella

2 G

While the vallied garden of our old neighbors was sweet with blossoms, my mother's garden bore a still fresher fragrance — that of green growing things; of "posies," lemon-balm, rose geranium, mint, and sage. I always associate with it in spring the scent of the strawberry bush, or calycanthus, and in summer of the fraxinella, which, with its tall stem of larkspur-like flowers, its still more graceful seed-vessels and its shining ash-like leaves, grew there in rich profusion and gave forth from leaf, stem, blossom, and seed a pure, a memory-sweet perfume half like lavender, half like anise.

Truly, much of our tenderest love of flowers comes from association, and many are lovingly recalled solely by their odors. Balmier breath than was ever borne by blossom is to me the pure pungent perfume of ambrosia, rightly named, as fit for the gods. Not the miserable weed ambrosia of the botany, but a lowly herb that grew throughout the entire summer everywhere in "our garden"; sowing its seeds broadcast from year to year; springing up unchecked in every unoccupied corner, and under every shrub and bushy plant; giving out from serrated leaf and irregular raceme of tiny pale-green flowers. a spicy aromatic fragrance if we brushed past it, or pulled a weed from amongst it as we strolled down the garden walk. And it is

our very own — I have never seen it elsewhere
than at my old home, and in the gardens of neighbors to whom its seeds were given by the gentle
hand that planted "our garden" and made it a
delight. Goethe says, "Some flowers are lovely to
the eye, but others are lovely to the heart." Ambrosia is lovely to my heart, for it was my mother's
favorite.

And as each "spring comes slowly up the way,"
I say in the words of Solomon, "Awake, O north
wind ; and come, thou south ; blow upon my garden, that the spices thereof may flow out" — that
the balm and mint, the thyme and southernwood,
the sweetbrier and ambrosia, may spring afresh and
shed their tender incense to the memory of my
mother, who planted them and loved their pure
fragrance, and at whose presence, as at that of Eve,
flowers ever sprung —

"And touched by her fair tendance gladlier grew."

Index

Abington, church vote in, 286.
Acrelius, Dr., quoted, 146.
Adams, Abigail, garden of, 435.
Adams, John, quoted, 71, 160; Sunday dinner of, 159–160; cider-drinking of, 161.
Adams, John Quincy, Mrs., straw bonnet of, 261.
Adams family, homes of, 22.
Albany, houses at, 9; deer in, 109; beer at, 161; bad boys in, 374–375; first church in, 385; cowherding in, 399.
Alchymy, 88.
Alewives, in New England waters, 120.
Ambrosia, a flower, 450.
Ames, quoted, 136.
Amherst, sign-board at, 360.
Andirons, 62.
Andover, church vote in, 286; bad boy in, 373.
Annapolis, dress in, 293.
Apostle spoons, 90.
Apples, culture of, 145; plenty in Maryland, 145; modes of cooking, 146; in pies, 146.
Apple-butter, 146–147.
Apple-paring, 146–147.
Apple-sauce, 146–147.
Architecture, of churches, 364 et seq., 385 et seq.
Arkamy, 88.
Axe-helves, 314–315.

Back-bar of fireplace, description, 53.
Bacon, quoted, 431.
Bagging, from coarse flax, 172.

Bake-kettle, 66.
Bake-shops, 147.
Ballots, of corn and beans, 141.
Balsam, as dye, 194.
Baltimore, dress in, 293; taverns in, 359.
Banyan, 294.
Barberry, root as dye, 194.
Basins, 106.
Bass, in New England waters, 120–121.
Bass-viols, in meeting, 378.
Bates of flax, 169.
Batteau, 329.
Batten, of loom, 220–221.
Baxter, 187.
Bayberry, description, 39; candles of, 39; wax of, 40; laws about, 40; soap from, 255.
Bead bags, 263.
Beam. See Warp-beam.
Beaming, in weaving, 218.
Beans, as ballots, 141; mode of cooking, 145.
Bed coverlet. See Coverlet.
Bedstead, alcove, 55; turn-up, 55–56.
Beer, among Dutch, 161.
Bees, called English flies, 111.
Beehives, 442.
Beetling of flax, 172.
Bell, as summons to meeting, 368.
Belt-loom. See Tape-loom.
Bennet, quoted, 123.
Berkeley, Gov., quoted, 111, 360–361.
Berries, 145.
Betty lamps, 43–44.
Beverages. See Drinks.
Bible, references to flax in, 177.

Biddeford, communal privileges in, 390.
Bier, in weaving, 220.
Birch-bark, doors of, 6; plates of, 83; baskets of, cans of, 253, 310.
Birch broom, making of, 301–303; price of, 302.
Blackjacks, 95–96.
Blazing, of trees, 330.
Bleaching, of flax thread, 175; of linen, 234; of straw bonnets, 261.
Bleeding-basins, 86.
Block-houses, 26.
Boards, scarcity of, 76.
Board cloth, 76–77.
Boardman Hill House, 22.
Bobbins, for weaving. See Quills.
Bobs, of flax, 168.
Bombards, 96.
Books of etiquette, 79.
Bore-staff of loom, 224.
Boston, fire-engine in, 19; early houses of, 19, 27; first fork in, 77; pigeons in, 110; fish in, 123; tea in, 164–165; coffee in, 165; chocolate in, 165; spinning schools in, 180; fulling-mill in, 187; dress in, 292–294; coach in, 331; stage-travel from, 350–351; night watch in, 363; meeting-houses in, 364, 366; restrictions of settlement in, 394; cows in, 400.
Bottles, of wood, 82; of pewter, 85; of glass, 92–93; of leather, 95.
Boucher, Jonathan, quoted, 382.
Bouncing-bet, 427, 447.
Bounty coats, 248.
Bouts, in weaving, 218.
Box-borders, a plea for, 430–431.
Boxing, of maple trees, 112.
Boylston, Nicholas, banyan of, 294.
Boys, clothing of, 287–288; wigs of, 297; seats in meeting for, 372 et seq.; misbehavior of, 372–373; in church, 384.
Braid-loom. See Tape-loom.
Bradford, Governor, quoted, 129–130.
Bread, white, 147; rye and Indian, 147.

Bread-peel, 67.
Breadtrough, 311.
Breakfast, or bread and milk, 148.
Breaking, of flax, 169–170; of hemp, 170.
Breaking out the winter roads, 412 et seq.
Breweries, in New York, 161.
Brewster, Elder, quoted, 117.
Brick, imported, 21.
British spinning and weaving school, 186.
Broach, 198.
Brooklyn, oysters in, 118–119; salting shad in, 124–125.
Brooms, of broom-corn, 256–257; of birch, 301–304; of hemlock, 304–305.
Broom-corn, 256–257.
Brown University, dress of first graduating class, 183.
Bucking, of flax thread, 175; of linen, 234.
Bull's-eye lamp, 45.
Bun, of flax, 169.
Bunch-thread, 251.
Bundling-mould. See Shingling-mould.
Burlers, in weaving, 252.
Bushnell, Horace, quoted, 246.
Busks, carved, 320.
Butter, price of, 149.
Buttermilk, for bleaching, 175.

Caches, for corn, 138.
Cage, for babies, 372; for bad boys, 385.
Calash, 289.
Calf-keeper, duties of, 400.
Cambridge, cowherding in, 399.
Campbell, Madam Angelica, coach of, 335.
Candles, cost of, 34; making of, 35–37; materials for, 38–39, 42.
Candle-arms, 42.
Candle-beams, 42.
Candle-box, 38.
Candle-dipping, 36.

Candle-moulds, 36–37.
Candle-prongs, 42.
Candle-rods, 36.
Candle-sticks, 42.
Candle-wood, 32.
Canoes, 325–327.
Canteens, of horn, 321.
Captain of the watch, duties of, 380.
Cards. See Wool-cards.
Carding described, 194–196.
Carding-machines, 206.
Card-setting. See Wool-cards.
Capuchins, 295.
Carolinas, sweet potatoes in, 145; hand-weaving in, 249–251; gardens in, 438–439.
Carpet. See Rag-carpet.
Carrots, 145.
Carving, terms in, 104–105; of wood, 320; of horn, 321–322.
Caves, description of, 2; for corn, 138.
Cave-dwellers, 1.
Cedar tops, for dyeing, 251.
Cellar of Dutch houses, 10.
Chain in weaving, 250.
Chair-seats, 310–311.
Chaise of Brother Jonathan, 353.
"Change-work," 417.
Chap-men, 300.
Chargers, 80, 84.
Charleston, flax manufacture in, 182–183; dress in, 293; gardens in, 438–439.
Charlevoix, Father, on canoes, 327.
Chaucer, quoted, on spinning, 179.
Chebobbin, 415.
Cheese, making of, 150.
Cheese-basket, 150–151.
Cheese-hoop, 312.
Cheese-ladder, 150–151, 312.
Cheese-press, 150–151, 312.
Chesapeake, turkeys on, 109; wild fowl on, 125.
Chicory, introduction of, 449.
Children, at table, 101–102; occupations of, 179–180, 182, 188–189, 203–204, 261–262; dress of, 287; in meeting, 372 et seq.; in noon-house, 376.
Chimney, catted, 15, 53; size of, 52, 68; description, 53; in Dutch houses, 55.
China, early use of, 100; importation of, 100–101.
Chinese stuffs, 294.
Chinking walls, 5.
Chopping-bee, 403 et seq.
Chorister, in Dutch churches, 386.
Churches, in Virginia, 381–383; in Albany, 385. See also Meeting-house.
Churns, few in New England, 149; examples of, 149–150; whittling of, 312.
Cider, use by children, 148–149, 161; use by students, 161; price of, 161; manufacture of, 161–162; generous use of, 161–163.
Clam-shells, use of, 308–309.
Clarionets, in meeting, 378.
Clavell-piece, 54.
Clay, for dyeing, 241.
Clergymen, in Virginia, 384.
Clocks, 299.
Clock-jack, 65.
Clock-reel, 174–175; price of, 177; for yarn, 200.
Clogs, 295.
Cloth, finishing of, 231–233.
Cloth bar, 224.
Clothes, durability of, 281; extravagance in, 281; laws about, 281 et seq.; of Massachusetts settlers, 286–287; of Virginia planters, 287; of children, 288 et seq.
Coaches, in Boston, 331, 353–354; in England, 354; Judge Sewall on, 354; in New York, 354–355. See also Stage-coach.
Coat-of-arms, on sampler, 267.
Coat roll, 248.
Cob irons, 62.
Cocoanut-cups, 96–97.

Codfish, early discoverers on, 115–116; plenty of, 115; in New England waters, 120–121; varieties of, 121; for Saturday dinner, 122; price in Boston, 123. See Fish and Fishing.

Coffee, substitutes for, 159; early use of, 165; queer mode of cooking, 165.

Colchester, girls' life in, 253.

Cold houses, 70–71.

Cold party, 419.

Colored herbs, 430.

Coloring, 23.

Combing, description of, 196.

Combing machine, 230.

Combs. See Wool-combs.

Comfortier, 69.

Common crops, 130.

Common herds. See Herding.

Common lands, 398.

Communal privileges, 390 et seq.

Conch-shell, as summons to meeting, 367–368.

Concord coaches, 352–353.

Concordance, 33.

Conestoga wagon, 339–343; shape of, 339; rates on, 340; great number of, 340.

Connecticut, tar-making in, 33; pumpkin bread in, 143; flax culture in, 179; straw manufacture in, 260.

Contributions in New England meetings, 378; in Dutch churches, 386–387.

Cooking, influence of Indian methods, 131–136; English modes of, 151; spices used in, 152; limitations in, 158–159.

Coöperation in olden times, 389 et seq.

Corbel roof, 9.

Coreopsis, persistence of, 448.

Corn, influence on colonists' lives, 126; in Virginia, 127–128; price of, 128, 138; scarcity of, 129; mode of cultivating, 130–131; Indian foods from, 131; Indian modes of preparing, 131; modes of cooking, 133–136; as currency, 138; profits on raising, 139; games with, 139; shelling of, 139–140; as ballots, 141; as national flower, 141.

Corn-cobs, use of, 141, 209.

Corn dances, 138.

Corn-husking, description of, 136.

Corn-sheller, 140–141.

Cotton, early use of, 206–207; cultivation of, 207; rarity of, 207–208; domestic manufacture, 209–210; Golden Age of, 230.

Cotton-gin, 208.

Cotton, John, quoted, 148, 285.

Coverlets, in Pennsylvania, 190; in Narragansett, 242–246.

Cows, herding of, 399–401.

Cowherds, duties of, 399–400; pay of, 399.

Cowkeeps, 399.

Cow-pens, 400.

Crabs, in Virginia, 118.

Crane, 53.

Creepers, 62.

Crocus, 237.

Crofting, of linen, 234.

Crown-imperial, 425.

Cups, 85, 90, 93–96.

Currency, corn as, 138.

"Cut-down," of trees, 405.

Cutler, Dr., quoted, 159.

Cut-tails, 122–123.

Daffodils, 426–427.

Dale, Sir Thomas, on corn-growing, 127; on Sunday observance, 380.

Danvers, Mass., house in, 30.

Daubing walls, 5.

Daughters of Liberty, 183–184.

Day's work in spinning, 185.

Deacons, in Dutch churches, 386–387.

Deacons' pew, 374.

"Deaconing" the psalm, 378.

Deaf pew, 374.

Dedham, Mass., house in, 22–23.

Deer, abundance of, 108–109; description of, 108.

Deerskin, clothing of, 288–289.

De La Warre, church attendance of, 382.

Delaware, house pie in, 146.

Delft ware, 100.

Dents, of sley, 219–220.

Designs, for weaving, 243–244, 250–251; of ancient Gauls, 242; for quilts, 272–273; for paper-cutting, 278–289.

Dew-retting, 169.

Dimity, 250.

Dinner, serving of, 104; primitive forms, 105–106; for Saturday, 122; in New York, 159; at John Adams' home, 159–160.

Discomforts of temperature, 70–71.

Distaff, in India, 178.

Dogs, in meeting, 374.

Dog-pelter, 374.

Dog-whipper, 374.

Donnison family, fire buckets of, 18.

Door latch, 11, 318.

Dorchester, windmill at, 133; corporation, laws in, 392, 394.

Double string-roaster, 64.

Drawing, in weaving, 219.

Drawing a bore, 224.

Dress. See Clothes.

Dresser, 68.

Drinking-cups, 85–96, 98.

Drinks, from curious materials, 163.

Drinking habits, 93–94, 161, 164.

Drinking-horns, 321.

Driver, 198.

Drugget, 250.

Drum, as summons to meeting, 367, 368.

Duck. See Wild fowl.

Duer, Colonel, dinner of, 159.

Dugouts, 326.

Dunfish, 121–122. Also see Codfish.

Durability of homespun, 238–239.

Durham, church discipline in, 372.

Dutch mode of serving meals, 106.

Dutch oven, 65.

Dyes, domestic, 155, 193–194, 250–251.

Dye-flower, 251.

Earmarks, 400.

Eastern Stage Company, 351.

Economy of colonists, 42, 185, 321–324; of Martha Washington, 237–238.

Eddis, quoted, 118.

Eels, method of catching, 117.

Egypt, flax in, 177–178; linen in, 178.

Embroidery. See Needlework.

Emerson, R. W., appointed hog-reeve, 403.

Endicott, Governor, sun-dial of, 443; his introduction of woad-wax, 448.

Entering, in weaving. See Drawing.

Ernst, C. W., quoted, 343, 345.

Etiquette for children, 100–102; of carving, 104–105.

Eye, of harness, 218.

Fairbanks, Jacob, house of, 22–23; sun-dial of, 443.

Fairs, instituted by Penn, 190; encouraged by Franklin, 191.

Faneuil, Miss, dress of, 292.

Fences, different varieties of, 25; common building of, 401–402; laws about, 401–402.

Fence-viewers, 401.

Ferries, by canoe, 330–331.

Finlay, Hugh, postal report of, 333–335.

Fireback, 54.

Fire-buckets, description, 16; use of, 17; of Donnison's, 18; of Quincy's, 18; of Oliver's, 19.

Fire-dogs, 62.

Fire-engine, first in Boston, 19; first in Brooklyn, 19.

Fire-hunting, 108–109.

Fire lanes, 16.

Fire laws, 15.

Fireplace of our fathers, 53.

Fire-plate, 54–55.

Fire-room, 7.

Fire-wardens, 15.

Fish, plenty of, 115–125; varieties of, in New England waters, 117; in Virginia waters, 119; in New York waters, 120; salted, 124–125; as fertilizer, 130; poisoned by flax, 169.

Fishing, King James on, 116; ill-success in, 117; supplies for, 117; in Virginia, 119–120; encouragement of, 121; laws on, 121; division of profit, 122, 123.

Fish-weirs, 121.

Flag, as summons to meeting, 368.

Flails, making of, 312; use of, 313–314.

Flannel sheets, 238.

Flax, patch of, 167; blossom of, 167; growth of, 168; weeding of, 168; ripening of, 168; pulling of, 168; spreading of, 168; rippling of, 168–169; watering of, 169; stacking of, 169; breaking of, 169–170; tenacity of, 171; swingling of, 171–172; beetling of, 172; hetcheling of, 172–173; spreading and drawing, 173; many manipulations of, 173; spinning of, 174; in Bible, 177; in Egypt, 177–178; in New England, 179–181, 186; in Pennsylvania, 181; in Virginia, 181, 182; in South Carolina, 182–183; in Ireland, 186; in Courtrai, 186; in England, 186.

Flax basket, 173.

Flax-brake, 169–170.

Flax hetchels, 172.

Flaxseed, how sown, 167; how gathered, 168, 176; how stored, 176.

Flax-thread, spinning of, 174; knotting of, 175; reeling of, 175; bleaching of, 175; backing of, 175.

Flax-wheel, revival of, 167; use of, 174; price of, 177.

Flint and steel, 48.

Flower, a national, 141.

Flowers, in churches, 383; old-time, 421 *et seq.;* folk-names of, 448; age of, 443–445; persistency of, 447; escaped from cultivation, 448.

Flower-seeds, sold by women, 440–441; old list of, 441.

Flutes, in meeting, 378.

Flying-machine, 345.

Fly-shuttle, 228.

Food, from forests, 108–114; from sea and river, 114–125; transportation of, 143; entirely from farm, 158; substitutes, 158–159.

Foot-mantle, 295.

Foot-paths, 329.

Foot-stoves, 375, 385.

Foot-treadle, of loom, 219.

Foot-wheel. See Flax-wheel.

Foote, Abigail, diary of, 253.

Forefathers' Dinner, 129.

Forests, destruction of, 52; riches of, 108–114.

Forms, 101.

Forks, use of, 77; first, 77.

Forts, as churches, 365, 385.

Fox, George, bequest of, 437.

Franklin, quoted, 53, 181; fairs encouraged by, 191; advertisement of, 292–293; as postmaster, 333; set milestones, 335; cyclometer of, 335–336; on canals, 353; in sedan-chair, 356.

Franklin stove, 70.

Fraxinella, 449.

Fringe-loom, 227.

Frocking, striped, 237.

Fulling-mill, in Boston, 188.

Fulling-stocks, 232.

Fulham jugs, 98.

Funerals, rings at, 298; gloves at, 298–299.

Furs, search for, 115.

Fustian, in America, 237; in Europe, 237.

Gallows-balke, 53.

Gallows-crooks, 53.

Gallows-frame. See **Tape-loom**.

Gambrels, 310.

Gambrel roof, description, 22.
Games, with corn, 139.
Garden, an old-time, 419 *et seq.;* in New England, 419 *et seq.;* in southern colonies, 438–439; in New York, 439–440.
Garnish of pewter, 85.
Garrison house, 26.
Garter-loom. See Tape-loom.
Geese, raising of, 257–258; pickings of, 257–259; noise of, 258.
Georgia, deer in, 109; turkeys in, 110; hand-weaving in, 249–251.
Georgius Rex jug, 99.
Germantown, flax-raising at, 181; flax-workers at, 181; seal of, 181; wool manufacture at, 190.
Gibcrokes, 53.
Gimlet, 305.
Giotto, loom of, 213.
Girdling, of trees, 403.
Girls, dress of, 289–292; seats in meeting for, 372.
Giskins, 96.
Glass, in windows, 23, 366; nailed in, 366; for lamps, 46; early use of, 92.
Gloucester, old house at, 70; fishing at, 122–123; communal privileges in, 390.
Gloves, given at funerals, 298–299.
Going a-leafing, 67.
Goldenrod, as dye, 193.
Goloe-shoes, 295.
Gookin, quoted, 137.
Goose-basket, 258.
Goose-neck andirons, 62.
Goose yoke, 258.
Gorse. See Woad-wax.
Gourds, cups of, 96; utensils of, 309.
Grant, Mrs. Anne, on Dutch gardens, 439.
Grapes, 145.
Grassing, of linen, 234.
Greeley, Horace, on canal-travel, 353.
Gridirons, 61.
Grist-mill, earliest, 133.

Guinea wheat, 129. See Corn.
Gun, as summons to meeting, 368.
Gundalow, 329.
Gutters of houses, 9.

Hackling. See Hetcheling.
Hadley, shad in, 123–124; potatoes in, 144; broom-making in, 256–257; restrictions of settlement in, 392–393; hay-ward in, 402.
Hakes, 53.
Half-faced camp, 3.
Hammond, John, quoted, 395.
Hamor, Ralph, quoted, 143.
Hancock House, knocker of, 28; on sampler, 268.
Hancock, John, hatred of pewter, 85; drinking cup of, 97; dress of, 293.
Hand-distaff. See Distaff.
Hand-loom. See Loom.
Hand-reel. See Niddy-noddy.
Hap-harlot, 242.
Harness. See Heddle.
Harvard College, standing salt of, 78–79; trenchers at, 81.
Hasty pudding, 135.
Hats, worn in meeting, 285; church votes about, 286.
Hay-wards, 402.
Heddle of loom, 219.
Heddle-frame. See Tape-loom.
Heel-pegs. See Shoe-pegs.
Hemlock, brooms of, 304–305; boxes of, 310.
Hemp, blossom of, 167; breaking of, 169.
Herding, of cows, 399–401; of sheep, 401; of swine, 403.
Hetcheling of flax, 172.
Hexe, of flax, 169.
Hides, use of, 109; tax on, 109.
Higginson, quoted, 33, 35, 117, 148.
Hind's-foot handle, 90.
Hinges, material of, 9, 318.
Hingham, church at, 365.
Hogarth, loom of, 213–214.

Hogs, as scavengers, 125; yokes of, 311; laws about, 402–403.
Hog-reeves, 402–403.
Homespun industries, 167; beneficent effect of, 179; foundation of liberty, 189.
Hominy, 131.
Honey, plenty of, 111.
Honey-locust, 163.
Horn, spoons of, 88; cups of, 96; as summons to meeting, 368.
Horse-blocks, in front of churches, 367.
Horse-bridges, 331.
Horse-laurel, as dye, 194.
Hose. See Stockings.
Hospitality, in Southern colonies, 395 et seq.
Hound handle, 100.
Hour-glass, in meeting, 376.
Housekeeper, qualifications of, 252–253.
House pie, 146.
House-raising. See Raising.
Hyperion tea, 165.

India china, 100.
Indians, houses of, 3–4; caves of, 138; corn dances of, 138; cultivation of corn by, 126–131; endurance of, 137; mode of cooking corn, 131–135; names of corn foods, 131–137; mode of drying pumpkins, 143; spoons of, 88; mode of cooking beans, 145; brooms of, 301–304; four best things, 304; modes of travel of, 325; boats of, 325; paths of, 329–330.
Indian corn. See Corn.
Indian pudding, 135.
Indigo, as dye, 193.
Inns. See Taverns.
Invention, of cotton-gin, 208; of fly-shuttle, 228; of spinning-jenny, 229; of throstle-spun yarn, 229; of combing-machine, 230; of flax-spinning machine, 230–231.

Ipswich, grist-mill at, 133.
Iris, as dye, 193.
Itineracies, old-time, 176, 300–301.

Jack-knife, 307-308.
Jacks, 64.
James I. on fishing, 116.
Jamestown, spinning-schools at, 182; summons to meeting at, 367.
Jeans, 250.
Jefferson, Thomas, quoted, 207, 256; hospitality of, 397; impoverishment of, 397–398.
Jewellery, slight wear of, 297.
Johnson, quoted, 143, 145, 188.
Johnson, Governor, baby clothes of, 265.
Johnny-cakes, 135.
Josselyn, quoted, 117; his list of plants in New England, 432 et seq.
Judd, Sylvester, quoted, 216, 237.
Jugs, of stoneware, 98.
Jumel, Madame, cave house of, 3.

Kalm, quoted, 39–40; on squirrels, 110; on bees, 111; on maize bread, 134; on canoes, 326–327; on the plantain, 436.
Kearsarge, Mount, romance of, 405.
Kentucky, hand-weaving in, 249.
Ketch, 328.
Kill-devil. See Rum.
Killing time, 153.
King Hooper house, 30.
Kitchen, description, 52; in rhyme, 73–75.
Knife. See Jack-knife.
Knife-racks, 68.
Knights, Madame, quoted, 8; on canoes, 327–328; journey of, 332; on sleighs, 355.
Knitting, 190; yarn for, 201; by children, 261–262; elaborate designs, 262.
Knitting machine, 190.
Knives, of flax brake, 170.

Knocker, Hancock house, 28; Winslow house, 29.
Knots, of flax thread, 175.
Krankbesoeckers, 385.

Labadist missionaries, quoted, 118-119.
Lad's lore, 428.
Lamps, 43-45.
Lathe. See Batten.
Latten ware, 58.
Laws, about flax culture, 179-180; about dress, 282-284; about ferries, 330-331; about mail, 334; about taverns, 357; on observance of Sunday, 378-379; of warning out, 392 *et seq.*; about fences, 401-402.
Lay, of loom. See Batten.
Laying a fire, 74.
Lays, of flax thread, 175.
Lean-to, description, 22.
Leashes, of heddle, 219.
Leather, utensils of, 95-96.
Letters. See Post.
Liberty Tea, 165.
Lincoln, Abraham, early home of, 4; rail-splitting, 25.
Linden, fibre from, 211.
Linen, manipulations of, 234; clothing of, 234; sentiment of, 234; price of, 234; checked, 238.
Lining the psalm, 378.
Litster, 187.
Livingstone, John, clothing of, 288.
Loaf-sugar. See Sugar-cones.
Lobsters, plenty of, 117; vast size of, 118.
Logan, Mrs., on flower-raising, 438.
Log cabin, forms of, 5.
Logging-bee, 416, 417.
Log-rolling, 389, 404, 406.
Longfellow, quoted, 327.
Long Island, bayberries on, 40; samp-mortars on, 133; wool raising on, 191; bad boys on, 373; Sunday observance on, 385; cowherding on, 400.

Long-short, 236-237.
Loom, antiquity of, 213-214; of Giotto, 213; of Hogarth, 213-214; description of, 214. See Power-loom, Tape-loom.
Loom-room, 212.
Louisiana, corn in, 128; petticoat rebellion in, 128; hand-weaving in, 250.
Lowell, quoted, 73.
Lucas, Governor, quoted, 182-183.
Lug-pole, 53.
Luxury, after the Revolution, 159-160.
Lye, making of, 254.

MacMaster, quoted, 207.
Madison, Dolly, dress of, 290.
Mail, of heddle, 219.
Mail. See Post.
Mail coaches, 344, 350.
Maine, windows in, 23; candle-wood in, 32; churns in, 149; axe-making in, 315.
Maize. See Corn.
Mandillion, 287.
Manhattan, bark houses on, 4; palisados on, 24.
Manners. See Etiquette.
Maple sugar, old description of, 111; manufacture of, 111-112.
Maple-wood, bowls of, 82, 318-320.
Marblehead, fishing at, 122-123.
Marigolds, 427.
Marmalades, 152.
Maryland, houses in, 11; wild fowl in, 125; apples in, 145; hospitality in, 396-397.
Masks, 290.
Massachusetts, cave dwellings in, 1; palisados in, 24; venison in, 109; fish in, 123; flax culture in, 179-180; wool-raising in, 188; bounty in, 205; sumptuary laws in, 281-284; outfit for settlers, 286-287; ferries in, 330-331.
Matches, first, 50-51.
Mazer, 319.

Mead, 163.
Meeting-house, in Boston, 364, 366; in Salem, 364; in Hingham, 365; descriptions of, 364, 366-369.
Metheglin, 163.
Metheglin cups, 85.
Metzel-soup, 419.
Milestones, 335-336.
Milford, Conn., palisados in, 24.
Milk, price of, 148; use as food, 148.
Milk pitchers, names of, 106.
Milkweed, for candle wicks, 35, 211.
Mill, Indian, 132.
Mince-pies, pioneer, 159.
Ministers, encourage fisheries, 121.
Mittens, fine knitting of, 262; quick knitting of, 262.
Modesty-piece, 270-271.
Molasses, for New England slave-trade, 163.
Monkey spoons, 90.
Moore, Thomas, quoted, 348.
Mortar, Indian, 132.
Morton, quoted, 120-121.
Moss-pink, 423.
Mount Vernon, description of, 13; weaving at, 237; garden at, 431.
Mourning rings. See Rings.
Mourning samplers, 268-269.
Muffs, worn by men, 298, 386.
Mutton, its disuse previous to Revolution, 189, 191.

Nails, scarcity of, 11.
Napkins, use of, 77.
Narragansett, hand-weaving in, 241-244; shift marriages in, 241-242; old quilt in, 275-276; threshing in, 313-314.
Needlework, stitches in, 264-265; delicacy of, 265; rules for, 265.
Neighborhood, title of settlement, 391.
Neighbors, old-time, 388 et seq., 395 et seq.
Netting, 263-264.
Nettles, fibre spun, 211.

New Amsterdam, first church in, 385; laws about fences in, 401-402.
Newman, Rev. Mr., manner of work, 33.
Newburyport, house at, 27; straw bleaching at, 261; sumptuary laws in, 283; fines in, 374.
New England, houses in, 15; candle-wood in, 32; lobsters in, 117; fisheries in, 117-124; Indian corn in, 127-136; mills in, 131-133; pumpkins in, 142-143; potatoes in, 144; squashes in, 144; milk and ministers in, 148; churns in, 149; cider in, 161-162; rum in, 163-164; slavery in, 164; wool-raising in, 188-189; taverns in, 356-357; watchmen in, 363; meeting-houses in, 365 et seq.; summons to meeting in, 368; Sunday observance in, 378 et seq.; "taste of dinner in," 418; old-time gardens in, 421 et seq.
New Hampshire, candle-wood in, 32; potatoes in, 144; pioneer mince-pies in, 159; wheelwrights in, 176; flax manufacture in, 180, 236; fine knitting in, 269; birch brooms in, 304.
New Haven, restrictions in, 392.
New London, mill at, 133.
Newport, box plants at, 430; garden in, 437-438.
New York, houses in, 8; candle-wood in, 32; first fork in, 78; venison in, 109; lobsters at, 118; fish in, 120; salting shad in, 124-125; suppawn in, 133; ale and beer in, 161; wool-raising in, 191; dress in, 292; turnpikes in, 349-350; coaches in, 354-355; sleighs in, 355; street lighting in, 362; watch in, 363; Sunday observance in, 384; cow-herding in, 399; gardens in, 439-440.
Niddy-noddy, 200-201; carved, 320.
Nightgowns, 294.
Nocake, description of, 137; use of, 137; Eliot's use of word, 137-138.

Noggins, 82.
Noil, 196.
Nokick. See Nocake.
Noon-houses, 374-375.
Noon-marks, 299.
Norridgewock, life-work of a citizen of, 407-408.
Northampton, sumptuary laws in, 283-284.
Northboro, spinning match at, 184.
North Saugus, house in, 21.
Norwich, naughty girl in, 373.
Notices, nailed on church doors, 367.
Nott, President, story of boyhood, 202-203.

Occamy, 88.
Occupations, of children, 179, 180, 182, 186, 437; of women, 187.
Oiled paper for windows, 23, 366.
Old South Church, on sampler, 268.
Old Ship, 365.
Old South, 366.
Opening in land, clearing, 406.
Ordinary, name for tavern, 356.
Osenbrigs, 288.
Otis, Hannah, sampler of, 268.
Overhang, in walls, 19-20.
Ovens, 67.
Ox-bows, 311.
Oxen, sign of distress in, 413.
Oysters, in Brooklyn, 118-119; in Virginia, 119; vast size of, 119.

Pace-weight, of loom, 224.
Pack-horses, use of, 336-339; pay for, 337; load of, 337-338.
Pails, early, 58.
Paint, not used, 23.
Pales. See Fences.
Palfrey, quoted, 122.
Palisado, description of, 24.
Pansy, folk-names of, 425-426.
Paper-cutting. See Papyrotamia.
Papyrotamia, 277-278.
Parley, Peter, reminiscence of, 140.

Parsnips, 145.
Pastorius, Father, his choice for seal, 181; his encouragement of gardening, 436.
Patchwork. See Quilt-piecing.
Patent, first to Americans, 138-139, 260.
Pattens, 295.
Paupers, in Narragansett, 313; treatment of, in New England, 324.
Pawn, 55.
Pawtucket, cotton thread in, 207.
Pay, for spinning, 185; for weaving, 230, 250; for cow-herding, 399; of swineherds, 403.
Peabody, Francis, house of, 31.
Peachy, 163.
Peas, 145.
Peel, 67.
Pegging, 262.
Pelisses, 295.
Penn, William, fairs instituted by, 190.
Pennsylvania, cave-dwellers in, 2; stoves in, 69; squirrels in, 110; wool manufacture in, 190; dress in, 292-293; mail in, 333; post-rider, 335; transportation in, 335-344; roads in, 339; turnpikes in, 349; coaching in, 350-351; metzel-soup in, 419; gardens in, 436-437.
Peonies, 421.
Perfumes, in cooking, 152; of old garden flowers, 424; of sweet-scented leaves, 449 et seq.
Periagua, 329.
Perry, 163.
Peter, Hugh, encourages fisheries, 121.
Petticoat rebellion, 128.
Petunias, 428.
Pews, described, 368 et seq.
Pewter, for lamps, 44-45; for utensils, 84-85; on dresser, 68; lids of, 100.
Phœbe-lamps, 44.
Philadelphia, early houses in, 15; luxurious dinners in, 160; straw manufacture in, 260; travel from, 347-350;

taverns in, 359; cow-herding in, 400–401.
Pickling, old-time, 152.
Pierce Garrison House, 26.
Pierpont, Rev. John, verses of, 306–307.
Pies, 146.
Pigeons, plenty of, 110; price of, 110.
Pilgrims, starvation of, 129.
Piling-bee, 406.
Pillions, 331–332.
Pillory, location of, 367.
Pinckney, Mrs., exchange of flowers of, 439.
Pinehurst, hand-weaving in, 250–251.
Pine-knots, use of, 32–33.
Pink, name of vessel, 328.
Pinks, varieties of, 427.
Pipe shelves, 68.
Pipe-tongs, 68–69.
Pitch-pipes, in meeting, 378.
Plantain, romance of, 135–136.
Plate-racks, 68.
Plate-warmer, 61.
Plymouth, vacant fields at, 130; sampler at, 266.
Pokeberry, as dye, 193.
Pompion. See Pumpkin.
Pones, 134.
Pop-corn, 135.
Poplar wood, use of, 81–82.
Porcelain. See China.
Porringers, 85–86.
Porter's fluid, 45.
Portsmouth, old house at, 21.
Portulaca, 429.
Posnet, 87.
Possing, of linen, 234.
Post, first, 332; duties of, 332–333; in Virginia, 333; report about, 333–335.
Potatoes, in New England, 144; queer modes of cooking, 144–145. See Sweet potatoes.
Potato-boiler, 57.
Pot-brakes, 53.
Pot-clips, 53.
Pot-crooks, 53.

Pot-hangers, 53.
Pothooks, 53.
Pots, cost of, 56; size of, 56.
Pound-keepers, 400.
Powder-horns, 320–321.
Powdering of hair, 297.
Powdering tub, 153.
Power-loom, 230.
Powhatan, teaches corn-planting, 127.
Prairie-schooner. See Conestoga wagon.
Prayers, length of, 376; with the sick, 419.
Preserving, old-time, 152.
Printer, dress of, 293.
Providence, straw manufacture in, 260; restrictions in, 392.
Psalm-singing, 376 et seq.
Puddings, of corn, 135.
Pudding-time, 104, 160.
Pue. See Pews.
Pulling of flax, 168.
Pulpits, 368, 385.
Pumpkin, tributes to, 143; modes of cooking, 143; their plenty, 143; shells of, 309.
Puncheon floor, 6.

Quakers, dress of, 258, 292.
Quarels, of glass, 9.
Quarnes, 133.
Quiddonies, 152.
Quills, for weaving, 216; from geese, 259.
Quilling-wheel, 216, 229.
Quilts, piecing of, 270–275; materials for, 272–274; patterns for, 272–275; quilting of, 273–274.
Quince drink, 96.
Quincy family, fire-buckets of, 18; samplers of, 266–267.
Quincy, Josiah, quoted, 341–342, 346.

Raddle, of loom, 219.
Rag carpet, 239–240.
Rail-fence, 25.

Raising, of a house, 408 *et seq.*
Rake. See Raddle.
Ramsay, quoted, 395–396.
Randolph, John, quoted, 205.
Raspberry leaves for tea, 158, 165.
Rattle-watch, 362.
Ravel. See Raddle.
Reading, communal privileges in, 391.
Recons, 53.
Reed. See Sley.
Reed-hook. See Sley-hook.
Reel, triple, 200. See Clock-reel and Niddy-noddy.
Revolution, influences towards success, 166–167, 189.
Rhode Island, stage-coach in, 346.
Rhode Island College. See Brown University.
Ribbon-beds, 445.
Ribbon-grass, 430.
Ride-and-tie system, 332.
Rings, wearing of, 297; at funerals, 298.
Rippling of flax, 168–169; of hemp, 169.
Rippling-comb, 168; of Egyptians, 178.
Roasting ears, 134.
Roasting-kitchens, 65.
Rock for spinning, in Egypt, 178; in India, 178; in New England, 179.
Rock-candy, 157.
Rocking-tree, of loom, 220.
Rochester, house-raising at, 410.
Rolliches, 154.
Rolling-roads, 330.
Rolling-up a house, 6.
Roof, of Dutch houses, 10; gambrel, 22.
Roquelaure, 295.
Rosselini, quoted, 178.
Roving, of yarn, 201.
Rowley, spinning match at, 184.
Ruffler for flax, 172.
Rum, manufacture of, 163; in New England, 163; in slave-trade, 163–164; at house-raisings, 410.

Rush, for scouring, 85.
Rushlight, 38.
Rutland, cave-dwellers in, 3.

Sabba-day house. See Noon-house.
Sabin Hall, 14.
Sack, law of sale, 357.
Sacjes, 386–387.
Saco, communal privileges in, 390.
Safeguards, 295.
Salem, coloring houses at, 23; lobsters at, 117; fisheries at, 121; milk in, 148; sumptuary laws in, 283; taverns at, 356–357; night-watch in, 363; meeting-house in, 364; seats for boys at meeting in, 372; swineherds in, 403.
Saler, 78.
Salisbury, meeting-house at, 369.
Salmon, price in Boston, 123; low regard of, 123; fishing for, 124.
Salt-cellar, 78–79.
Salting of fish, 124; of meat, 153.
Samp, mode of preparing, 131–132, 134; porridge of, 134.
Samplers, 265–268.
Samp-mills, 133.
Samp-mortars, 133.
Sap-buckets, 112.
Sap-yoke, 113.
Sassafras, as dye, 194; for soap, 255.
Sausages, making of, 154–155.
Sausage-gun, 154.
Save-alls, 42.
Scaffold, name for pulpit, 368.
Scarne. See Skarne.
Sconces, 42.
Scouring-rush, 85.
Scutching. See Swingling.
Scythe snathe, 309–312.
Seal of Germantown, 181.
Seating the meeting, 370–371.
Seats, at table, 101; in New England meetings, 369; in Virginia churches, 383–384; in Dutch churches, 386–387.

2 H

Section. See Bout.
Sedan-chairs, 356.
Sermons, length of, 376.
Sewall, Samuel, quoted, 354–356; 'character of, 418.
Shad, low regard of, 123–124; price of, 124; fishing for, 124; salting of, 124.
Shallop, 328,
Shed, in weaving, 221.
Sheep, in Massachusetts, 188; laws about, 188, 189; herding of, 409.
Sheep-folds, 401.
Sheep-herds, 401.
Sheep-ranges, 401.
Shelburne, girls work in, 262.
Shepster, 187.
Sherry-vallies, 296.
Shingles, making of, 316–317.
Shingle-bolts, 318.
Shingle-mould, 317.
Shoe-pegs, 315–316.
Shuttles, for loom, 224–225.
Sign-boards, name on, 358–359; historical value of, 359; of Philadelphia, 359; of Baltimore, 359.
Sigourney, Mrs., quoted, 277–278.
Silk-grass, 211.
Silver, use of, 89–92.
Skarne, 216–217.
Skeins, of flax thread, 175.
Skillet, 50.
Skilts, 236.
Slave-kitchen, 54.
Slave quarters, 14.
Slavery, in New England, 163; in Virginia, 164.
Sleds, 343.
Sleighs, in New York, 355.
Sley, of loom, 219–220; price of, 224.
Slice, 67.
Slippings, of flax thread, 175.
Smith, John, quoted, 115–116; plants corn, 127; description of first Virginia church, 381–382.
Smoke-house, 153.

Smoke-jack, 65.
Smoking tongs, 68–69.
Snake-fence, 25.
Sneak-cups, 106.
Snow, name of vessel, 328.
Snowstorm, in New England, 410 et seq.
Snuffers, 42.
Snuffers tray, 42.
Soap, making of, 253–255.
Society house, 396.
Sorrel, as dye, 194.
South Carolina. See Carolinas.
Southernwood, 428.
Spatter-dashes, 296.
Spelling, varied, of squashes, 144.
Spenser, quoted, 319.
Spermaceti, 42.
Spices, in cooking, 153; ground at home, 158.
Spice-mills, 158.
Spice-mortars, 158.
Spinning, of flax, 174, 230; pay for, 175; in Egypt, 178; in India, 178; in New England, 179–180; in Pennsylvania, 181; in France, 230–231; day's work in, 185; in modern times, 186; of wool, 196–198, 229–230; new materials for, 211; race between weaving and, 228–229; a by-industry, 228.
Spinning classes, 180.
Spinning-cup, 174.
Spinning-jenny, 229.
Spinning-matches, 184–185.
Spinning-school, 180, 182.
Spinning-wheel. See Flax-wheel and Wool-wheel.
Spinster, legal title of women, 187.
Splint brooms. See Birch brooms.
Spool-holder. See Skarne.
Spoons, use of, 87; material of, 87–88; types of, 89–90.
Spoon-moulds, 87–88.
Spoon-racks, 68.
Spreading of flax, 168.
Spunks, 50.

Squadrons, of spinners, 189.
Squanto, teaches fishing, 117; teaches corn-planting, 130.
Squashes, varied names of, 144.
Squirrels, abundance of, 110; premium on, 110.
Stage-coaches, in Great Britain, 331, 345-346; in America, 345-346.
Stage-wagon, 345.
Staircases, 27.
Standing salt, 78-79.
Standish, Lorea, sampler of, 266.
Starting a fire, 48-50.
Starving times, in Virginia, 127; in New England, 129.
Staves, 316.
Stays, 291.
Steeples, 366.
Steep-pool, for flax, 169.
Stepping-stones. See Horse-blocks.
Stitches, names of, 264-265.
St.-John's-Wort, as dye, 194.
Stockings, knitting of, 190, 262-263; weaving of, 190.
Stocks, location of, 367.
Stone-bee, 407.
Stone-hauling, 407.
Stone walls, 407.
Stoves, first, 69; in Dutch churches, 385.
Strachey, quoted, 119.
Strangers, harboring of, forbidden in New England, 393-394.
Stratford, tithing-man in, 372.
Straw manufacture, 259-261.
Streets, condition of, 362; lighting of, 362; washing of, 363.
Strikes, of flax, 172.
Striking a light, 47.
Stump-pulling, 407.
Sturgeon, great catch of, 120; in New York, 120.
Substitutes for imported foods, 158-159.
Succotash, 134.
Sudbury, tavern at, 357-358.
Sugar, substitutes for, 110, 111, 147, 157, 158; cutting of, 155-156.

Sugar-bowls, names for, 106.
Sugar-cones, 155.
Sugar-cutters, 155-156.
Summer-piece, 8.
Sunday, observance of, by Puritans, 378 et seq.; by Rev. John Cotton, 379; by Virginians, 380; by the Dutch, 384; duration of, 379.
Sun-dials, 299, 442-443; inscriptions on, 443; materials of, 443.
Suppawn, use of, 133.
Sweep and mortar mill, 132.
Sweet potatoes, modes of cooking, 145.
Swifts, 215-216.
Swineherds. See Hog-reeves.
Swingling of flax, 171-172.
Swingling block, 171.
Swingling knives, 171, 312.
Swingle-tree hurds, 172.
Swingling tow, bonfires of, 177.
Swing-sign. See Sign-board.

Table, description of, 76.
Table-board, 76, 81.
Table-cloths, 77.
Tallow, lack of, 34.
Tambour work, 269.
Tankards, original meaning, 83; of wood, 83-84; of silver, 99.
Tapping-gauge, 112.
Tape-loom, various names of, 225; described, 225-227.
Tap-room, of Wayside Inn, 357-358.
Tarboggin. See Chebobbin.
Tar-making, 33.
Taste of a dinner, 418.
Tasters, 86-87.
Taverns, establishment of, 356; titles for, 356; prices at, 357; values about, 357; names of rooms at, 357; in southern colonies, 360; in New Netherland, 361.
Tea, substitutes for, 158-159; first sales of, 164; queer mode of cooking, 165.
Teazels, 232.
Teazeling, of cloth, 232.

Temperature, of houses, 70–71; of churches, 374.
Temple, of loom, 223.
Tennessee, hand-weaving in, 249.
Tenting, of cloth, 232.
Terbobbin. See Chebobbin.
Terrapin, 120.
Thatch, for roofs, 15.
Threshing, 313–314.
Thumbing, in weaving, 218.
Thumb-rings, 298.
Tin, slight use of, 58.
Tinder, 48.
Tinder-box, 48.
Tinder-mill, 50.
Tinder-wheel, 49.
Tithing-men, 372, 373.
Titles, old-time, for women, 187.
Toasting-forks, 60.
Tobacco, as currency, 189; use forbidden near meeting-house, 379.
Tomble. See Temple.
Tongs, 236.
Tow, garments of, 235–236.
Town, unit in New England, 390; narrow feeling of, 391.
Townsend, revolutionary story of, 203.
Toys, of wood, 306.
Trammels, 53.
Transportation, on horseback, 176, 336 et seq.; by wagons, 339 et seq.
Trees, girdling of, 403; drive of, 404; under-cutting of, 404.
Trenchers, description, 80; material, 82.
Trivets, 60.
Troughs, making of, 311.
Trumbull, Jonathan, chaise of, 353.
Trunks, 348.
Trunk pedler, 300.
Tumble. See Temple.
Tummings, 195.
Turkeys, wild, 109; size of, 109–110; price of, 110.
Turkey wheat, 129. See Corn.
Turkey-wings, 309.

Turnips, 145.
Turnpikes, 349–350.
Turnspit dog, 65.
Tusser, Thomas, quoted, 35, 168, 255, 321–322.
Twifflers, 106.

Van der Donck, quoted, 118, 119, 120.
Van Tienhoven, quoted, 2.
Veils, interference about, 285.
Venison. See Deer.
Vermont, candle-wood in, 32; broom-making in, 303.
Victualling, name for tavern, 356.
Violins, in meeting, 378.
Virginia, early houses in, 11; palisados in, 24; candle-wood in, 32; first fork in, 78; silver in, 91; table furnishings in, 104; deer in, 108–109; birds and fowl in, 110; lobsters in, 118; crabs in, 118; oysters in, 119; plenty of fish in, 118–119; corn in, 127; massacre in, 127; windmills in, 133; toll in, 133; starvation in, 127, 144; pumpkins in, 143; locust groves in, 163; flax culture in, 181–182; wool culture in, 189–190; cloths in, 237; broom-corn in, 256; sumptuary laws in, 285; outfit of settlers, 289; roads in, 331; taverns in, 361; Sunday observance in, 380; churches in, 381–382; cows in, 400; fences in, 402.
Virginia fence, 25.
Voiders, 106–107.
Voorleezer, duties of, 386.

Waffle-irons, 61.
Wagon. See Conestoga wagon.
Warming-pans, 72.
Warning out, 392; a mystery in, 393.
Warp, 218.
Warp-beam, 214.
Warping, 217–218.
Warping-bars, 217–218.
Warping-needle, 219.
Warp-threads. See Warp.

Washing, domestic, 255.

Washington, George, home of, 13; outfit of his stepdaughter, 291; dress of, 293; as canal promoter, 353.

Washington, Martha, thrift of, 237–238; netting of, 265.

Watches, 299.

Watch-chains, 263.

Water, as beverage, 147.

Watering of flax, 169.

Water-fowl, plenty of, 125; enumerated, 125.

Watertown, windmill at, 133; restrictions of settlement in, 393.

Wax, candles of, 37; bayberry, 39–40.

Waynesville, hand-weaving in, 250.

Wayside Inn, 357–358.

Weather-skirt, 295.

Weavers, status of, 212–213; seat of, 221; working-hours of, 228; in Narragansett, 241–244.

Weaving, noise of, 212, 220; three motions in, 221–222; disappearance of, 227; on tape-looms, 225–227; race between spinning and, 228–230; of linens, 230–231; of rag-carpet, 239–240; of coverlets, 242–246; during Civil War, 249. See Loom.

Weaving-room. See Loom-room.

Webster, 187.

Weeds, once garden flowers, 435–436, 447–449.

Weight-timbers, 11.

Weld, quoted, 348–349.

Well-sweep, 443–444.

Westmoreland Revival, 227.

Whale-fishing, 41.

"Whang," 417.

Wheat, planting of, 147.

Wheel. See Flax-wheel and Wool-wheel.

Wheel-peg, 198.

Wheelwrights, early use of wood, 176.

Whipping-post, location of, 367.

White-Ellery House, 19.

White-weed, in America, 449.

Whitney, Eli, invention of, 208.

Whittemore, Amos, invention of, 205.

Whittier, quoted, 73–74, 181, 370, 413, 436; homespun attire of, 248.

Whittling, 321–323.

Wicks for candles, 34, 45.

Wigs, wearing of, 296–297; denounced, 296; names of, 296–299; cost of, 297.

Wigwams, 3.

William and Mary College, tax for, 109.

Williams, Roger, quoted, 134, 137, 285.

Windmills, Indian fear of, 130; first erected, 133; of John Winthrop, 133; in Virginia, 133.

Windows, of glass, 23; of oiled paper, 23.

Windsor, boys' pews in, 372.

Wine-taster, 87.

Winslow house, knocker of, 29.

Winthrop, John, fork of, 77; jug of, 98; his use of water as beverage, 148; pick-a-back, 329; sedan-chair of, 356.

Winthrop, John, Jr., quoted, 32; mill of, 133.

Woad-wax, in Massachusetts, 448.

Woburn, long services at, 376.

Wolfskin bags in meeting, 374.

Wolves' heads, nailed on meeting-houses, 364–365.

Wood, trenchers of, 80–81; utensils of, 82; spoons of, 88; for shuttles, 225; unusual uses of, 305; toys of, 306; natural shapes in, 308–311.

Wood, quoted, 32–33, 137.

Wool, an ancient industry, 187; early culture of, 187–193; manufacture of, 187–193; restraints on manufacture, 191–192; in England, 192; preparation of, 193; dyeing of, 193–194; carding of, 194–195; combing of, 196; spinning of, 196–198. See Yarn.

Wool-cards, described, 194–195; history of, 204–206.

Wool-combs, 196.

Wool-wheel, price of, 177.

Wordsworth, quoted, on spinning, 179.

Worsted stuffs, 233.

Wrathe. See Raddle.

Yarn, spinning of, 197–198, 201, 229; winding of, 198; skeining of, 199; cleansing of, 202; water-twist, 229.

Yarn beam. See Warp-beam.

Yarn roll. See Warp-beam.